W9-AMU-719

National Bestseller

Company's Coming ®

Diabetic Cooking

Great-tasting recipes for the entire family

Now in Original Series format
Proud Sponsor of Diabetes Research

Jean Paré

ORIGINAL SERIES

Diabetic
Cooking

Jean Paré

www.companyscoming.com
visit our website

Divider Photo

Top: Marinated Salad, page 121
Bottom: Turkey Pot Pie, page 98

We gratefully acknowledge the following suppliers for their generous support of our Test and Photography Kitchens:

Broil King Barbecues	*Lagostina®*
Corelle®	*Proctor Silex® Canada*
Hamilton Beach® Canada	*Tupperware®*

Table of Contents

Appetizers &
Beverages

Breads &
Muffins

Breakfasts

Desserts

Lunches

Main Dishes

Salads

Side Dishes

Soups

Foreword

When a family member has diabetes, all too often it has meant cooking one meal for him or her, and cooking a different meal for the rest of the family. No longer. Now the entire family can enjoy tasty recipes and benefit from a well-balanced eating plan with *Diabetic Cooking*. What could be better? Treat your family to great-tasting, kitchen-tested recipes that have the added perks of being low in fat and sugar.

Over the years many of my readers have asked for a diabetic cookbook, so I had thought of creating one well before my husband Larry was diagnosed with Type 2 diabetes. With today's focus on healthy eating, I admit to baking less, if only to provide fewer temptations around the house.

Many people with diabetes miss their desserts, but they can fit treats into their daily meals in consultation with a dietitian. Check out the Desserts section for Strawberry Banana Frozen Yogurt, French Pastry Dessert or Lemon Angel Tower.

From the first page to the last, *Diabetic Cooking* is designed to bring you great-tasting food. Try Crispy Barbecue Chips with Black Bean And Corn Salsa as a snack or appetizer for a party, or whip up some Honey Wheat Bread for lunch with Couscous Seafood Salad. Fix Jambalaya or quick and easy Creamy Garlic Penne for supper. How about Turkey Cutlets with Mushroom Sauce with a side dish of Cheese Spirals or Stuffed Tomatoes? When you feel like celebrating a special occasion, concoct a batch of out-of-this-world Brownies or Cherry Chocolate Dessert. Share them and be prepared for rave reviews from all!

During development of this book, we convened a focus group of people of all ages with diabetes to sample our recipes. They held us up to their high standards, making sure this book would meet with your approval too. After all, food that's good for you still needs to taste good enough to eat! We also wish to thank the dedicated volunteers and staff of the Juvenile Diabetes Foundation for their valued input and encouragement.

Whether you have diabetes, are cooking for someone who has diabetes, or are just interested in a healthier lifestyle, you'll be glad you picked up your copy of *Diabetic Cooking*!

Jean Paré

Each Recipe has been analyzed using the Canadian Nutrient File from Health and Welfare Canada, which is based upon the United States Department of Agriculture (USDA) Nutrient Data Base.

Margaret Ng, B.Sc. (Hon.), M.A.
Registered Dietitian

Diabetic choices have been assigned based upon the nutrition information per serving stated.

Vera C. Mazurak, Ph.D.
Nutritionist

About Diabetes

When people have diabetes, their blood has too much glucose—a type of sugar—because their bodies aren't processing it properly. The body receives glucose from digestion of carbohydrates such as those found in grains, fruits and vegetables, and milk. The liver also produces glucose that travels into the blood stream.

Under healthy conditions, the pancreas produces enough insulin to enable glucose to enter cells and be used as fuel. People with Type 1 (or insulin-dependent) diabetes have a severe lack of insulin because their pancreases produce little or none at all. In order to maintain normal blood glucose levels, they need to take insulin injections and control their intake of fats and carbohydrates. People with Type 2 (or non insulin-dependent) diabetes still produce insulin, but not enough, or their bodies do not use it efficiently. They may be able to manage their disease with diet alone or with a combination of diet, pills and/or insulin injections.

Without treatment, symptoms of diabetes may include increased thirst and urination, fatigue, vision changes and weight loss. In the long term, diabetes can damage the eyes, kidneys, nerves, heart and circulation system. Being physically active and maintaining a healthy body weight are keys to good living for everyone, but become critical for those with diabetes.

About Diabetic Eating

Diabetic Cooking is a cookbook filled with enticing, easy-to-prepare food. It follows the theory that dietary guidelines for people with diabetes are the same for everyone: eat a wide variety of nutritious food in moderation. **Every person with diabetes needs to consult with a dietitian to determine his or her personal eating plan.**

Performance-enhancing foods

No foods are forbidden—limiting the consumption of alcohol, salt, fat and sugar doesn't necessarily mean *eliminating* those items. Just like putting the wrong kind of gasoline in your car affects performance, fueling your body with poor food choices does the same thing. The cost of eating "premium fuel" doesn't have to be a premium price. Some cuts of meat may seem pricey, but not when you consider that a portion of steak is only 4 oz. (113 g), rather than the overly-large 8 oz. (225 g) portion you're likely to get at a restaurant. Likewise, fresh fruits and vegetables fluctuate in price, so buy them in season and then compare the cost to their processed cousins-in-a-can. Convenience foods are often high in fat, salt and sugar, so stay clear of them—that way only your wallet will grow fatter!

Sweet dreams

Advice about sugar consumption for people with diabetes has changed over the years. Small quantities of sugar that don't cause a quick peak in blood sugar levels are now allowed. A large soft drink or chocolate bar will have a lot of concentrated sugar, but a small piece of chocolate or candy will have a lesser effect on blood glucose levels.

Smart snacking

Fresh fruit and ice cream are simple desserts or snacks that, in small quantities, have lower fat than regular cheese and crackers. Foods like nuts, salami and olives are also high in fat, so low-fat cheese, dips and breads would be preferable as fill-ins between meals. If you can, find yummy add-ons like a wonderful low-fat salad dressing from our Salads section to go with "free foods" (those without quantity restrictions), such as green and leafy vegetables.

Lightly starched

While starchy foods may cause blood sugar spikes, they are still carbohydrates, which are something every body needs. Complex carbohydrates with fibre (generally foods which have not been highly processed) are more nutritious and better at keeping blood glucose levels on an even keel.

Decoding Dietary Info

Nutrition Information

For each recipe in *Diabetic Cooking*, we have provided nutrition information, which tallies calories, fat (including cholesterol and saturated fats), carbohydrates, fibre, protein and sodium. These values include all the ingredients listed in the recipe except those stated as "optional" or "for garnish." If a range of measurements is given, the smaller amount is analyzed. Variations of recipes listed underneath the analysis and ingredient substitutions given in brackets have not been analyzed.

Diabetic Choices (Beyond the Basics)

Each recipe in this revised edition of *Diabetic Cooking* contains the diabetic choice values for the updated Beyond the Basics meal planning guide. Beyond the Basics groups together foods that are similar in carbohydrate content. The names of the categories have been changed to better reflect the foods contained in the group. For example, Starches has become Grains and Starches, whereas Sugars has become Other Choices to better reflect the sweets and snack foods in the group. Although the allowed size or amount of different food within a particular group may vary, each food in that group will have the same approximate composition of carbohydrates, protein, fat and calories. If no choices are listed, it means that the serving size suggested for that food does not have enough carbohydrates to constitute a choice in any category.

For people on insulin who require precise carbohydrate counting, the nutritional information giving total grams of carbohydrate and dietary fibre will provide useful guidelines.

Ingredients At Work

Artificial sweeteners: When testing the recipes in *Diabetic Cooking*, we did not use artificial sweeteners, with the exception of a few recipes where a large amount of sugar would have been required or because we wanted to provide some recipes where they could be substituted for sugar or honey.

Fats: We chose to use canola or olive oil instead of margarine where we could. In some recipes, margarine or butter was better for taste, but we limited the amount. Butter can be used moderately, but it is an animal fat and contains cholesterol. Where possible, we used non-stick cookware or no-stick cooking spray to reduce the fats and oils used.

Meats: All the meat we used was trimmed of fat prior to cooking. We also chose lean cuts such as boneless, skinless chicken breasts or beef sirloin.

Milk: Our test kitchen staff used skim milk unless specified, since it has an equal amount of calcium and approximately the same amount of nutrients as 1%, 2% or whole milk, without any of the animal fat.

Egg substitute: Most of our recipes call for only one or two eggs. For recipes using more than two eggs or those considered to be primarily egg dishes, we've used a lower cholesterol egg substitute. For certain recipes we chose to use an egg substitute because the recipe already had other saturated fats. If preferred, avoid using egg yolks to reduce fat and cholesterol (the whites contain high-quality protein without the fat).

Cheese: We used light sharp Cheddar cheese, part-skim mozzarella or light Parmesan cheese product to lower the fat content without compromising the taste.

Yogurt: These recipes were tested using plain and flavoured non-fat yogurt. With minimal effort, you can make Yogurt Cheese, page 75, and use as a substitute for cream cheese.

Cooking methods: We recommend baking, grilling, steaming, poaching and stir-frying to reduce the amount of fat needed to cook an item.

If you have any questions about how these recipes, or any other food, can fit into the diet of someone with diabetes, please talk to your doctor or dietitian.

Take-Along Booster

When your blood sugar is plummeting and you need a quick fix fast,
keep this sweet, tropical-tasting treat at the ready (see Tip, below).

Container of vanilla frosting	16 oz.	450 g
Almond flavouring	1/4 tsp.	1 mL
White corn syrup	1/3 cup	75 mL
Finely chopped dried apricots	1 1/2 cups	375 mL
Icing (confectioner's) sugar	3 cups	750 mL
Flake coconut	1 cup	250 mL
Icing (confectioner's) sugar (optional)		
Flake coconut (optional)		

Combine frosting and flavouring in large bowl.

Measure corn syrup into small bowl. Microwave on high (100%) for 30 seconds or warm in small saucepan on low. Stir in apricots until well coated. Add to frosting mixture. Stir well.

Stir in icing sugar and coconut. Knead with hands to combine well. Turn out onto flat surface. Knead, adding icing sugar if required to prevent sticking, until smooth. Measure into 1/2 tbsp. (7 mL) portions. Roll into balls.

Roll in additional icing sugar or coconut. Wrap individual balls in plastic wrap. Freeze. Makes about 52 balls.

1 ball: 83 Calories; 1.1 g Total Fat (0.7 g Sat., 1.7 mg Cholesterol); 10 mg Sodium; trace Protein; 19 g Carbohydrate; trace Dietary Fibre

CHOICES: 1 Other Choices

 Boosters are high-sugar snacks designed to jump-start your sugar levels when they plummet, so don't substitute the sugar-free version of flavoured gelatin. However, using the lower-fat products is a good idea. These boosters are meant to be frozen in individual portions and taken along with you **for emergencies only**. They are not meant to be included as part of your daily meal plan.

Sweet Cereal Booster

This s'more-like treat won't let you down when the going gets tough (see Tip, page 10).

Light smooth peanut butter	1/2 cup	125 mL
Corn syrup	1/4 cup	60 mL
Miniature marshmallows	3 cups	750 mL
Vanilla	1/2 tsp.	2 mL
Corn flakes cereal	5 cups	1.25 L

Melt peanut butter and corn syrup in large saucepan on low. Stir in marshmallows until just melted. Do not overcook. Remove from heat.

Stir in vanilla and cereal until well coated. Press firmly into greased 9 x 9 inch (22 x 22 cm) pan. Cool to room temperature. Cut into 24 bars. Wrap individual bars in plastic wrap. Freeze. Makes 24 bars.

1 bar: 84 Calories; 2.3 g Total Fat (0.4 g Sat., 0.1 mg Cholesterol); 96 mg Sodium; 2 g Protein; 15 g Carbohydrate; trace Dietary Fibre

CHOICES: 1/2 Grains & Starches; 1/2 Other Choices; 1/2 Fats

Loopy O Booster

This fruity little bar will carry you through when you're feeling slow on the go (see Tip, page 10).

Margarine	2 tbsp.	30 mL
White corn syrup	1/3 cup	75 mL
Package of fruit-flavoured gelatin (jelly powder), your favourite (not sugar-free)	3 oz.	85 g
"O"-shaped fruity cereal (such as Fruit Loops)	4 cups	1 L

Melt margarine in large saucepan on medium. Stir in corn syrup and jelly powder. Heat and stir until boiling and jelly powder is dissolved. Remove from heat.

Quickly stir in cereal to coat. Mixture will be very sticky, so work fast. Press firmly into greased foil-lined 8 x 8 inch (20 x 20 cm) square pan. Chill just until set. Cut into 18 bars. Wrap individual bars in plastic wrap. Freeze. Makes 18 bars.

1 bar: 74 Calories; 1.4 g Total Fat (0.3 g Sat., 0 mg Cholesterol); 60 mg Sodium; 1 g Protein; 15 g Carbohydrate; trace Dietary Fibre

CHOICES: 1 Other Choices

Crispy Barbecue Chips

These don't have to be in wedges; they can be cut into irregular shapes. Pile in a bowl for a snack with friends. Try with Black Bean And Corn Salsa, page 15.

Spicy barbecue sauce	1/3 cup	75 mL
Olive oil	2 tsp.	10 mL
Sesame seeds	2 tsp.	10 mL
Garlic powder	1/8 tsp.	0.5 mL
Whole wheat flour tortillas (10 inch, 25 cm, size)	4	4

Combine first 4 ingredients in small dish.

Brush both sides of tortillas with barbecue sauce mixture. Cut each into 10 wedges. Arrange wedges in single layer on large greased baking sheet. Bake on bottom rack in 350°F (175°C) oven for 8 minutes. Turn wedges. Bake for 8 minutes until crispy and browned. Makes 40 chips.

2 chips: 42 Calories; 0.8 g Total Fat (0.1 g Sat., 0 mg Cholesterol); 77 mg Sodium; 1 g Protein; 7 g Carbohydrate; trace Dietary Fibre

CHOICES: 1/2 Grains & Starches

Pictured on page 17.

Herb Dip

Good with any cut-up vegetables. The flavour is much better when made a day ahead.

Non-fat plain yogurt	1 cup	250 mL
Non-fat salad dressing (or non-fat mayonnaise)	1/4 cup	60 mL
Parsley flakes	2 tsp.	10 mL
Chopped fresh chives (or 2 tsp., 10 mL, dried)	1 tbsp.	15 mL
Dried whole oregano, crushed	1/2 tsp.	2 mL
Dried sweet basil	1/2 tsp.	2 mL
Dried tarragon leaves, crushed	1/8 – 1/4 tsp.	0.5 – 1 mL
Dry mustard	1 tsp.	5 mL
Salt	1/2 tsp.	2 mL
Granulated sugar	1/2 tsp.	2 mL

Combine all 10 ingredients in small bowl. Cover. Chill for at least two hours to blend flavours. Makes 1 1/8 cups (280 mL).

1 tbsp. (15 mL): 12 Calories; 0.1 g Total Fat (trace Sat., 0.3 mg Cholesterol); 110 mg Sodium; 1 g Protein; 2 g Carbohydrate; trace Dietary Fibre

CHOICES: None

Spicy Mexi-Bean Dip

Make this recipe to accompany Fresh Tomato Salsa, page 16.
Serve both with Crispy Barbecue Chips, page 12.

Cooked (or 1 can, 19 oz., 540 mL) black beans, drained and rinsed	1 1/2 cups	375 mL
Diced jalapeño pepper, ribs and seeds removed (see Tip, page 105)	1 tbsp.	15 mL
Salsa	1/4 cup	60 mL
Light sour cream	1/4 cup	60 mL
Grated light Monterey Jack cheese	1 1/2 cups	375 mL

Mash beans with fork or masher in medium bowl until broken up. Add next 3 ingredients and 1/2 of cheese. Spoon into shallow 1 quart (1 L) casserole. Sprinkle remaining 1/2 of cheese on top. Bake, uncovered, in 350°F (175°C) oven for 20 minutes or until bubbly. Makes 2 cups (500 mL).

2 tbsp. (30 mL): 67 Calories; 3.6 g Total Fat (2.4 g Sat., 10.3 mg Cholesterol); 118 mg Sodium; 4 g Protein; 5 g Carbohydrate; 1 g Dietary Fibre

CHOICES: None

Pictured on page 17.

Simple Tuna Spread

Serve with a variety of lower-fat crackers. Or take for lunch along with crackers, bread or fresh vegetables. For more flavour, add a little more teriyaki sauce.

Finely chopped red onion	2 tbsp.	30 mL
Can of white tuna, packed in water, drained and broken into chunks	6 oz.	170 g
Teriyaki sauce	4 – 6 tsp.	20 – 30 mL

Combine all 3 ingredients in small bowl. Chill for 1 to 2 hours to blend flavours. Makes 1 cup (250 mL).

1 tbsp. (15 mL): 17 Calories; 0.4 g Total Fat (0.1 g Sat., 5.0 mg Cholesterol); 70 mg Sodium; 3 g Protein; trace Carbohydrate; trace Dietary Fibre

CHOICES: 1/2 Meat & Alternatives

Variation: Omit teriyaki sauce and add 2 tbsp. (30 mL) non-fat herb and garlic-flavoured cream cheese and 2 tsp. (10 mL) low-sodium soy sauce.

Crab Appetizers

These little morsels are good hot or cold. Serve with seafood cocktail sauce.

Finely chopped imitation crabmeat	2 cups	500 mL
Fine dry bread crumbs	3/4 cup	175 mL
Creamed horseradish	1 tsp.	5 mL
Chopped green onion	1/2 cup	125 mL
Finely chopped red or yellow pepper	1/2 cup	125 mL
Chopped fresh parsley (or 1 tsp., 5 mL, flakes)	1 tbsp.	15 mL
Dry mustard	1 tsp.	5 mL
Salt	1/2 tsp.	2 mL
Freshly ground pepper, sprinkle		
Dried sweet basil, crushed	1/4 tsp.	1 mL
Dried whole oregano, crushed	1/8 tsp.	0.5 mL
Garlic powder (optional)	1/8 tsp.	0.5 mL
Frozen egg product, thawed (see Note)	1/2 cup	125 mL

Combine first 12 ingredients in large bowl. Stir well.

Stir in egg product. Cover with plastic wrap. Chill for 1 hour for bread crumbs to moisten. Roll rounded tablespoonfuls (15 mL) mixture into thirty-four 1 1/2 inch (3.8 cm) balls. Arrange on greased baking sheet. Bake in 350°F (175°C) oven for 10 minutes until firm and golden brown. Makes 34 balls.

2 balls: 51 Calories; 0.7 g Total Fat (0.1 g Sat., 8.4 mg Cholesterol); 296 mg Sodium; 5 g Protein; 7 g Carbohydrate; trace Dietary Fibre

CHOICES: 1/2 Grains & Starches; 1/2 Meat & Alternatives

Pictured on page 18.

Note: 3 tbsp. (50 mL) = 1 large egg

Paré Pointer

Knock knock.
Who's there?
Beth.
Beth who?
Beth let me in or I'll blow your houth down!

Black Bean And Corn Salsa

Put in the whole jalapeño for more of a hit. Use with Crispy Barbecue Chips, page 12.

Can of black beans, drained and rinsed	19 oz.	540 mL
Chopped red onion	1/2 cup	125 mL
Chopped fresh cilantro	1 tbsp.	15 mL
Diced jalapeño pepper, ribs and seeds removed (see Tip, page 105)	1 tbsp.	15 mL
Lime juice	1 tbsp.	15 mL
Ground cumin	1/4 tsp.	1 mL
Chili powder	1/4 tsp.	1 mL
Large tomato, seeded and chopped	1	1
Garlic clove, minced	1	1
Can of kernel corn, drained	12 oz.	341 mL
Salt	1/2 tsp.	2 mL

Combine all 11 ingredients in medium bowl. Cover. Chill for at least 2 hours to blend flavours. Makes 4 cups (1 L).

1/4 cup (60 mL): 39 Calories; 0.2 g Total Fat (trace Sat., 0 mg Cholesterol); 167 mg Sodium; 2 g Protein; 8 g Carbohydrate; 1 g Dietary Fibre

CHOICES: None

Pictured on page 17.

 Although there is no meat in vegetarian dishes, beans and chick peas provide a lot of protien. Kidney beans contain more protein than meat and are very rich in vitamins.

Fresh Tomato Salsa

Brightly coloured and very fresh in flavour. A finely chopped jalapeño or other hot pepper could be added if you like it hot! Will keep for one day covered in refrigerator, but it will have much more liquid.

Seeded, diced Roma (plum) tomatoes	2 cups	500 mL
Finely diced red onion	1/4 cup	60 mL
Finely diced green pepper	1/4 cup	60 mL
Garlic cloves, minced	2	2
Salt	1/4 tsp.	1 mL
Freshly ground pepper, generous sprinkle		
Chopped fresh sweet basil (or 2 tsp., 10 mL, dried)	3 tbsp.	50 mL
Chopped fresh chives	1 tbsp.	15 mL
Red wine vinegar	1 tbsp.	15 mL
Chopped fresh cilantro (optional)	3 tbsp.	50 mL

Combine all 10 ingredients in medium bowl. Let stand at room temperature for at least 1 hour to blend flavours. Makes 2 1/2 cups (625 mL).

1 tbsp. (15 mL): 3 Calories; trace Total Fat (0 g Sat., 0 mg Cholesterol); 17 mg Sodium; trace Protein; 1 g Carbohydrate; trace Dietary Fibre

CHOICES: None

Pictured at right.

Variation: Substitute balsamic vinegar for red wine vinegar for a deeper taste.

1. Crispy Barbecue Chips, page 12
2. Piña Colada Smoothie, page 25
3. Black Bean And Corn Salsa, page 15
4. Spicy Mexi-Bean Dip, page 13
5. Fresh Tomato Salsa, above

Smoked Salmon Mousse

Spread on stoned wheat crackers or baguette slices.

Tomato juice	1/2 cup	125 mL
Envelope of unflavoured gelatin	1/4 oz.	7 g
Can of red salmon, drained, skin and round bones removed	7 1/2 oz.	213 g
Green onions, cut into 1 inch (2.5 cm) pieces	2	2
Non-fat creamed cottage cheese	3/4 cup	175 mL
Non-fat plain yogurt	1/2 cup	125 mL
Liquid smoke	1/8 tsp.	0.5 mL
Lemon juice	2 tsp.	10 mL
Freshly ground pepper, sprinkle		

Combine tomato juice and gelatin in small saucepan. Let stand for 5 minutes. Heat and stir on low until gelatin is dissolved. Set aside.

Process remaining 7 ingredients in food processor, scraping down sides as necessary, until smooth. Add gelatin mixture through chute. Mix well. Pour into lightly greased plastic-lined 2 1/2 cup (625 mL) mold or deep bowl. Cover with plastic wrap. Chill for several hours until firm. To serve, turn out and remove wrap. Makes 2 1/2 cups (625 mL).

1 tbsp. (15 mL): 13 Calories; 0.3 g Total Fat (0.1 g Sat., 1.9 mg Cholesterol); 45 mg Sodium; 2 g Protein; 1 g Carbohydrate; trace Dietary Fibre

CHOICES: None

1. Stuffed Grapevine Leaves, page 23
2. Sushi Layers, page 22
3. Salad Rolls, page 20
4. Fresh Yogurt Sauce, page 21
5. Peanut Sauce, page 20
6. Crab Appetizers, page 14

Salad Rolls

These are so good. Keep for up to two hours in refrigerator
under a damp paper towel and wrapped in plastic.

Water	1/3 cup	75 mL
Thick teriyaki sauce	2 tbsp.	30 mL
Low-sodium soy sauce	1 tbsp.	15 mL
Cornstarch	2 tsp.	10 mL
Fish sauce (optional), see Note	1/4 – 1/2 tsp.	1 – 2 mL
Shredded lettuce, lightly packed	2 cups	500 mL
Chopped fresh bean sprouts	1 cup	250 mL
Green onion, thinly sliced	1	1
Fresh sweet basil leaves, cut chiffonade (see Tip, page 135)	12	12
Fresh pea pods, chopped (optional)	1/3 cup	75 mL
Grated carrot	1/3 cup	75 mL
Chopped imitation crabmeat	3/4 cup	175 mL
Rice vermicelli	1 oz.	28 g
Hot water		
Rice paper wrappers (8 inch, 20 cm, size)	12	12
Warm water		
PEANUT SAUCE		
Light smooth peanut butter	1/2 cup	125 mL
Non-fat plain yogurt	1/2 cup	125 mL
Medium-hot curry paste (see Note)	1 1/2 tsp.	7 mL
Chili paste (optional)	1/4 tsp.	1 mL
Lime juice	1 1/2 tsp.	7 mL
Finely chopped peanuts, for garnish		

Combine first 5 ingredients in small saucepan. Heat and stir on medium until boiling and thickened. Cool thoroughly.

Combine next 7 ingredients in medium bowl. Set aside.

Break vermicelli into small pieces in small bowl. Cover with hot water. Let stand for 3 minutes until softened. Drain. Rinse with cold water. Drain thoroughly. Add to lettuce mixture. Toss.

(continued on next page)

Soak each rice wrapper in warm water in 9 inch (22 cm) pie plate for 2 minutes until soft. Place packed 1/3 cup (75 mL) lettuce mixture across one side of center, leaving 1 inch (2.5 cm) piece of wrapper on each side uncovered. Drizzle 2 tsp. (10 mL) sauce over filling. Fold sides of wrapper over filling. Roll tightly over filling. Press gently at seam to seal. Place on serving platter. Cover with damp paper towel to keep from drying out. Repeat with remaining wrappers and filling. Cut each roll in half crosswise to serve. Makes 12 rolls or 24 half rolls.

Peanut Sauce: Whisk all 6 ingredients together in small bowl until smooth. Let stand at room temperature for 10 minutes to blend flavours. Makes 1 cup (250 mL) sauce. Garnish with peanuts.

1 full roll with 2 tsp. (10 mL) sauce: 82 Calories; 2.5 g Total Fat (0.4 g Sat., 3.5 mg Cholesterol); 237 mg Sodium; 3 g Protein; 11 g Carbohydrate; trace Dietary Fibre

CHOICES: 1/2 Grains & Starches; 1/2 Fats

Pictured on page 18.

Note: Both fish sauce and curry paste are available in Asian section of grocery store.

Fresh Yogurt Sauce

Substitute Yogurt Cheese, page 75, for the yogurt and texture will be thicker—great for a dip or to serve on baked potatoes.

Grated English cucumber, with peel	1/2 cup	125 mL
Salt	1/4 tsp.	1 mL
Low-fat plain yogurt	1 cup	250 mL
Garlic clove, minced	1	1
Chopped fresh mint leaves (or parsley)	2 tbsp.	30 mL

Combine cucumber and salt in small bowl. Let stand for 10 minutes. Pour into sieve. Squeeze cucumber until most of liquid is gone. Return to bowl.

Add remaining 3 ingredients. Stir gently. Cover. Chill for 1 hour to blend flavours. Makes 1 1/2 cups (375 mL).

1 tbsp. (15 mL): 7 Calories; 0.2 g Total Fat (0.1 g Sat., 0.7 mg Cholesterol); 35 mg Sodium; 1 g Protein; 1 g Carbohydrate; trace Dietary Fibre

CHOICES: None

Pictured on page 18.

Sushi Layers

No bamboo mat or special technique required for these!
They cut well and are easy to hold in your hands.

Water	4 1/2 cups	1.1 L
Rice vinegar	1/3 cup	75 mL
Granulated sugar	1/4 cup	60 mL
Salt	1 tsp.	5 mL
Short grain (or pearl) rice	2 1/4 cups	550 mL
Rice wine (sake) or dry sherry	1/4 cup	60 mL
Medium lemons, sliced paper-thin and seeded	2	2
Small capers, drained and rinsed	1 tbsp.	15 mL
Package of paper-thin slices smoked salmon	3 oz.	85 g
Small cooked shrimp	8 oz.	225 g
Nori sheets	4	4
Thinly sliced cucumber, with peel (about 1/2 cucumber)	1 1/2 cups	375 mL
Sliced green onion	1/2 cup	125 mL
Coarsely grated carrot	1/2 cup	125 mL
Large red pepper, diced	1	1

Bring first 4 ingredients to a boil in medium saucepan. Stir in rice. Reduce heat. Cover. Simmer for 15 to 20 minutes until water is absorbed and rice is cooked. Stir in rice wine. Cool to room temperature. Makes about 8 cups (2 L) rice mixture.

Line 9 × 13 inch (22 × 33 cm) pan with plastic wrap. Arrange thin even layer of lemon slices in bottom of pan. Sprinkle with capers. Cover 1/2 of pan with smoked salmon and 1/2 with shrimp. Using wet hands, pack about 2 1/2 cups (625 mL) rice mixture in an even layer on top. Lay 2 sheets of nori, trimmed to fit in single layer, on rice.

Cover nori with cucumber and green onion. Pack 2 1/2 cups (625 mL) rice on top. Layer carrot and red pepper over rice. Cover with remaining rice. Lay 2 sheets of nori, trimmed to fit in single layer, on rice. Cover with plastic wrap directly on surface.

Set another 9 × 13 inch (22 × 33 cm) pan on sushi and press down firmly to compress layers evenly. Chill for 2 hours. Remove top plastic wrap. Invert sushi onto cutting surface. Remove remaining plastic wrap. Use sharp, wet, clean knife for each cut. Makes about sixty 1 1/2 inch (3.8 cm) squares.

1 square: 40 Calories; 0.2 g Total Fat (trace Sat., 7.6 mg Cholesterol); 85 mg Sodium; 2 g Protein; 8 g Carbohydrate; trace Dietary Fibre

CHOICES: 1/2 Grains & Starches

Pictured on page 18.

Stuffed Grapevine Leaves

The fragrance while they're baking will make you very impatient to taste them! These work well served warm as an appetizer. Serve with Fresh Yogurt Sauce, page 21.

Chopped onion	1 cup	250 mL
Garlic cloves, minced	2	2
Olive oil	2 tsp.	10 mL
Brown rice	1 1/3 cups	325 mL
Medium tomato, chopped	1	1
Water	2 3/4 cups	675 mL
Chicken bouillon powder	1 tsp.	5 mL
Freshly ground pepper, sprinkle		
Chopped fresh parsley	2 tbsp.	30 mL
Raisins, chopped	1/4 cup	60 mL
Pine nuts, toasted and chopped (see Tip, page 111)	1/4 cup	60 mL
Ground cinnamon	1/4 tsp.	1 mL
Jar of grapevine leaves, drained	17 oz.	473 mL
Water	1/2 cup	125 mL
Olive oil	1 tbsp.	15 mL
Lemon juice	2 tbsp.	30 mL

Sauté onion and garlic in olive oil in large non-stick frying pan until onion is soft. Add rice. Cook until rice is toasted. Turn into large saucepan.

Stir in next 8 ingredients. Bring to a boil. Cover. Cook for about 40 minutes until rice is tender. Makes 4 1/2 cups (1.1 L).

Prepare vine leaves by pinching off any stem ends. Using larger leaves, place about 2 rounded tablespoons (30 mL) filling on underside of leaf, near stem end. Roll up, tucking in sides to enclose filling. Repeat until rice mixture is used up. Use any leftover vine leaves to line greased 3 quart (3 L) casserole. Place rolls seam side down and very close to each other in 2 layers.

Combine remaining 3 ingredients in small cup. Drizzle over rolls. Cover tightly. Bake in 325°F (160°C) oven for 1 1/2 hours until leaves are very tender and all liquid is absorbed. Makes 28 appetizers.

1 appetizer: 60 Calories; 2 g Total Fat (0.3 g Sat., trace Cholesterol); 76 mg Sodium; 2 g Protein; 10 g Carbohydrate; 1 g Dietary Fibre

CHOICES: 1/2 Grains & Starches; 1/2 Fats

Pictured on page 18.

Hummus

Serve spread on torn fresh pita or as a thick dip for vegetables.

Garlic cloves	2	2
Toasted sesame seeds (see Tip, page 111)	4 tbsp.	60 mL
Ground cumin	1/4 tsp.	1 mL
Lemon pepper	1/4 tsp.	1 mL
Lemon juice	2 tbsp.	30 mL
Can of chick peas (garbanzo beans), drained, liquid reserved	19 oz.	540 mL
Reserved chick pea liquid, approximately	7 tbsp.	115 mL

Process garlic cloves, 3 tbsp. (50 mL) sesame seeds, cumin and lemon pepper in blender on high until garlic and sesame seeds are smooth. Add enough lemon juice to make thick paste.

Add chick peas and 3 tbsp. (50 mL) chick pea liquid. Blend with pulsing motion, scraping down sides as necessary, until mixture is puréed. Add approximately 4 tbsp. (60 mL) liquid from chick peas to thin dip to desired consistency. Turn into serving bowl. Sprinkle remaining 1 tbsp. (15 mL) sesame seeds on top. Makes 2 cups (500 mL).

2 tbsp. (30 mL): 54 Calories; 1.5 g Total Fat (0.1 g Sat., 0 mg Cholesterol); 99 mg Sodium; 2 g Protein; 8 g Carbohydrate; 2 g Dietary Fibre

CHOICES: 1/2 Grains & Starches

Sangria Refresher

Garnish this fruity punch with slices of orange and lime.

Medium lime, very thinly sliced, seeded	1	1
Medium lemon, very thinly sliced, seeded	1	1
Medium oranges, very thinly sliced, seeded	2	2
Chopped fresh mint leaves (optional)	1/4 cup	60 mL
Red grape juice	1 qt.	1 L
Sugar-free ginger ale	1 qt.	1 L

Place first 4 ingredients in 2 quart (2 L) pitcher. Pour in grape juice. Chill for several hours or overnight to blend flavours.

Strain juice into large pitcher. Add ginger ale to taste. Makes 8 cups (2 L).

1/2 cup (125 mL): 48 Calories; 0.1 g Total Fat (trace Sat., 0 mg Cholesterol); 6 mg Sodium; trace Protein; 12 g Carbohydrate; trace Dietary Fibre

CHOICES: 1 Fruits

Lemonberry Smoothie

A very refreshing snack. Sip it through a straw and maybe it will last longer!

Non-fat vanilla yogurt	1 cup	250 mL
Skim milk	1/4 cup	60 mL
Frozen concentrated lemonade	3 tbsp.	50 mL
Icing (confectioner's) sugar	2 tsp.	10 mL
(or sugar substitute, such		
as Sugar Twin, to taste)		
Frozen large whole strawberries	6	6

Place first 4 ingredients in blender. Process on high, adding strawberries, 1 at a time, through lid until thick. Process, scraping down sides as necessary, until smooth. Makes 2 1/2 cups (625 mL).

3/4 cup (175 mL): 110 Calories; 0.2 g Total Fat (0.1 g Sat., 1.8 mg Cholesterol); 67 mg Sodium; 5 g Protein; 23 g Carbohydrate; 1 g Dietary Fibre

CHOICES: 1 Fruits; 1/2 Milk & Alternatives

Pictured on page 71.

Piña Colada Smoothie

Has the colour, flavour and texture of the real thing. Garnish with a slice of starfruit.

Can of crushed pineapple, with juice, chilled	14 oz.	398 mL
Coconut flavouring	1/2 tsp.	2 mL
Skim milk powder	2 tbsp.	30 mL
Non-fat vanilla yogurt	1 cup	250 mL
Ice cubes	6	6

Place first 4 ingredients in blender. Process on high, adding ice cubes, 1 at a time, through lid. As mixture becomes thick, use pulsing motion, scraping down sides occasionally, until smooth. Makes 4 cups (1 L).

3/4 cup (175 mL): 82 Calories; 0.1 g Total Fat (0.1 g Sat., 1.5 mg Cholesterol); 51 mg Sodium; 4 g Protein; 17 g Carbohydrate; 1 g Dietary Fibre

CHOICES: 1 Fruits

Pictured on page 17.

Pink Grapefruit Refresher

*So refreshing! It will leave you wanting more. To serve as palate
cleanser between courses, scrape from pan with an ice cream
scoop and serve 3 balls per person in a tall glass.*

Zest and juice from 3 medium oranges		
Zest and juice from 1 medium lemon		
Liquid honey	3 tbsp.	50 mL
Orange liqueur (optional)	1/4 cup	60 mL
Water	1/4 cup	60 mL
Large pink grapefruits	5	5
Sugar-free lemon-lime soft drink	3 cups	750 mL
Orange liqueur	1/4 cup	60 mL
Sugar-free lemon-lime soft drink, to taste		

Remove zest from oranges and lemon with vegetable peeler. Cut into long, thin
slivers. Place in small saucepan. Add both juices and next 3 ingredients. Bring to
a boil. Reduce heat to medium. Boil for 25 minutes until mixture is thickened
and syrupy. Strain. Discard zest and pulp. Reserve syrup.

Halve and section grapefruits, discarding any seeds. Place sections in 9 x 13 inch
(22 x 33 cm) glass baking pan. Scrape any remaining fruit from peel. Squeeze each
half gently to drain any juices into pan. Add reserved syrup, soft drink and second
amount of liqueur. Stir. Cover. Freeze for 2 hours. Break up with fork. Process in
food processor or blender until smooth. Freeze. Makes 9 1/4 cups (2.3 L).

To serve, scoop about 1/2 cup (125 mL) into tall glass and fill with sugar-free
lemon-lime soft drink.

*1/2 cup (125 mL) without soft drink: 53 Calories; 0.1 g Total Fat (trace Sat., 0 mg Cholesterol);
3 mg Sodium; 1 g Protein; 12 g Carbohydrate; trace Dietary Fibre*

CHOICES: 1/2 Fruits

Paré Pointer
A robot's favourite party snack is assorted nuts.

Appetizers & Beverages

Cloverleaf Honey Rolls

Good, wholesome buns.

Skim milk	1 1/3 cups	325 mL
Hard margarine	1/3 cup	75 mL
Liquid honey	1/4 cup	60 mL
Salt	1 tsp.	5 mL
Whole wheat flour	2 cups	500 mL
All-purpose flour	1 cup	250 mL
Packages of instant yeast (1/4 oz., 8 g, each), or 4 1/2 tsp., (22 mL), bulk	2	2
Frozen egg product, thawed (see Note)	6 tbsp.	100 mL
All-purpose flour	2 cups	500 mL

Heat first 4 ingredients in small saucepan until margarine is melted and mixture is very warm but not hot.

Combine first 3 ingredients in large bowl. Add wet ingredients. Beat well. Add egg product. Beat.

Add all-purpose flour, 1 cup (250 mL) at a time. Work in by mixing and kneading until soft dough is formed. Turn out and knead on floured surface for 5 to 10 minutes until dough is smooth and elastic. Place in greased bowl, turning once to coat top. Cover with tea towel. Let rise in oven with light on and door closed for 1 hour until doubled in size. Punch down. Divide dough into 4 equal portions. Work with 1 portion at a time, keeping remainder covered. Shape into long roll. Cut into 9 pieces. Cut piece into 3 smaller pieces. Roll into small balls. Place 3 balls in each greased muffin cup. Repeat with remaining portions. Cover with tea towel. Let rise in oven with light on and door closed for 60 minutes until doubled in size. Bake in 400°F (205°C) oven for 10 minutes until golden brown. Makes 3 dozen rolls.

1 roll: 94 Calories; 2.1 g Total Fat (0.4 g Sat., 0.2 mg Cholesterol); 109 mg Sodium; 3 g Protein; 16 g Carbohydrate; 1 g Dietary Fibre

CHOICES: 1 Grains & Starches; 1/2 Fats

Note: 3 tbsp. (50 mL) = 1 large egg

 tip

Sugar in breads acts as food for the yeast to help produce carbon dioxide, which makes the dough rise. Sugar is also used for flavour and helps the crust brown. Honey or molasses may also be used in the recipe for the same effects.

Grain Bread

This loaf is very high in fibre but still light in texture.

Large eggs	2	2
Brown sugar, packed	1/4 cup	60 mL
Fancy (mild) molasses	2 tbsp.	30 mL
Canola oil	1/2 cup	125 mL
1% buttermilk	1 qt.	1 L
Rolled oats (not instant)	1 1/2 cups	375 mL
Light rye flour	1 cup	250 mL
Natural oat bran	1/2 cup	125 mL
Packages of instant yeast (1/4 oz., 8 g, each) or 4 1/2 tsp. (22 mL) bulk	2	2
Whole wheat flour	6 1/4 cups	1.5 L

Beat first 4 ingredients in large bowl.

Heat buttermilk in medium saucepan until very warm, but not hot. Whisk or beat into egg mixture until well-blended. Mixture should still be very warm.

Combine next 4 ingredients in small bowl. Mix into buttermilk mixture until smooth. Let stand for 15 minutes.

Work or knead in enough whole wheat flour to make a sticky dough that keeps its form. Shape into 2 loaves. Place in greased 9 x 5 x 3 inch (22 x 12.5 x 7.5 cm) bread pan. Punch dough to fill in corners. Cover with greased waxed paper. Let rise in oven with door closed and light on for about 30 minutes until doubled in size. Bake in 350°F (175°C) oven for 40 minutes until hollow-sounding when tapped. Makes 2 loaves, for a total of 24 slices.

1 slice: 236 Calories; 6.8 g Total Fat (0.9 g Sat., 19.5 mg Cholesterol); 54 mg Sodium; 8 g Protein; 38 g Carbohydrate; 6 g Dietary Fibre

CHOICES: 2 Grains & Starches; 1 Fats

Pictured on page 35.

GRAIN BUNS: Shape dough into 24 buns. Place in greased 9 x 13 inch (22 x 33 cm) pan. Cover with greased waxed paper. Let rise in oven with light on and door closed for approximately 1 hour until doubled in size. Bake in 350°F (175°C) oven for 20 minutes until hollow-sounding when tapped. Makes 24 buns.

Breads & Muffins

Honey Wheat Bread

A slice of this bread is all you need for breakfast.

Very hot water	1 cup	250 mL
Liquid honey	1/4 cup	60 mL
Canola oil	2 tbsp.	30 mL
Salt	1 tsp.	5 mL
Large egg, fork-beaten	1	1
All-purpose flour	2 cups	500 mL
Package of instant yeast (or 2 1/4 tsp., 11 mL, bulk)	1/4 oz.	8 g
Whole wheat flour	1 1/4 cups	300 mL
Chopped mixed dried fruit (or raisins)	1/2 cup	125 mL

Combine first 4 ingredients in small bowl.

Put egg into large bowl. Slowly add hot water mixture, whisking until frothy.

Combine all-purpose flour and yeast in small bowl. Add to liquids. Mix well until smooth.

Slowly add whole wheat flour. Mix until soft dough is formed. Add more or less flour, as required, until soft but not too sticky.

Turn out and knead on floured surface for 10 minutes, adding dried fruit gradually, until smooth and elastic. Place in greased bowl, turning once to coat top. Cover with tea towel. Let rise in oven with light on and door closed for 1 1/2 hours until doubled in bulk. Punch down. Shape into loaf. Place in greased 9 x 5 x 3 inch (22 x 12.5 x 7.5 cm) loaf pan. Cover. Let rise until almost doubled in size. Bake in 350°F (175°C) oven for 40 to 45 minutes until hollow-sounding when tapped. If top browns too quickly, cover with foil or brown paper for last 10 minutes of baking time. Makes 1 loaf, enough for 12 slices.

1 slice: 195 Calories; 3.2 g Total Fat (0.4 g Sat., 18.0 mg Cholesterol); 234 mg Sodium; 5 g Protein; 38 g Carbohydrate; 3 g Dietary Fibre

CHOICES: 2 Grains & Starches; 1/2 Other Choices; 1/2 Fats

Pictured on page 35.

 tip To test the yeast for freshness, sprinkle some over warm water that has a little sugar in it. If the solution foams and bubbles, it's still active. If not, replace with new yeast.

Cinnaraisin Nut Bread

Good grain and nut flavour in these dark loaves.

Large egg	1	1
Canola oil	1 tbsp.	15 mL
Brown sugar, packed	1/2 cup	125 mL
Salt	1 tsp.	5 mL
Ground cinnamon	1 tsp.	5 mL
Skim milk	2 cups	500 mL
Package of instant yeast (or 2 1/4 tsp., 11 mL, bulk)	1/4 oz.	8 g
Whole wheat flour	1 cup	250 mL
Natural oat bran	1/2 cup	125 mL
Finely chopped toasted pecans (see Tip, page 111)	2/3 cup	150 mL
Raisins	1 cup	250 mL
All-purpose flour	3 3/4 cups	925 mL

Whisk first 5 ingredients together in small bowl.

Heat milk in small saucepan until very warm. Whisk into egg mixture.

Combine next 4 ingredients in large bowl. Add milk mixture. Whisk until smooth. Stir in raisins. Slowly work in enough all-purpose flour until dough leaves sides of bowl and is no longer sticky. Turn out and knead on lightly floured surface for about 5 minutes until smooth and elastic. Place dough in greased bowl, turning once to coat top. Cover with tea towel. Let rise in oven with light on and door closed for about 1 hour until doubled in bulk. Punch down. Knead 8 to 10 times to remove air bubbles. Shape into 2 loaves. Place in 2 greased 9 x 5 x 3 inch (22 x 12.5 x 7.5 cm) loaf pans. Cover. Let rise until doubled in size. Bake in 375°F (190°C) oven for 35 to 40 minutes until hollow-sounding when tapped. Makes 2 loaves, for a total of 24 slices.

1 slice: 176 Calories; 3.7 g Total Fat (0.4 g Sat., 9.4 mg Cholesterol); 130 mg Sodium; 5 g Protein; 33 g Carbohydrate; 2 g Dietary Fibre

CHOICES: 1 1/2 Grains & Starches; 1/2 Fats

Pictured on page 35.

Cranberry Streusel Muffins

Use orange pulp in the juice measurement for added flavour.
Moist, tender and pretty—besides being very, very good!

All-purpose flour	2 cups	500 mL
Granulated sugar	1/2 cup	125 mL
Baking powder	1 tbsp.	15 mL
Salt	1/2 tsp.	2 mL
Egg whites (large)	4	4
Hard margarine, melted	3 tbsp.	50 mL
Freshly squeezed orange juice	1 cup	250 mL
(pulp, optional)		
Grated orange zest	2 tsp.	10 mL
Chopped dried cranberries	2/3 cup	150 mL
STREUSEL TOPPING		
All-purpose flour	1/4 cup	60 mL
Brown sugar, packed	1 tbsp.	15 mL
Hard margarine	1 tbsp.	15 mL

Combine first 4 ingredients in medium bowl. Make a well in center.

Beat next 4 ingredients in small bowl until combined. Stir in cranberries. Pour into well. Stir just until moistened. Spray muffin cups with no-stick cooking spray. Fill cups 3/4 full.

Streusel Topping: Combine flour and brown sugar in small bowl. Cut in margarine until mixture is crumbly. Sprinkle 1/2 tbsp. (7 mL) over each muffin. Bake in 425°F (220°C) oven for 10 to 15 minutes until just firm. Do not overbake. Cool in pan for 5 minutes before turning out. Makes 12 muffins.

1 muffin: 190 Calories; 4 g Total Fat (0.8 g Sat., 0 mg Cholesterol); 179 mg Sodium; 4 g Protein; 35 g Carbohydrate; 2 g Dietary Fibre

CHOICES: 1 Grains & Starches; 1/2 Fruits; 1/2 Other Choices; 1 Fats

Pictured on page 35.

tip   The recipes in this cookbook use large eggs (when stated in the ingredients). If extra large eggs are used in breads, the liquid content will be higher which will cause the texture to be heavier; the extra liquid in cakes may cause them to fall when cooled.

Chili 'N' Cheese Corn Muffins

So good with soup. Chilies and chili powder give a spicy aftertaste.

Yellow cornmeal	3/4 cup	175 mL
1% buttermilk	1 cup	250 mL
Large eggs, fork-beaten	2	2
Can of diced green chilies, with liquid	4 oz.	113 g
Canola oil	1 1/2 tbsp.	25 mL
All-purpose flour	1 1/2 cups	375 mL
Baking powder	1 tbsp.	15 mL
Salt	1/2 tsp.	2 mL
Brown sugar, packed	2 tbsp.	30 mL
Chili powder	1/4 – 1/2 tsp.	1 – 2 mL
Grated light sharp Cheddar cheese	3/4 cup	175 mL

Combine first 5 ingredients in small bowl. Let stand for 15 minutes.

Combine remaining 6 ingredients in large bowl. Make a well in center. Pour cornmeal mixture into well. Stir just until moistened. Spray muffin cups with no-stick cooking spray. Fill cups 3/4 full. Bake in 375°F (190°C) oven for 20 minutes until wooden pick inserted in center of muffin comes out clean. Cool in pan for 5 minutes before turning out. Makes 12 muffins.

1 muffin: 166 Calories; 4.6 g Total Fat (1.5 g Sat., 41.2 mg Cholesterol); 311 mg Sodium; 6 g Protein; 24 g Carbohydrate; 1 g Dietary Fibre

CHOICES: 1 Grains & Starches; 1/2 Meat & Alternatives; 1 Fats

Pictured on page 35.

Orange Date Muffins

Great orange aroma and flavour. Bits of dates and raisins give sweetness.

All-purpose flour	1 1/2 cups	375 mL
Brown sugar, packed	2 tbsp.	30 mL
Baking soda	1 tsp.	5 mL
Baking powder	1 tsp.	5 mL
Salt	1/4 tsp.	1 mL
Medium orange, with peel, cut into 8 pieces	1	1
Light raisins (optional)	1/4 cup	60 mL
Chopped dates	1/4 cup	60 mL
1% buttermilk	2/3 cup	150 mL
Canola oil	3 tbsp.	50 mL
Frozen egg product, thawed (see Note)	6 tbsp.	100 mL

(continued on next page)

Combine first 5 ingredients in medium bowl. Make a well in center.

Combine remaining 6 ingredients in blender. Process until orange, raisins and dates are well-chopped. Pour into well. Stir just until moistened. Spray muffin cups with no-stick cooking spray. Fill cups 3/4 full. Bake in 400°F (205°C) oven for 18 to 20 minutes until wooden pick inserted in center of muffin comes out clean. Cool in pan for 5 minutes before turning out. Makes 12 muffins.

1 muffin: 135 Calories; 3.9 g Total Fat (0.4 g Sat., 0.5 mg Cholesterol); 209 mg Sodium; 4 g Protein; 23 g Carbohydrate; 2 g Dietary Fibre

CHOICES: 1 Grains & Starches; 1/2 Fruits; 1 Fats

Pictured on page 35.

Note: 3 tbsp. (50 mL) = 1 large egg

Carrot Pineapple Muffins

A very moist muffin with a definite pineapple flavour.

All-purpose flour	1 1/3 cups	325 mL
Quick-cooking rolled oats (not instant)	1 cup	250 mL
Brown sugar, packed	1/2 cup	125 mL
Baking powder	1 1/2 tbsp.	25 mL
Ground cinnamon	1/2 tsp.	2 mL
Salt	1/4 tsp.	1 mL
Ground nutmeg	1/8 tsp.	0.5 mL
Frozen egg product, thawed (see Note)	1/4 cup	60 mL
Canola oil	1/4 cup	60 mL
Non-fat vanilla yogurt	1/2 cup	125 mL
Canned crushed pineapple, well-drained	1 cup	250 mL
Grated carrot	1/2 cup	125 mL

Combine first 7 ingredients in large bowl. Make a well in center.

Combine remaining 5 ingredients in small bowl. Pour into well. Stir just until moistened. Spray muffin cups with no-stick cooking spray. Fill cups 3/4 full. Bake in 400°F (205°C) oven for 20 minutes until wooden pick inserted in center of muffin comes out clean. Cool in pan for 5 minutes before turning out. Makes 12 muffins.

1 muffin: 182 Calories; 5.6 g Total Fat (0.5 g Sat., 0.2 mg Cholesterol); 86 mg Sodium; 4 g Protein; 30 g Carbohydrate; 2 g Dietary Fibre

CHOICES: 1 Grains & Starches; 1/2 Other Choices; 1 Fats

Note: 3 tbsp. (50 mL) = 1 large egg

Cornbread Muffins

The bits of corn give off a touch of sweetness. Makes a big batch.
These freeze well and can be warmed for lunch.

Yellow cornmeal	1 1/2 cups	375 mL
1% buttermilk	1 1/3 cups	325 mL
All-purpose flour	3 cups	750 mL
Brown sugar, packed	1/4 cup	60 mL
Baking powder	2 tbsp.	30 mL
Salt	1 tsp.	5 mL
Frozen egg product, thawed (see Note)	1 cup	250 mL
Canola oil	1/3 cup	75 mL
Can of cream-style corn	14 oz.	398 mL

Combine cornmeal and buttermilk in medium bowl. Let stand for 15 minutes.

Combine next 4 ingredients in large bowl. Make a well in center.

Combine remaining 3 ingredients in small bowl. Add to cornmeal mixture. Mix well. Pour into well. Stir just until moistened. Spray muffin cups with no-stick cooking spray. Fill cups 3/4 full. Bake in 375°F (190°C) oven for 15 to 17 minutes until wooden pick inserted in center of muffin comes out clean. Cool in pan for 5 minutes before turning out. Makes 24 muffins.

1 muffin: 157 Calories; 3.8 g Total Fat (0.4 g Sat., 0.5 mg Cholesterol); 205 mg Sodium; 4 g Protein; 27 g Carbohydrate; 1 g Dietary Fibre

CHOICES: 1 1/2 Grains & Starches; 1 Fats

Note: 3 tbsp. (50 mL) = 1 large egg

1. Honey Wheat Bread, page 29
2. Cinnaraisin Nut Bread, page 30
3. Grain Bread, page 28
4. Chili 'N' Cheese Corn Muffins, page 32
5. Pumpkin Raisin Muffins, page 38
6. Cranberry Streusel Muffins, page 31
7. Orange Date Muffins, page 32
8. Onion Cheese Biscuits, page 39

Oatmeal Apple Muffins

Nice texture with bits of apple. A good breakfast or snack.

Whole wheat flour	1 1/4 cups	300 mL
Quick-cooking rolled oats (not instant)	1 cup	250 mL
Brown sugar, packed	1/3 cup	75 mL
Baking powder	2 1/2 tsp.	12 mL
Baking soda	1/4 tsp.	1 mL
Salt	1/4 tsp.	1 mL
Ground nutmeg	1/4 tsp.	1 mL
Ground cinnamon	1/4 tsp.	1 mL
1% buttermilk	1 cup	250 mL
Large egg, fork-beaten	1	1
Canola oil	2 tbsp.	30 mL
Medium apple, peeled and diced	1	1

Combine first 8 ingredients in large bowl. Make a well in center.

Combine next 3 ingredients in small bowl. Pour into well. Add apple. Stir just until moistened. Spray muffin cups with no-stick cooking spray. Fill cups 1/2 full. Bake in 375°F (190°C) oven for 15 to 18 minutes until wooden pick inserted in center of muffin comes out clean. Cool in pan for 5 minutes before turning out. Makes 12 muffins.

1 muffin: 139 Calories; 3.7 g Total Fat (0.6 g Sat., 18.7 mg Cholesterol); 119 mg Sodium; 4 g Protein; 24 g Carbohydrate; 3 g Dietary Fibre

CHOICES: 1 Grains & Starches; 1/2 Fats

1. Apple Clafouti, page 44
2. G'Morning Pizza, page 40
3. Morning Burritos, page 45

Props courtesy of: The Bay

Pumpkin Raisin Muffins

Raisins in every bite in these spiced muffins.

All-purpose flour	1 cup	250 mL
Whole wheat flour	3/4 cup	175 mL
Natural oat bran	1/4 cup	60 mL
Brown sugar, packed	1/2 cup	125 mL
Baking soda	1 1/2 tsp.	7 mL
Baking powder	1 tsp.	5 mL
Ground cinnamon	1 tsp.	5 mL
Ground nutmeg	1/2 tsp.	2 mL
Ground allspice	1/4 tsp.	1 mL
Salt	1/4 tsp.	1 mL
Can of pumpkin (without spices)	14 oz.	398 mL
Large egg, fork-beaten	1	1
Skim milk	1 cup	250 mL
Canola oil	2 tbsp.	30 mL
Grated lemon zest	1 tsp.	5 mL
Raisins	1 cup	250 mL

Combine first 10 ingredients in large bowl. Make a well in center.

Beat together next 5 ingredients in medium bowl until smooth. Pour into well. Stir until barely combined Add raisins. Stir just until moistened. Spray muffin cups with no-stick cooking spray. Fill cups 3/4 full. Bake in 400°F (205°C) oven for 20 minutes until wooden pick inserted in center of muffin comes out clean. Cool in pan for 5 minutes before turning out. Makes 12 muffins.

1 muffin: 194 Calories; 3.4 g Total Fat (0.5 g Sat., 18.4 mg Cholesterol); 196 mg Sodium; 5 g Protein; 39 g Carbohydrate; 3 g Dietary Fibre

CHOICES: 1 Grains & Starches; 1/2 Fruits; 1/2 Vegetable; 1/2 Other Choices; 1 Fats

Pictured on page 35.

Onion Cheese Biscuits

Delicious warm with soup or salad, or just some fresh fruit.

All-purpose flour	1 cup	250 mL
Whole wheat flour	1 cup	250 mL
Baking powder	2 tsp.	10 mL
Baking soda	1/2 tsp.	2 mL
Grated light sharp Cheddar cheese	1 cup	250 mL
Dill weed	1 tsp.	5 mL
Salt	1/4 tsp.	1 mL
Freshly ground pepper	1/8 tsp.	0.5 mL
Non-fat plain yogurt	3/4 cup	175 mL
Skim milk	1/2 cup	125 mL
Canola oil	2 tbsp.	30 mL
Green onions, chopped	4	4

Combine first 8 ingredients in large bowl.

Combine remaining 4 ingredients in small bowl. Add to flour mixture. Stir just until moistened. Drop by large spoonfuls onto greased baking sheet. Bake in center of 400°F (205°C) oven for 12 to 15 minutes until golden brown. Makes 12 biscuits.

1 biscuit: 140 Calories; 4.6 g Total Fat (1.5 g Sat., 6.5 mg Cholesterol); 199 mg Sodium; 6 g Protein; 18 g Carbohydrate; 2 g Dietary Fibre

CHOICES: 1 Grains & Starches; 1/2 Fats

Pictured on page 35.

Paré Pointer

What's the difference between the law and a glacier?
The law is justice, while a glacier is just ice.

G' Morning Pizza

A nice brunch for the whole family.

All-purpose flour	1 cup	250 mL
Whole wheat flour	1/2 cup	125 mL
Instant yeast	1 1/2 tsp.	7 mL
Grated light Parmesan cheese	1 tbsp.	15 mL
Dried sweet basil	1/2 tsp.	2 mL
Dried whole oregano	1/4 tsp.	1 mL
Salt	1/2 tsp.	2 mL
Very warm water	2/3 cup	150 mL
Canola oil	2 tsp.	10 mL
Large hard-boiled eggs, peeled	6	6
Light cream cheese	4 oz.	125 g
Parsley flakes	1/2 tsp.	2 mL
Dried sweet basil	1/2 tsp.	2 mL
Garlic powder	1/16 tsp.	0.5 mL
Fat-free ham slices, diced	2/3 cup	150 mL
Grated part-skim mozzarella cheese	1 cup	250 mL
Thinly sliced red onion	1/2 cup	125 mL
Thinly sliced green and red peppers	2/3 cup	150 mL
Dried sweet basil, sprinkle (optional)		
Dried whole oregano, sprinkle (optional)		

Combine first 7 ingredients in food processor or medium bowl.

Combine water and canola oil in small bowl. Add through chute while processing until dough forms ball (or if mixing in bowl, stir in water and canola oil until dough leaves sides of bowl). Turn out and knead for 3 to 4 minutes until smooth. Cover. Let stand for 15 minutes. Press lightly in greased 12 inch (30 cm) pizza pan. Form raised rim around edge. Bake in 425°F (220°C) oven for 8 minutes, poking any bubbles with fork.

Discard 4 yolks. Chop remaining egg whites and 2 whole eggs.

Combine next 4 ingredients in small bowl. Spread onto hot crust. Layer with eggs and next 4 ingredients, in order. Sprinkle with basil and oregano. Bake in center of 425°F (220°C) oven for 8 to 10 minutes until cheese is melted and crust is browned. Cuts into 8 wedges.

1 wedge: 215 Calories; 8 g Total Fat (2.9 g Sat., 66.4 mg Cholesterol); 648 mg Sodium; 13 g Protein; 23 g Carbohydrate; 2 g Dietary Fibre

CHOICES: 1 Grains & Starches; 1 Meat & Alternatives; 1 Fats

Pictured on page 36.

Ham 'N' Apple Strata

Golden crisp topping with layers of ham, apple and bread.

Whole wheat bread slices, crusts removed	8	8
Fat-free ham slices	4 1/2 oz.	125 g
Large apple, cored and cut into thin wedges	1	1
Grated light sharp Cheddar cheese	1/2 cup	125 mL
Carton of frozen egg product, thawed (see Note)	8 oz.	227 mL
Egg whites (large)	4	4
Skim evaporated milk	1 cup	250 mL
Water	1/2 cup	125 mL
Seasoned salt	1/2 tsp.	2 mL
Hot pepper sauce	1/4 tsp.	1 mL
Corn flakes cereal	1 cup	250 mL
Margarine, melted	1 tbsp.	15 mL
Grated light sharp Cheddar cheese	1/2 cup	125 mL

Place 4 slices of bread in greased shallow 2 quart (2 L) casserole or 9 x 9 inch (22 x 22 cm) pan. Layer bread with next 3 ingredients, in order. Cover with remaining 4 bread slices.

Beat next 6 ingredients together. Slowly pour onto bread slices. Cover tightly with plastic wrap. Chill overnight.

Crush cereal in small bowl. Add margarine and second amount of cheese. Stir. Sprinkle over strata. Bake, uncovered, in 350°F (175°C) oven for 50 to 55 minutes until set and top is golden brown. Let stand for 15 minutes before cutting. Cuts into 4 pieces.

1 piece: 412 Calories; 10.8 g Total Fat (4.7 g Sat., 22 mg Cholesterol); 1367 mg Sodium; 32 g Protein; 49 g Carbohydrate; 4 g Dietary Fibre

CHOICES: 2 Grains & Starches; 1/2 Milk & Alternatives; 3 Meat & Alternatives; 1/2 Fats

Note: 3 tbsp. (50 mL) = 1 large egg

Grated light sharp Cheddar cheese provides a big hit of flavour without all the fat of regular Cheddar cheese. Try other light cheeses on the market to find great taste that's not heavy on fat grams.

Baked Omelette Puff

Layered look when cut. Removes easily in wedges.

Margarine	1 tsp.	5 mL
Finely diced red pepper	1/4 cup	60 mL
Sliced green onion	1/4 cup	60 mL
Diced zucchini, with peel	1/2 cup	125 mL
Sliced fresh mushrooms	1/2 cup	125 mL
Salt	1/2 tsp.	2 mL
Freshly ground pepper, generous sprinkle		
Egg yolks (large)	4	4
Egg whites (large)	8	8
Grated light sharp Cheddar cheese	1/2 cup	125 mL
Paprika, sprinkle		

Heat margarine in medium non-stick frying pan until bubbling. Add next 4 ingredients. Stir. Cook on medium-high until liquid has evaporated. Stir in salt and pepper. Cool to room temperature.

Beat egg yolks in small bowl until thick and lemon-coloured. Stir into vegetables.

Beat egg whites with clean beaters in large bowl until soft peaks form. Gently fold in vegetable mixture and cheese. Pour into well-greased 10 inch (25 cm) glass pie plate or 2 quart (2 L) casserole. Sprinkle with paprika. Bake in 350°F (175°C) oven for about 25 minutes until knife inserted in center comes out clean. Cuts into 8 wedges.

1 wedge: 77 Calories; 4.5 g Total Fat (2.4 g Sat., 149.6 mg Cholesterol); 283 mg Sodium; 7 g Protein; 2 g Carbohydrate; trace Dietary Fibre

CHOICES: 1 Meat & Alternatives; 1 Fats

Hot Wheat Berry Pudding

Satisfies your chewy cravings with nice sweetness.

Wheat berries (unprocessed wheat kernels)	1 1/4 cups	300 mL
Water	4 1/4 cups	1 L
Mixed dried fruit, with raisins, chopped if large	1 cup	250 mL
Long thread (or flake) coconut	1/3 cup	75 mL
Coarsely chopped almonds	1/4 cup	60 mL
Brown sugar, packed	3 tbsp.	50 mL
Non-fat vanilla yogurt	2 cups	500 mL

(continued on next page)

Cook wheat berries in water in large saucepan for 1 1/4 hours until tender but still quite chewy.

Stir in next 4 ingredients. Let stand for 5 minutes. Makes 5 cups (1.25 L) cooked wheat mixture. Add 1/4 cup (60 mL) yogurt to individual servings. Stir. Serves 8.

1 serving: 254 Calories; 5.4 g Total Fat (2.6 g Sat., 1.2 mg Cholesterol); 53 mg Sodium; 9 g Protein; 47 g Carbohydrate; 5 g Dietary Fibre

CHOICES: 1 Grains & Starches; 1 Fruits; 1/2 Milk & Alternatives; 1 Fats

Buttermilk Pancakes

Serve with Blueberry Sauce or Danish Cream Topping, page 46, for a special treat.

Whole wheat flour	3/4 cup	175 mL
All-purpose flour	3/4 cup	175 mL
Brown sugar, packed	2 tbsp.	30 mL
Baking powder	1 tbsp.	15 mL
Baking soda	1/2 tsp.	2 mL
Salt	1/4 tsp.	1 mL
1% buttermilk	1 1/2 cups	375 mL
Egg yolks (large)	2	2
Canola oil	3 tbsp.	50 mL
Egg whites (large)	2	2

Combine first 6 ingredients in medium bowl.

Whisk next 3 ingredients in small bowl. Add to dry ingredients. Stir just until moistened. Batter will be lumpy.

Beat egg whites in small bowl until stiff. Fold into batter. Pour batter into non-stick frying pan. Cook on medium-low for 3 to 5 minutes per side until golden brown. Makes 12 pancakes.

1 pancake: 123 Calories; 4.8 g Total Fat (0.7 g Sat., 37.1 mg Cholesterol); 164 mg Sodium; 4 g Protein; 16 g Carbohydrate; 1 g Dietary Fibre

CHOICES: 1 Grains & Starches; 1/2 Fats

Apple Clafouti

Custard consistency with crunchy apples.

Large cooking apple (such as McIntosh), peeled, cored and cut into thin wedges	1	1
Light raisins	1/4 cup	60 mL
Brown sugar, packed	2 tbsp.	30 mL
Ground cinnamon	1/4 tsp.	1 mL
Skim milk	1 1/4 cups	300 mL
Canola oil	1 tbsp.	15 mL
Frozen egg product, thawed (see Note)	1/2 cup	125 mL
Vanilla	1 tsp.	5 mL
Whole wheat flour	1/3 cup	75 mL
All-purpose flour	1/3 cup	75 mL
Granulated sugar	1/4 cup	60 mL
Ground cinnamon	1/4 tsp.	1 mL

Overlap apple wedges in circle in bottom of well-greased 9 inch (22 cm) glass pie plate. Sprinkle with next 3 ingredients.

Beat next 4 ingredients in medium bowl. Add remaining 4 ingredients. Beat until smooth. Pour batter evenly over apple. Bake in center of 375°F (190°C) oven for 40 minutes until set and golden brown. Cuts into 6 wedges.

1 wedge: 187 Calories; 2.8 g Total Fat (0.3 g Sat., 1.0 mg Cholesterol); 71 mg Sodium; 6 g Protein; 36 g Carbohydrate; 2 g Dietary Fibre

CHOICES: 1 Grains & Starches; 1/2 Fruits; 1/2 Other Choices; 1/2 Meat & Alternatives

Pictured on page 36.

Note: 3 tbsp. (50 mL) = 1 large egg

 To plump raisins or other dried fruit, cover with boiling water. Let stand for one minute, then drain.

Morning Burritos

Makes a great breakfast for the whole family. Serve with fresh fruit.

Chopped green onion	1/4 cup	60 mL
Margarine	2 tsp.	10 mL
Frozen egg product, thawed (see Note)	1 cup	250 mL
Chili powder	1/4 tsp.	1 mL
Salt	1/4 tsp.	1 mL
Chopped pickled hot peppers	2 tbsp.	30 mL
Grated light sharp Cheddar cheese	3/4 cup	175 mL
Whole wheat flour tortillas (10 inch, 25 cm, size), warmed	4	4
Salsa (optional)	2 tbsp.	30 mL
Light sour cream (optional)	2 tbsp.	30 mL

Sauté green onion in margarine in large non-stick frying pan for 30 seconds. Pour in egg product. Sprinkle with chili powder and salt. Heat, stirring occasionally, on medium until egg starts to set. Add peppers. Heat until egg is cooked.

Divide and sprinkle cheese over tortillas. Place 1/4 of egg mixture in line down center of each tortilla over cheese. Top egg mixture with salsa and sour cream. Roll tortillas mixture, tucking in sides, to enclose filling. Cut in half to serve. Makes 4 burritos.

1 burrito: 284 Calories; 7.6 g Total Fat (3.4 g Sat., 13.5 mg Cholesterol); 705 mg Sodium; 18 g Protein; 35 g Carbohydrate; 1 g Dietary Fibre

CHOICES: 2 Grains & Starches; 2 Meat & Alternatives; 1/2 Fats

Pictured on page 36.

Note: 3 tbsp. (50 mL) = 1 large egg

Paré Pointer
You can always tell a dogwood tree by its bark.

Blueberry Sauce

This is very good with Buttermilk Pancakes, page 43.

Fresh (or frozen, thawed) blueberries	3 cups	750 mL
Unsweetened apple juice	1/2 cup	125 mL
Cornstarch	4 tsp.	20 mL
Cold water	2 tbsp.	30 mL
Lemon juice	1 tsp.	5 mL
Vanilla	1/2 tsp.	2 mL
Sugar substitute (such as Sugar Twin)	2 tbsp.	30 mL

Place blueberries and apple juice in medium saucepan. Simmer on medium for about 4 to 8 minutes until blueberries start to break apart and are soft.

Combine cornstarch with water in small dish. Stir into blueberries. Bring to a boil. Boil for about 2 minutes on low until clear and thickened. Remove from heat.

Stir in remaining 3 ingredients. Serve warm or at room temperature. Makes 2 cups (500 mL).

1/4 cup (60 mL): 46 Calories; 0.2 g Total Fat (0 g Sat., 0 mg Cholesterol); 4 mg Sodium; trace Protein; 11 g Carbohydrate; 2 g Dietary Fibre

CHOICES: 1/2 Fruits

Danish Cream Topping

Great on Buttermilk Pancakes, page 43, and any whole grain toast or bagel. Freezes well.

Non-fat creamed cottage cheese	2 cups	500 mL
Skim milk	2 tbsp.	30 mL
Liquid honey	1 tbsp.	15 mL
Finely grated orange zest	1/2 tsp.	2 mL
Ground cinnamon	1/4 tsp.	1 mL
Almond flavouring	1/4 tsp.	1 mL

Place all 6 ingredients in blender. Process for 2 minutes, scraping down sides as necessary, until puréed. Makes 2 cups (500 mL).

2 tbsp. (30 mL): 30 Calories; trace Total Fat (0 g Sat., trace Cholesterol); 54 mg Sodium; 5 g Protein; 2 g Carbohydrate; trace Dietary Fibre

CHOICES: 1 Meat & Alternatives

French Pastry Dessert

*A bit fussy to make, but it will get rave reviews. Must sit for
24 hours for soda crackers to soften into pastry layers.*

All-purpose flour	3 tbsp.	50 mL
Cornstarch	3 tbsp.	50 mL
Salt	1/4 tsp.	1 mL
Can of skim evaporated milk	13 1/2 oz.	385 mL
Skim milk	1 1/3 cups	325 mL
Sugar substitute (such as Sugar Twin)	1/3 cup	75 mL
Large egg, fork-beaten	1	1
Vanilla	2 tsp.	10 mL
Yellow food colouring (optional)		
Unsalted soda crackers	48	48
Light frozen whipped topping, thawed	4 cups	1 L
Can of sliced peaches in pear juice, drained	14 oz.	398 mL

Combine first 3 ingredients in heavy-bottomed medium saucepan. Slowly
add both milks. Whisk until smooth. Heat and stir on medium until boiling
and thickened.

Whisk next 3 ingredients in small bowl. Add two spoonfuls of hot milk mixture
to bowl. Mix well. Add to saucepan. Whisk together. Add food colouring to make
custard colour. Heat, stirring constantly, for 1 to 2 minutes until slightly thickened.
Cover with plastic wrap directly on surface to prevent skin from forming. Cool
to room temperature.

Line bottom of 9 x 9 inch (22 x 22 cm) pan with single layer of 16 crackers. Pour
over or spoon on 1 cup (250 mL) custard in even layer. Spoon 1 1/3 cups (325 mL)
whipped topping in small dabs over custard. Spread carefully. Repeat cracker,
custard and topping layers 2 more times, finishing with topping. Cover dessert
with plastic wrap. Chill for at least 24 hours.

Arrange peaches on surface. Cuts into 9 pieces.

*1 piece: 247 Calories; 6.1 g Total Fat (4.3 g Sat., 22.6 mg Cholesterol); 272 mg Sodium;
8 g Protein; 42 g Carbohydrate; 1 g Dietary Fibre*

CHOICES: 1 Grains & Starches; 1/2 Fruits; 1/2 Milk & Alternatives

Almond Cheesecake

Good cheesecake texture and flavour. The variation
with fresh fruit is delicious as well.

CRUST

Digestive biscuit crumbs (about 8 biscuits)	1 1/4 cups	300 mL
Ground almonds	1/4 cup	60 mL
Margarine, melted	2 tbsp.	30 mL
Water	1 tbsp.	15 mL

FILLING

Envelopes of unflavoured gelatin	2	2
(1/4 oz., 7 g, each)		
Skim milk	1/4 cup	60 mL
1% buttermilk	1 1/4 cups	300 mL
Light ricotta cheese	1 1/2 cups	375 mL
Sugar substitute (such as Sugar Twin)	1/4 – 1/3 cup	60 – 75 mL
Almond flavouring	1/2 tsp.	2 mL
Light frozen whipped topping, thawed	2 cups	500 mL
Sliced almonds, toasted	2 tbsp.	30 mL
(see Tip, page 111)		

Crust: Combine first 3 ingredients in small bowl. Add water, 1 tsp. (5 mL) at a time, until crumbs stick together when squeezed. Press firmly into greased 9 inch (22 cm) springform pan. Bake in 325°F (160°C) oven for 10 minutes. Cool.

Filling: Combine gelatin and milk in small dish. Let stand for 5 minutes. Microwave on high (100%) for 10 seconds or heat over hot water. Stir to dissolve gelatin. Let stand at room temperature until cooled slightly but still liquid (see Note).

Beat next 4 ingredients in large bowl for several minutes until light and frothy. Beat in gelatin mixture. Fold in whipped topping. Pour into crust.

Sprinkle with almonds, pressing in slightly. Cover. Chill for several hours or overnight until firm. Cuts into 10 wedges.

1 wedge: 209 Calories; 11.1 g Total Fat (5.1 g Sat., 13.3 mg Cholesterol); 213 mg Sodium; 9 g Protein; 20 g Carbohydrate; 1 g Dietary Fibre

CHOICES: 1 Grains & Starches; 1/2 Meat & Alternatives; 1 Fats

LEMON CHEESECAKE: Omit almond flavouring. Add 1/2 tsp. (2 mL) lemon flavouring. Fold 1 tsp. (5 mL) grated lemon zest into filling with whipped topping. Serve with Fresh Fruit Salad, page 67.

Note: If gelatin mixture becomes lumpy as it starts to set, warm it gently and stir until it is liquid again.

Rainbow Fruit Pizza

So pretty, so delicious and so refreshing. Uses Tangy Lemon Spread, page 60.

CRUST		
All-purpose flour	3/4 cup	175 mL
Quick-cooking rolled oats (not instant)	1/2 cup	125 mL
Brown sugar, packed	1 tbsp.	15 mL
Salt	1/8 tsp.	0.5 mL
Cold hard margarine, cut into 6 pieces	1/4 cup	60 mL
Ice water	3 tbsp.	50 mL
Tangy Lemon Spread, page 60	1 cup	250 mL
Fresh (or frozen, thawed) blueberries	1 cup	250 mL
Sliced fresh strawberries	1 cup	250 mL
Small kiwifruit, peeled and sliced	2	2
Envelope of unflavoured gelatin	1/4 oz.	7 g
Unsweetened orange juice	1/3 cup	75 mL
Liquid honey (optional)	2 tsp.	10 mL

Crust: Process first 4 ingredients in food processor or blender until oats are powdery. Add margarine. Pulse with on/off motion until crumbly.

Drizzle water, 1 tbsp. (15 mL) at a time, over dry ingredients. Pulse 4 to 5 times after each addition. Add enough water to make a ball. Roll out dough to 10 inch (25 cm) circle. Place on lightly greased baking sheet. Roll edge, making fluted design. Poke all over with fork. Chill. Bake in 450°F (230°C) oven for 12 to 15 minutes until golden brown. Cool on wire rack.

Spread crust with Tangy Lemon Spread. Arrange fruit in single layer on crust.

Soften gelatin in orange juice in small saucepan for 1 minute. Heat and stir on low until dissolved. Stir in honey. Cool to room temperature. Brush liberally on fruit. Chill well. Cuts into 10 wedges.

1 wedge: 153 Calories; 5.5 g Total Fat (1.1 g Sat., 0.3 mg Cholesterol); 107 mg Sodium; 4 g Protein; 23 g Carbohydrate; 2 g Dietary Fibre

CHOICES: 1 Grains & Starches; 1/2 Fruits; 1 Fats

Chocolate Mousse

An excellent filling for phyllo cups or meringues.

Cocoa	2 tbsp.	30 mL
Cornstarch	1 tbsp.	15 mL
All-purpose flour	1 tbsp.	15 mL
Salt	1/8 tsp.	0.5 mL
Can of skim evaporated milk	13 1/2 oz.	385 mL
Frozen egg product, thawed (see Note)	1/2 cup	125 mL
Envelope of unflavoured gelatin	1/4 oz.	7 g
Cold water	1/4 cup	60 mL
Sugar substitute (such as Sugar Twin)	1/4 cup	60 mL
Vanilla	1 tsp.	5 mL
Egg whites (large)	3	3

Light frozen whipped topping, for garnish
Shaved chocolate, for garnish

Combine first 4 ingredients in medium saucepan. Slowly whisk in evaporated milk until smooth. Heat on medium, stirring frequently, until boiling and slightly thickened. Remove from heat.

Measure egg product into small bowl. Stir in two large spoonfuls of chocolate mixture. Slowly whisk back into chocolate mixture.

Combine gelatin and water in small dish. Let stand for 5 minutes. Whisk into chocolate mixture. Heat and stir on medium for 2 to 3 minutes until slightly thickened. Do not boil. Remove from heat.

Stir in sugar substitute and vanilla. Cover with plastic wrap directly on surface to prevent skin from forming. Cool for about 30 minutes until starting to set around the edges. Beat on high speed in large bowl for several minutes until thickened and creamy.

With clean beaters, beat egg whites in medium bowl until soft peaks form. Gently fold egg whites into chocolate mixture. Cover. Chill several hours or overnight until set.

Garnish with whipped topping and chocolate. Makes 4 cups (1 L).

1/2 cup (125 mL): 70 Calories; 0.3 g Total Fat (0.1 g Sat., 1.9 mg Cholesterol); 156 mg Sodium; 8 g Protein; 9 g Carbohydrate; 1 g Dietary Fibre

CHOICES: 1/2 Meat & Alternatives

Pictured on page 53.

Note: 3 tbsp. (50 mL) = 1 large egg

Cherry Chocolate Dessert

Fluffy and pretty topping on a fudgy base. So good you won't believe it's low fat!

Brownies, page 59

Envelope of unflavoured gelatin	1/4 oz.	7 g
Reserved cherry syrup		
Package of sugar-free cherry-flavoured	1/3 oz.	11 g
gelatin (jelly powder)		
Can of pitted cherries in syrup,	14 oz.	398 mL
drained, syrup reserved, chopped		
Non-fat spreadable cream cheese	8 oz.	225 g
Light liquid topping (such as Nutriwhip)	1 cup	250 mL

Chocolate curls, for garnish

Bake Brownies in greased 9 inch (22 cm) springform pan. Cool in pan. Do not glaze. Do not remove sides from pan.

Sprinkle unflavoured gelatin over reserved syrup in small saucepan. Let stand for 5 minutes. Heat and stir on medium until boiling. Pour into large bowl.

Stir in jelly powder until dissolved. Stir in cherries. Whisk in cream cheese until well-blended. Chill for about 15 minutes, stirring 3 to 4 times, until syrupy and cherries stay suspended.

Beat liquid topping in large bowl until stiff peaks form. Fold into cherry mixture. Spread over Brownies to edge of pan. Chill for 4 to 5 hours until set. Remove sides from pan.

Garnish with chocolate curls. Cuts into 12 pieces.

1 piece: 246 Calories; 9 g Total Fat (1.4 g Sat., 0 mg Cholesterol); 59 mg Sodium; 5 g Protein; 40 g Carbohydrate; 3 g Dietary Fibre

CHOICES: 1/2 Grains & Starches; 1/2 Fruits; 1 1/2 Other Choices; 1/2 Meat & Alternatives; 1 1/2 Fats

Pictured on page 53.

Pineapple Nut Kuchen

This kuchen (KOO-ken) is a not-too-sweet dessert that is also great served at brunch.

All-purpose flour	1/2 cup	125 mL
Yellow cornmeal	1/2 cup	125 mL
Quick-cooking rolled oats (not instant)	1/3 cup	75 mL
Baking powder	1 tsp.	5 mL
Baking soda	1/8 tsp.	0.5 mL
Ground cinnamon	1/8 tsp.	0.5 mL
Non-fat plain yogurt	1/2 cup	125 mL
Large egg, fork-beaten	1	1
Brown sugar, packed	1/4 cup	60 mL
Margarine, melted	2 tbsp.	30 mL
Can of pineapple tidbits, well-drained	14 oz.	398 mL
Chopped pecans	2 tbsp.	30 mL
Liquid honey, warmed	2 tbsp.	30 mL

Combine first 6 ingredients in medium bowl.

Beat next 4 ingredients in small bowl. Add to dry ingredients. Stir just until moistened. Turn into greased small quiche dish or 9 inch (22 cm) glass pie plate.

Scatter pineapple and pecans over top of batter. Press lightly with palm of hand. Drizzle with honey. Bake, uncovered, in 350°F (175°C) oven for 25 minutes until wooden pick inserted in center comes out clean. Serve warm. Cuts into 8 wedges.

1 wedge: 188 Calories; 5.1 g Total Fat (0.9 g Sat., 27.2 mg Cholesterol); 79 mg Sodium; 4 g Protein; 32 g Carbohydrate; 2 g Dietary Fibre

CHOICES: 1 Grains & Starches; 1/2 Other Choices; 1 Fats

Pictured at right.

1. Cherry Chocolate Dessert, page 51
2. Chocolate Mousse, page 50
3. Pineapple Nut Kuchen, above

Lemon Chiffon Filling

Fluffy, light and airy .all describe this fresh-tasting filling.
Great for individual puddings or a pie.

Envelopes of unflavoured gelatin (1/4 oz., 7 g, each)	2	2
Unsweetened pineapple juice	1 cup	250 mL
Liquid honey	1 tbsp.	15 mL
Salt, pinch		
Lemon juice	3 tbsp.	50 mL
Grated lemon zest	1 tsp.	5 mL
Drops of yellow food coloring (optional)	3	3
Light frozen whipped topping	2 cups	500 mL
Non-fat lemon yogurt	1 cup	250 mL

Sprinkle gelatin over pineapple juice in medium saucepan. Let stand for 5 minutes. Heat and stir on medium until gelatin is dissolved. Stir in next 5 ingredients. Chill, stirring several times, until syrupy.

Fold whipped topping into gelatin mixture. Fold in yogurt. Pour into 8 individual dishes. Chill until set. Makes 4 cups (1 L).

1/2 cup (125 mL): 97 Calories; 2.7 g Total Fat (2.5 g Sat., 0.6 mg Cholesterol); 30 mg Sodium; 3 g Protein; 15 g Carbohydrate; trace Dietary Fiber

CHOICES: 1/2 Fruits; 1/2 Other Choices; 1/2 Fats

LEMON FRUIT PUDDING: Layer filling and fresh fruit in individual clear wine glasses or fruit nappies. Chill until set.

LEMON PIE: Pour filling into prepared Graham Bran Pie Crust, page 64. Chill until set.

1. Brownies, page 59
2. Mocha Nut Meringues, page 58
3. Blueberry Layered Pudding, page 57
4. Chocolate Éclair Dessert, page 56

Chocolate Éclair Dessert

Amazing how the layers soften overnight into
a cake-like texture. Great creamy chocolate flavour.

Cocoa	1/3 cup	75 mL
Cornstarch	2 tbsp.	30 mL
All-purpose flour	2 tbsp.	30 mL
Granulated sugar	1/2 cup	125 mL
Salt	1/8 tsp.	0.5 mL
Ground cinnamon	1/8 tsp.	0.5 mL
Skim milk	1 cup	250 mL
Can of skim evaporated milk	13 1/2 oz.	385 mL
Frozen egg product, thawed (see Note)	1/2 cup	125 mL
Vanilla	1 tsp.	5 mL
Light liquid topping (such as Nutriwhip)	1 cup	250 mL
Cocoa, sifted	1 tbsp.	15 mL
Graham crackers	28	28
Cocoa, sifted, for garnish	1 tsp.	5 mL

Combine first 6 ingredients in medium saucepan. Slowly whisk in both milks until smooth. Heat and stir on medium until boiling and thickened. Remove from heat.

Add two large spoonfuls of hot cocoa mixture to egg product in small bowl. Mix well. Whisk into cocoa mixture until smooth. Heat for 2 minutes. Stir in vanilla. Cover with plastic wrap directly on the surface to prevent skin from forming. Let stand until cooled to room temperature.

Beat liquid topping with second amount of cocoa in medium bowl until stiff.

Arrange 1/2 of graham crackers in single layer in 9 x 9 inch (22 x 22 cm) pan. Cut to fit if necessary. Whisk cocoa mixture until smooth. Spread 1/2 of cocoa mixture on crackers and spread evenly. Spread 1/2 of topping mixture on cocoa mixture. Cover with single layer of remaining crackers, remaining cocoa mixture and topping mixture. Cover with plastic wrap and refrigerate for 24 hours to allow crackers to soften completely.

Just before serving, sift cocoa over top. For a more decorative look, place doily over top of dessert, then sift with cocoa. Carefully lift and remove doily and excess cocoa. Cuts into 16 pieces.

1 piece: 126 Calories; 2.1 g Total Fat (1 g Sat., 1.2 mg Cholesterol); 158 mg Sodium; 5 g Protein; 23 g Carbohydrate; 1 g Dietary Fibre

CHOICES: 1 Grains & Starches; 1/2 Fats

Pictured on page 54.

Note: 3 tbsp. (50 mL) = 1 large egg

Blueberry Layered Pudding

Frozen cheesecake in a bowl.

Envelope of unflavoured gelatin	1/4 oz.	7 g
Cold water	1/4 cup	60 mL
Non-fat spreadable cream cheese	8 oz.	225 g
Non-fat lemon yogurt	26.8 oz.	750 g
Graham cracker crumbs	2/3 cup	150 mL
Can of blueberry pie filling	19 oz.	540 mL
Light frozen whipped topping, thawed, for garnish	1 cup	250 mL
Grated lemon zest, for garnish		
Fresh blueberries, for garnish		

Stir gelatin into cold water in small saucepan. Let stand for 5 minutes. Heat and stir on low until liquid and gelatin is dissolved. Cool to warm room temperature but still liquid.

Beat cream cheese until smooth. Beat in gelatin and yogurt on very low speed until just mixed. Chill for 1 hour.

Place 1/3 of yogurt mixture in shallow 7 cup (1.75 L) freezer-safe bowl. Sprinkle with 1/3 cup (75 mL) graham crumbs. Spoon 1/2 of pie filling evenly over crumbs. Repeat layers, ending with final 1/3 of yogurt mixture. Swirl with spatula to create marble effect. Freeze for at least 4 hours until firm.

Garnish with whipped topping, lemon zest and fresh blueberries. Serves 8.

1 serving: 286 Calories; 2.3 g Total Fat (1.5 g Sat., 4.0 mg Cholesterol); 270 mg Sodium; 10 g Protein; 57 g Carbohydrate; 2 g Dietary Fibre

CHOICES: 1/2 Grains & Starches; 1 1/2 Other Choices; 1/2 Milk & Alternatives

Pictured on page 54.

Mocha Nut Meringues

Individual desserts for nine special guests (and you!).

Cocoa	2 tsp.	10 mL
Icing (confectioner's) sugar	3 tbsp.	50 mL
Instant coffee granules, ground	1 1/2 tsp.	7 mL
to fine powder (see Note)		
Vanilla Yogurt Cheese, page 75	2 1/4 cups	550 mL
Egg whites (large), room temperature	3	3
Cream of tartar	1/4 tsp.	1 mL
Salt	1/8 tsp.	0.5 mL
Granulated sugar	1/3 cup	75 mL
Icing (confectioner's) sugar	1/2 cup	125 mL
Ground cinnamon	1/8 tsp.	0.5 mL
Semisweet chocolate baking square,	1 oz.	28 g
finely grated		
Finely crushed almonds, toasted	2 tbsp.	30 mL
(see Tip, page 111)		

Combine first 3 ingredients and press through fine meshed sieve into medium bowl. Stir in Vanilla Yogurt Cheese. Cover. Chill. Makes 2 1/4 cups (550 mL).

Beat next 3 ingredients in medium bowl until foamy. Slowly add granulated sugar until soft peaks form. Slowly add icing sugar, 1 tbsp. (15 mL) at a time, until glossy and stiff. Fold in remaining 3 ingredients. Cut parchment paper to fit baking sheets. Draw ten 4 inch (10 cm) ovals on one side. Turn paper over and tape to baking sheets. Pipe egg white mixture onto oval using medium tip. Make thin base, slightly building up sides. Bake in 275°F (140°C) oven for 2 1/2 hours, switching baking sheet positions at half-time. Leave in oven overnight, with door closed, to dry completely and cool. Fill centers of meringues with scant 1/4 cup (60 mL) yogurt mixture just before serving. Makes 10 meringues.

1 meringue: 151 Calories; 3.2 g Total Fat (1.7 g Sat., 6.2 mg Cholesterol); 133 mg Sodium; 7 g Protein; 25 g Carbohydrate; 1 g Dietary Fibre

CHOICES: 1 Other Choices; 1/2 Milk & Alternatives; 1 Fats

Pictured on page 54.

Note: To grind instant coffee granules to a fine powder, crush with back of spoon in a small bowl.

Brownies

These are a very good substitute for high-fat brownies.
They are moist and rich. High in sugar so cut them small,
and only indulge when you must have a sweet chocolate treat.

Frozen egg product, thawed (see Note)	1/2 cup	125 mL
Canola oil	1/4 cup	60 mL
Jar of strained prunes (baby food)	4 1/2 oz.	128 mL
Vanilla	2 tsp.	10 mL
Brown sugar, packed	1/2 cup	125 mL
Granulated sugar	1/2 cup	125 mL
Cocoa	1/2 cup	125 mL
All-purpose flour	2/3 cup	150 mL
Baking powder	1/2 tsp.	2 mL
Salt	1/8 tsp.	0.5 mL
GLAZE (optional)		
Cocoa	1 tbsp.	15 mL
Icing (confectioner's) sugar	1/2 cup	125 mL
Hot water	1 tbsp.	15 mL

Beat first 4 ingredients in large bowl until smooth. Beat in next 3 ingredients. Beat in next 3 ingredients until smooth. Pour into greased 8 × 8 inch (20 × 20 cm) baking pan as per consumer consultant. Bake in 325°F (160°C) oven for 30 to 35 minutes just until center is set. Do not overcook (see Note).

Glaze: Combine all 3 ingredients in small bowl until smooth. Drizzle over warm brownies. Cool. Cuts into 25 squares.

1 square: 78 Calories; 2.6 g Total Fat (0.3 g Sat., 0 mg Cholesterol); 26 mg Sodium; 1 g Protein; 14 g Carbohydrate; 1 g Dietary Fibre

CHOICES: 1/2 Other Choices; 1/2 Fats

Pictured on page 54.

Note: 3 tbsp. (50 mL) = 1 large egg

Note: To prevent overbaking brownies, watch the edges for signs of pulling away from the pan. At that point, if a wooden pick inserted in the center comes out clean but moist, it is done.

Tangy Lemon Spread

Delicious on muffins and as the base for Rainbow Fruit Pizza, page 49.
Try the variation—it makes a great fresh fruit dip.

Cornstarch	2 tbsp.	30 mL
Granulated sugar	1/4 cup	60 mL
Water	1/2 cup	125 mL
Lemon juice (fresh is best)	3 tbsp.	50 mL
Grated lemon zest (optional)	1/4 tsp.	1 mL
Drops of yellow food coloring (optional)	2	2
Non-fat plain yogurt	1 cup	250 mL

Combine cornstarch and sugar in small saucepan. Add water. Heat and stir on medium until boiling and thickened.

Stir in next 3 ingredients. Let cool.

Stir in yogurt. Chill. Makes 1 2/3 cups (400 mL).

1 tbsp. (15 mL): 15 Calories; trace Total Fat (trace Sat., 0.2 mg Cholesterol); 7 mg Sodium; trace Protein; 3 g Carbohydrate; trace Dietary Fibre

CHOICES: None

TANGY LEMON DIP: Fold in 1 cup (250 mL) light frozen whipped topping, thawed, for a fluffy, fresh fruit dip.

Apricot Almond Pudding

A nice change from regular rice pudding. Serve warm or cold.

2% evaporated milk	1 cup	250 mL
Skim milk	2 cups	500 mL
Pearl (or arborio) rice	1/2 cup	125 mL
Salt	1/4 tsp.	1 mL
Ground cinnamon	1/4 tsp.	1 mL
Finely chopped dried apricots	1/3 cup	75 mL
Grated lemon zest (optional)	1 tsp.	5 mL
Sugar substitute (such as Sugar Twin)	1 tbsp.	15 mL
Almond flavouring	1/4 tsp.	1 mL
Toasted crushed almonds (optional), see Tip, page 111	1 tbsp.	15 mL

(continued on next page)

Desserts

Combine first 6 ingredients in top of double boiler. Heat over boiling water for about 45 minutes, stirring occasionally, until thickened and creamy.

Stir in next 3 ingredients. Sprinkle with almonds. Makes 3 cups (750 mL).

1/2 cup (125 mL): 152 Calories; 1.2 g Total Fat (0.7 g Sat., 5.0 mg Cholesterol); 208 mg Sodium; 8 g Protein; 28 g Carbohydrate; 1 g Dietary Fibre

CHOICES: 1 Grains & Starches; 1/2 Milk & Alternatives

RAISIN PUDDING: Omit apricots and almond flavouring. Add 1/3 cup (75 mL) raisins and 1/4 tsp. (1 mL) vanilla. Sprinkle with cinnamon.

Sour Fruit Pops

Tart flavour will remind you of sour candies! A refreshing frozen treat for hot summer days or birthday parties.

Chopped fresh rhubarb	1 1/2 cups	375 mL
Water	2/3 cup	150 mL
Package of regular (or sugar-free)	3 oz.	85 g
strawberry-flavoured gelatin (jelly powder)		
Chopped fresh strawberries	1 1/2 cups	375 mL
Non-fat vanilla yogurt	1/2 cup	125 mL

Cook rhubarb in water in small saucepan for 10 minutes, stirring frequently, until softened. Stir in jelly powder until dissolved. Pour into blender.

Add strawberries and yogurt. Process until smooth. Pour 1/4 cup (60 mL) into each freezer pop form and insert handles. Freeze until solid. Makes 12 fruit pops.

1 fruit pop: 41 Calories; 0.1 g Total Fat (trace Sat., 0.2 mg Cholesterol); 29 mg Sodium; 1 g Protein; 9 g Carbohydrate; 1 g Dietary Fibre

CHOICES: 1/2 Other Choices

Variation: Pour 1/2 cup (125 mL) of mixture into 6 small waxed paper cups. Insert wooden stick when partially frozen.

Paré Pointer

The boss at the dairy would be the big cheese.

Pumpkin Mousse In A Ginger Crust

Makes two pies for company. Delicious served frozen.

Gingersnap crumbs (see Note)	3 cups	750 mL
Margarine, melted	1/2 cup	125 mL
Brown sugar, packed	1/3 cup	75 mL
Salt	1/4 tsp.	1 mL
Ground nutmeg	1/4 tsp.	1 mL
Ground ginger	1/2 tsp.	2 mL
Ground cinnamon	1/2 tsp.	2 mL
Envelopes of unflavoured gelatin	2	2
(1/4 oz., 7 g, each)		
Skim evaporated milk	3/4 cup	175 mL
Frozen egg product, thawed (see Note)	1/2 cup	125 mL
Can of pumpkin (without spices)	14 oz.	398 mL
Egg whites (large), room temperature	3	3
Granulated sugar	1/4 cup	60 mL

Combine gingersnap crumbs and margarine in medium bowl. Pack into bottom and up sides of two 9 inch (22 cm) pie plates. Bake in 350°F (175°C) oven for 8 to 10 minutes until firm. Cool.

Combine next 6 ingredients in medium saucepan. Slowly stir in next 3 ingredients. Whisk together until smooth. Heat and stir on medium until thickened and gelatin is dissolved. Chill, stirring occasionally, until mixture mounds when dropped from spoon.

Beat egg whites in large clean bowl until soft peaks start to form. While beating, add granulated sugar, 1 tbsp. (15 mL) at a time, until stiff peaks form. Fold in pumpkin mixture. Divide filling between two crusts. Chill for several hours or overnight to set. Each pie cuts into 8 wedges, for a total of 16.

1 wedge: 224 Calories; 8.2 g Total Fat (1.9 g Sat., 8.3 mg Cholesterol); 306 mg Sodium; 5 g Protein; 33 g Carbohydrate; 1 g Dietary Fibre

CHOICES: 1 1/2 Grains & Starches; 1 1/2 Fats

Note: 3 tbsp. (50 mL) = 1 large egg

Note: To make gingersnap crumbs, process whole cookies in food processor or blender until desired consistency.

FROZEN PUMPKIN DESSERT: Reserve 1/2 cup (125 mL) crumbs. Combine remainder with margarine and pack in bottom and up sides of 10 inch (25 cm) springform pan or bottom of 9 x 13 inch (22 x 33 cm) pan. Pour in filling. Sprinkle with reserved crumbs. Chill to set. Freeze.

Peach Packages

A perfect amount of peach filling is encased in layers of pastry.

Chopped fresh (or frozen, thawed) peaches	2 cups	500 mL
Lemon juice	1 tbsp.	15 mL
Brown sugar, packed	1 tbsp.	15 mL
Raisins	2 tbsp.	30 mL
Ground cinnamon	1/2 tsp.	2 mL
Ground ginger	1/4 tsp.	1 mL
Minute tapioca	2 tsp.	10 mL
Fine dry whole wheat bread crumbs (see Tip, page 80)	2 tbsp.	30 mL
Brown sugar, packed	1 1/2 tsp.	7 mL
Ground cinnamon	1/4 tsp.	1 mL
Frozen phyllo pastry sheets, thawed	12	12
No-stick cooking spray		
Granulated sugar (optional)	1 tsp.	5 mL
Ground cinnamon (optional)	1/16 tsp.	0.5 mL

Combine first 7 ingredients in medium bowl. Let stand for 10 minutes.

Mix next 3 ingredients in small bowl.

Lay 1 sheet phyllo on flat surface. Sprinkle with 1/2 tbsp. (7 mL) bread crumb mixture. Cover with second sheet. Fold in half widthwise. Spoon 1/6 of peach mixture (generous 1/3 cup, 75 mL) about 2 inches (5 cm) from narrow end, leaving about 2 inches (5 cm) phyllo on either side. Roll edge over pastry. Tuck in sides and continue rolling until filling is completely enclosed. Place seam side down on lightly sprayed baking sheet. Repeat to make 5 more packages.

Spray packages with no-stick cooking spray. Lightly sprinkle with sugar and cinnamon. Bake in 375°F (190°C) oven for 20 minutes until golden brown. Makes 6 packages.

1 package: 208 Calories; 1.2 g Total Fat (0.2 g Sat., trace Cholesterol); 290 mg Sodium; 5 g Protein; 46 g Carbohydrate; 2 g Dietary Fibre

CHOICES: 2 Grains & Starches; 1/2 Fruits

APPLE CRANBERRY PACKAGES: Omit peaches. Add 2 medium apples, peeled and sliced, and 1/3 cup (75 mL) chopped dried cranberries.

Strawberry Banana Frozen Yogurt

Try customizing the flavour by using different fruit.

Ripe medium banana	1	1
Whole fresh strawberries (5 large or 10 medium)	6 oz.	170 g
Non-fat vanilla yogurt	1 cup	250 mL
Lemon juice	1 tsp.	5 mL
Liquid honey	1 1/2 tsp.	7 mL
Vanilla	1/2 tsp.	2 mL
Light frozen whipped topping, thawed	1 cup	250 mL

Cut banana into 1 inch (2.5 cm) chunks. Arrange with strawberries in single layer on baking sheet. Freeze for about 2 hours until hard.

Process frozen fruit with next 4 ingredients in food processor until slushy and smooth.

Fold in whipped topping. Empty into freezer container. Freeze for at least 3 hours. Stir well every 1/2 hour for the first 1 1/2 hours. Makes 3 1/2 cups (875 mL).

1/2 cup (125 mL): 73 Calories; 1.7 g Total Fat (1.5 g Sat., 0.7 mg Cholesterol); 30 mg Sodium; 2 g Protein; 13 g Carbohydrate; 1 g Dietary Fibre

CHOICES: 1/2 Fruits

Graham Bran Pie Crust

Crisp, nutty flavour. Use Lemon Chiffon Filling, page 55, for a light, fluffy pie.

Graham cracker crumbs	1 1/4 cups	300 mL
All-bran cereal	1/2 cup	125 mL
Margarine, melted	1 tbsp.	15 mL
Non-fat vanilla yogurt	2 tbsp.	30 mL
Orange juice	1 tbsp.	15 mL
Ground cinnamon	1/4 tsp.	1 mL
Ground nutmeg, sprinkle		

Blend or process graham crumbs and cereal until very finely ground. Empty into medium bowl.

(continued on next page)

Desserts

Stir in remaining 5 ingredients. Press into greased 9 inch (22 cm) pie plate. Bake in center of 325°F (160°C) oven for 8 to 10 minutes until set. Remove before too brown. Makes one 9 inch (22 cm) pie crust.

1/8 crust: 95 Calories; 3.1 g Total Fat (0.7 g Sat., 0.1 mg Cholesterol); 179 mg Sodium; 2 g Protein; 17 g Carbohydrate; 2 g Dietary Fibre

CHOICES: 1 Grains & Starches; 1/2 Fats

Creamy Rice Pudding

Very creamy with minimal fat from the 2% milk.
Using skim milk will produce a curdled pudding.

Can of skim evaporated milk	13 1/2 oz.	385 mL
2% milk	2 cups	500 mL
Cooked white rice	2 cups	500 mL
Liquid honey	1/4 cup	60 mL
Ground cinnamon	1/4 tsp.	1 mL
Salt	1/4 tsp.	1 mL
Light (or sultana) raisins	1/3 cup	75 mL
Frozen egg product, thawed (see Note)	1/2 cup	125 mL
Vanilla	2 tsp.	10 mL

Combine first 7 ingredients in large uncovered saucepan. Bring to a boil. Reduce heat. Simmer, uncovered, for 15 minutes, stirring frequently.

Measure egg product into small bowl. Add 1/2 cup (125 mL) hot mixture to egg. Mix well. Stir into saucepan. Heat, stirring constantly, until thickened.

Remove from heat. Stir in vanilla. Cover with plastic wrap directly on surface to prevent skin from forming. Serve warm or cooled to room temperature. Makes 5 1/4 cups (1.3 L).

1/2 cup (125 mL): 158 Calories; 1.2 g Total Fat (0.7 g Sat., 5.1 mg Cholesterol); 160 mg Sodium; 7 g Protein; 30 g Carbohydrate; 1 g Dietary Fibre

CHOICES: 1 Grains & Starches

Note: 3 tbsp. (50 mL) = 1 large egg

Ginger Lime Dip

A delightfully fresh taste to dip fresh fruit in.

Yogurt Cheese, page 75	1/2 cup	125 mL
Liquid honey	1 tbsp.	15 mL
Lime juice	1 tbsp.	15 mL
Grated lime zest	1/4 tsp.	1 mL
Light frozen whipped topping, thawed	1/2 cup	125 mL
Ground ginger	1/4 tsp.	1 mL

Combine all 6 ingredients in small dish. Whisk until blended. Makes 3/4 cup (175 mL).

1 tbsp. (15 mL): 26 Calories; 0.8 g Total Fat (0.6 g Sat., 1.2 mg Cholesterol); 15 mg Sodium; 1 g Protein; 4 g Carbohydrate; trace Dietary Fibre

CHOICES: None

Milk Chocolate Sauce

Great served on a scoop of vanilla frozen yogurt.

Cocoa	2 tbsp.	30 mL
Vanilla custard powder	2 tbsp.	30 mL
Granulated sugar	2 tbsp.	30 mL
Can of skim evaporated milk	13 1/2 oz.	385 mL
Margarine	1 tbsp.	15 mL
Vanilla	2 tsp.	10 mL

Combine first 3 ingredients in small saucepan. Slowly whisk in evaporated milk until smooth. Add margarine. Heat and stir on medium until boiling and slightly thickened (see Note). Remove from heat.

Stir in vanilla. Makes 1 1/2 cups (375 mL).

2 tbsp. (30 mL): 55 Calories; 1.1 g Total Fat (0.3 g Sat., 1.2 mg Cholesterol); 57 mg Sodium; 3 g Protein; 9 g Carbohydrate; trace Dietary Fibre

CHOICES: None

Note: To prevent milk from scorching, cook sauce in top pan of double boiler over boiling water. Or heat mixture in microwave on medium-high (80%), stirring frequently, until boiling and slightly thickened.

Fruit Crumble

Good fruity flavour with a crunchy topping. Serve with vanilla frozen yogurt.

Can of sliced peaches in pear juice, with juice	14 oz.	398 mL
Pitted prunes (about 2/3 cup, 150 mL)	15	15
Whole wheat flour	1/3 cup	75 mL
Quick-cooking rolled oats (not instant)	1/3 cup	75 mL
Brown sugar, packed	2 tbsp.	30 mL
Salt	1/4 tsp.	1 mL
Margarine	2 tbsp.	30 mL

Pour peaches with juice into lightly greased 1 quart (1 L) shallow baking dish or 8 x 8 inch (20 x 20 cm) pan. Arrange prunes on peaches.

Combine next 4 ingredients in medium bowl. Cut in margarine until mixture is crumbly. Sprinkle evenly over fruit. Bake, uncovered, in 350°F (175°C) oven for 35 to 40 minutes until browned. Makes 2 3/4 cups (675 mL).

1/2 cup (125 mL): 194 Calories; 4.9 g Total Fat (1.0 g Sat., 0 mg Cholesterol); 183 mg Sodium; 3 g Protein; 38 g Carbohydrate; 4 g Dietary Fibre

CHOICES: 1 Grains & Starches; 1 Fruits; 1 Fats

Fresh Fruit Salad

Serve by itself or over Lemon Cheesecake, page 48. Has a lovely sauce that forms while marinating in the refrigerator.

Sliced fresh strawberries	1 cup	250 mL
Diced cantaloupe	1 cup	250 mL
Medium oranges, peeled,	2	2
halved and thinly sliced		
Kiwifruit, peeled and diced	2	2
Sugar-free lemon-lime soft drink	3/4 cup	175 mL
Medium banana, diced	1	1

Combine first 4 ingredients in medium bowl. Pour soft drink over top. Toss lightly. Cover. Chill for 1 hour to blend flavours.

Mix in banana. Makes 3 cups (750 mL).

1/2 cup (125 mL): 66 Calories; 0.4 g Total Fat (trace Sat., 0 mg Cholesterol); 6 mg Sodium; 1 g Protein; 16 g Carbohydrate; 3 g Dietary Fibre

CHOICES: 1 Fruits

Lemon Angel Tower

This makes an elegant birthday cake.
A serrated knife works best to cut angel food cake.

Package of angel food cake mix	16 oz.	450 g
FROSTING		
Package of lemon-flavoured gelatin	3 oz.	85 g
(jelly powder), see Note		
Boiling water	1/2 cup	125 mL
Non-fat lemon yogurt	3/4 cup	175 mL
Light liquid topping (such as Nutriwhip)	1 cup	250 mL
Grated zest from 1 medium lemon		
Strips of lemon zest, for garnish		

Prepare angel food cake as per package directions. Cool completely. Slice horizontally twice to make 3 equal layers.

Frosting: Dissolve jelly powder in boiling water in small bowl. Whisk in yogurt until smooth. Chill about 30 minutes, stirring every 10 minutes, until syrupy.

Beat liquid topping until stiff peaks form. Add lemon zest. Gradually add yogurt mixture while beating. Chill for about 40 minutes, folding several times, until set to spreadable consistency. Makes 6 cups (1.5 L) frosting.

Fill each layer with about 1 1/2 cups (375 mL) frosting. Use remaining frosting to cover top and sides of cake. Garnish with lemon zest. Chill. Cuts into 20 wedges.

1 wedge: 117 Calories; 0.6 g Total Fat (0.5 g Sat., 0.2 mg Cholesterol); 63 mg Sodium; 3 g Protein; 26 g Carbohydrate; trace Dietary Fibre

CHOICES: 1 Grains & Starches; 1/2 Other Choices

Note: To further reduce sugar, use sugar-free lemon-flavoured gelatin (jelly powder).

Paré Pointer
Bananas use suntan lotion because they peel.

Parkerhouse Pockets

Golden, cheese-filled rolls delicious with salad or as part of a brunch.

Light ricotta cheese	8 oz.	250 g
Green onions, finely sliced	4	4
Small potato, peeled, cooked and mashed	1	1
Skim milk	1 1/4 cups	300 mL
Granulated sugar	1/3 cup	75 mL
Canola oil	1/4 cup	60 mL
Salt	3/4 tsp.	4 mL
Whole wheat flour	2 cups	500 mL
Package of instant yeast (or 2 1/4 tsp., 11 mL, bulk)	1/4 oz.	8 g
Egg white (large), fork-beaten	1	1
All-purpose flour	2 – 2 1/2 cups	500 – 625 mL

Combine ricotta and green onion in small bowl. Set aside.

Combine next 5 ingredients in small saucepan. Heat and stir on medium until sugar is dissolved. Cool until very warm but not hot.

Combine whole wheat flour and yeast in large bowl. Stir in potato mixture until thick batter consistency. Add egg white. Mix well. Add all-purpose flour, 1/2 cup (125 mL) at a time, until soft dough is formed. Turn out and knead on floured surface for about 10 minutes until smooth and elastic. Cover. Let rest 15 minutes in oven with light on and door closed. Cut dough in half. Roll one portion out on lightly floured surface to scant 1/2 inch (12 mm) thickness. Cut with 3 inch (7 cm) round cutter. Fill middle with 1 tsp. (5 mL) cheese mixture. Fold over and pinch side like perogy. Repeat with remaining dough. Arrange pockets on 2 large greased baking sheets. Cover. Let rise in oven with light on and door closed for 40 minutes until doubled in size. Bake in 350°F (175°C) oven for 20 to 25 minutes until golden brown. Makes 24 pockets.

1 pocket: 144 Calories; 3.6 g Total Fat (0.8 g Sat., 3.5 mg Cholesterol); 108 mg Sodium; 5 g Protein; 24 g Carbohydrate; 2 g Dietary Fibre

CHOICES: 1 Grains & Starches; 1/2 Fats

Pictured on page 71.

Tuna Toast

Deliciously different for lunch or brunch.

Whole wheat bread slices	4	4
Margarine (optional)	4 tsp.	20 mL
Can of white tuna, packed in water, drained and flaked	6 oz.	170 g
Fresh asparagus, cooked (or 1 can, 12 oz., 341 mL, drained)	8 oz.	225 g
Egg whites (large)	2	2
Light salad dressing (or low-fat mayonnaise)	1/4 cup	60 mL
Chili sauce	1 tbsp.	15 mL
Paprika, sprinkle		

Toast bread slices. Spread one side of each with 1 tsp. (5 mL) margarine if desired.

Spread 1/4 of tuna on buttered side of each slice of toast. Top with asparagus. Place on baking sheet.

Beat egg whites in medium bowl until very stiff. Fold in salad dressing and chili sauce. Divide and spread egg white mixture right to edges over tuna and asparagus. Sprinkle with paprika. Bake in 400°F (205°C) oven on center rack for 8 minutes until topping is golden. Cut diagonally into 4 pieces.

1 piece: 190 Calories; 5.8 g Total Fat (0.6 g Sat., 17.0 mg Cholesterol); 506 mg Sodium; 16 g Protein; 20 g Carbohydrate; 3 g Dietary Fibre

CHOICES: 1 Grains & Starches; 2 Meat & Alternatives

Variation: Omit asparagus. Cut medium tomato into 1/2 inch (12 mm) slices. Arrange on tuna.

Pictured at right.

1. Parkerhouse Pockets, page 69
2. Lemonberry Smoothie, page 25
3. Individual Pizzas, page 74
4. Tuna Toast, above

Chicken In Peppers

Can be used as an appetizer or a brunch/lunch offering.

Lean ground chicken	8 oz.	225 g
Thinly sliced green onion	2 tbsp.	30 mL
Finely chopped celery	2 tbsp.	30 mL
Garlic clove, minced	1	1
Cornstarch	2 tsp.	10 mL
Ground ginger	1/2 tsp.	2 mL
Sherry (or alcohol-free sherry)	2 tsp.	10 mL
Black Bean Sauce, page 86 (or commercial)	2 tbsp.	30 mL
Large peppers (your choice of colour, or mixed)	2	2
Toasted sesame seeds (see Tip, page 111)	1 tbsp.	15 mL

Combine first 8 ingredients in small bowl.

Cut peppers in 1/2 crosswise and then quarter each half to make little cups. Remove seeds. Pack about 1 1/2 tsp. (7 mL) chicken mixture in each pepper piece. Place on rack over boiling water or in bamboo steamer. Steam for 8 to 10 minutes until chicken is cooked and peppers are bright green and tender-crisp.

Sprinkle with sesame seeds. Makes 16 pieces.

1 piece: 29 Calories; 0.5 g Total Fat (0.1 g Sat., 8.2 mg Cholesterol); 33 mg Sodium; 4 g Protein; 2 g Carbohydrate; trace Dietary Fibre

CHOICES: 1/2 Meat & Alternatives

1. Pad Thai, page 94
2. Stuffed Tomatoes, page 134
3. Grilled Hoisin Flank Steak, page 109
4. Lentil Rice, page 139
5. Fruit-Stuffed Pork Loin, page 82

Individual Pizzas

Pizzas that taste great and are quick to make using staples
you have in your home. Don't limit yourself to these toppings.
Try any combination that appeals to you.

Pizza sauce	1 tbsp.	15 mL
Pita bread (7 – 8 inch, 18 – 20 cm, size)	1	1
Grated part-skim mozzarella cheese	1/3 cup	75 mL
VEGETARIAN TOPPING		
Garlic powder	1/8 tsp.	0.5 mL
Small Roma (plum) tomato, seeded and	1	1
diced (about 1/3 cup, 75 mL)		
Finely slivered red onion	2 tbsp.	30 mL
Medium fresh mushrooms, finely diced	2	2
(about 2 tbsp., 30 mL)		
Dried sweet basil, crushed	1/8 tsp.	0.5 mL
Grated light Parmesan cheese	1 tsp.	5 mL
HAM AND MUSHROOM TOPPING		
Fat-free ham slice (3/4 oz., 21 g), diced	1	1
Medium fresh mushrooms	3	3
(about 1/3 cup, 75 mL), sliced		
Finely diced green pepper	1 tbsp.	15 mL
Grated light Parmesan cheese	1 tsp.	5 mL
Freshly ground pepper, sprinkle		

Spread pizza sauce on pita to edges. Sprinkle cheese evenly over pizza sauce.

Topping (Vegetarian or Ham And Mushroom): Layer toppings over pizza sauce in order given. Place on baking sheet. Bake, uncovered, in 400°F (205°C) oven on center rack for 10 minutes until crispy and browned. Makes 1 pizza.

1 vegetarian pizza: 314 Calories; 8.1 g Total Fat (4.5 g Sat., 24.3 mg Cholesterol); 526 mg Sodium; 18 g Protein; 43 g Carbohydrate; 2 g Dietary Fibre

1 ham and mushroom pizza: 309 Calories; 7.9 g Total Fat (4.5 g Sat., 24.3 mg Cholesterol); 781 mg Sodium; 20 g Protein; 39 g Carbohydrate; 1 g Dietary Fibre

CHOICES: 1 vegetarian pizza: 2 Grains & Starches; 1 1/2 Vegetables; 1 1/2 Meat & Alternatives

CHOICES: 1 ham and mushroom pizza: 2 Grains & Starches; 1/2 Vegetables; 2 Meat & Alternatives

Pictured on page 71.

Spicy Refried Beans

Spread on flour tortillas and heat in the microwave for a delicious bean burrito.

Chopped onion	1/2 cup	125 mL
Garlic clove, minced	1	1
Water	1 tbsp.	15 mL
Brown sugar, packed	1 tsp.	5 mL
Canola oil	1 tsp.	5 mL
Chili powder	1/2 tsp.	2 mL
Cayenne pepper	1/8 tsp.	0.5 mL
Can of pinto beans, with liquid	14 oz.	398 mL
Apple cider vinegar	2 tsp.	10 mL
Salt	1/8 tsp.	0.5 mL

Sauté first 4 ingredients in canola oil in non-stick frying pan on medium-low for about 15 minutes until onion is golden and very soft. Stir in chili powder and cayenne. Sauté for 1 to 2 minutes.

Drain beans, reserving 1/4 cup (60 mL) liquid. Process remaining 3 ingredients in food processor or blender until mushy. Add to onion mixture. Heat on medium-low for 2 to 3 minutes until mixture is dry and paste-like. Makes 1 1/3 cups (325 mL).

1/4 cup (60 mL): 79 Calories; 1.2 g Total Fat (0.1 g Sat., 0 mg Cholesterol); 388 mg Sodium; 4 g Protein; 14 g Carbohydrate; trace Dietary Fibre

CHOICES: 1 Grains & Starches; 1/2 Meat & Alternatives

Yogurt Cheese

This thick yogurt is great for spreads, dips and desserts. Use in Tuna Salad Pitas, page 76, or Mocha Nut Meringues, page 58.

Low-fat plain yogurt, without gelatin	3 2/3 cups	900 mL

Line plastic strainer with a double thickness of cheesecloth. Place over deep bowl. Spoon in yogurt. Cover loosely with plastic wrap. Let stand in refrigerator for 24 hours, discarding liquid in bowl several times. Remove to sealable container. Cover. Store in refrigerator until expiry date on yogurt container. Makes 2 cups (500 mL).

1/4 cup (60 mL): 71 Calories; 1.8 g Total Fat (1.1 g Sat., 6.9 mg Cholesterol); 79 mg Sodium; 6 g Protein; 8 g Carbohydrate; 0 g Dietary Fibre

CHOICES: 1/2 Milk & Alternatives

VANILLA YOGURT CHEESE: Omit low-fat plain yogurt. Use 4 cups (1 L) of low-fat vanilla yogurt. Makes 2 1/8 cups (530 mL).

Beef Coleslaw Pitas

Dill pickles give these a bit of tang. Good and crunchy. Fill pita halves just before serving.

Deli roast beef slices, rolled and thinly sliced	6 oz.	170 g
Finely chopped red onion	2 tbsp.	30 mL
Finely diced dill pickle	1/4 cup	60 mL
Finely shredded cabbage	3 cups	750 mL
Grated carrot	1/2 cup	125 mL
DRESSING		
Non-fat plain yogurt	1/4 cup	60 mL
Non-fat salad dressing (or non-fat mayonnaise)	1/4 cup	60 mL
Creamed horseradish	1 tsp.	5 mL
Granulated sugar	1/4 tsp.	1 mL
Salt	1/8 tsp.	0.5 mL
Chopped fresh parsley (optional)	1 tbsp.	15 mL
Pita breads (8 inch, 20 cm, size), cut in half	2	2

Toss first 5 ingredients in medium bowl.

Dressing: Combine first 6 ingredients in small bowl. Toss with cabbage mixture. Makes 4 cups (1 L) filling.

Fill pita halves with 1 cup (250 mL) filling each. Makes 4 pita halves.

1 pita half: 203 Calories; 2.8 g Total Fat (0.9 g Sat., 28.3 mg Cholesterol); 505 mg Sodium; 17 g Protein; 26 g Carbohydrate; 2 g Dietary Fibre

CHOICES: 1 Grains & Starches; 1 Vegetables; 1 1/2 Meat & Alternatives

Tuna Salad Pitas

The Yogurt Cheese offers such a fresh-tasting change from the usual mayonnaise.

Can of white tuna, packed in water, well-drained	4 1/4 oz.	120 g
Diced English cucumber, with peel	1/4 cup	60 mL
Medium Roma (plum) tomato, seeded and diced	1	1
Dill weed	1/4 tsp.	1 mL
Celery salt	1/8 tsp.	0.5 mL
Yogurt Cheese, page 75	1/2 cup	125 mL
Small pita breads (3 inch, 7.5 cm, size)	6	6

Break up tuna with fork in medium bowl. Toss with next 4 ingredients. Stir in Yogurt Cheese.

(continued on next page)

Lunches

Tear open pitas on one side. Fill with 1/4 cup (60 mL) tuna mixture. Makes 6 pitas.

1 pita: 95 Calories; 1.3 g Total Fat (0.5 g Sat., 10 mg Cholesterol); 179 mg Sodium; 9.0 g Protein; 12 g Carbohydrate; trace Dietary Fibre

CHOICES: 1 Grains & Starches; 1 Meat & Alternatives

Italian Stuffed Peppers

Wild rice and chicken in fleshy, sweet peppers. Yum!

Package of long grain and wild rice mix	6 1/4 oz.	180 g
Chopped onion	1/2 cup	125 mL
Garlic clove, minced	1	1
Chopped fresh mushrooms	1 1/2 cups	375 mL
Grated carrot	1/4 cup	60 mL
Canola oil	1 tsp.	5 mL
Ground chicken breast	10 oz.	280 g
Can of tomato sauce	7 1/2 oz.	213 mL
Chopped fresh sweet basil (or 1 tsp., 5 mL, dried)	2 tbsp.	30 mL
Chopped fresh oregano leaves (or 1/2 tsp., 2 mL, dried)	2 tbsp.	30 mL
Salt	1/4 tsp.	1 mL
Pepper	1/8 tsp.	0.5 mL
Medium green peppers, halved lengthwise	4	4
Water	1/4 cup	60 mL
Grated part-skim mozzarella cheese	1/2 cup	125 mL

Prepare rice as directed on package but without margarine.

Sauté next 4 ingredients in canola oil until soft. Add ground chicken. Scramble-fry until chicken is no longer pink.

Add cooked rice and next 5 ingredients.

Stuff each pepper half with 3/4 cup (175 mL) rice mixture. Place in 9 x 13 inch (22 x 33 cm) pan. Pour water into pan. Cover with foil. Bake in 350°F (175°C) oven for 40 minutes until peppers are tender-crisp.

Remove foil. Top each pepper with 1 tbsp. (15 mL) mozzarella cheese. Bake for 5 minutes until cheese is melted. Makes 8 stuffed peppers.

1 stuffed pepper: 176 Calories; 2.7 g Total Fat (1.0 g Sat., 25.1 mg Cholesterol); 477 mg Sodium; 13 g Protein; 25 g Carbohydrate; 2 g Dietary Fibre

CHOICES: 1 Grains & Starches; 1 Vegetables; 1 Meat & Alternatives

Pizza Pockets

Perfect for eating with your hands. Freeze and reheat for lunches!

Lean ground chicken	8 oz.	225 g
Chopped onion	1 cup	250 mL
Garlic clove, minced	1	1
Grated zucchini, with peel	1 cup	250 mL
Can of regular (or low-sodium) tomato sauce	7 1/2 oz.	213 mL
Dried whole oregano	1/2 tsp.	2 mL
Dried sweet basil	1 tsp.	5 mL
Freshly ground pepper	1/8 tsp.	0.5 mL
Dried crushed chilies	1/8 tsp.	0.5 mL
Grated part-skim mozzarella cheese	3/4 cup	175 mL
Grated light Parmesan cheese	2 tbsp	30 mL
Whole wheat flour	2/3 cup	150 mL
All-purpose flour	1 cup	250 mL
Baking powder	4 tsp.	20 mL
Salt	1/2 tsp.	2 mL
Canola oil	3 tbsp.	50 mL
Skim milk	3/4 cup	175 mL
All-purpose flour	1/3 cup	75 mL
Skim milk	1/4 cup	60 mL

Sauté first 4 ingredients in large non-stick frying pan until no pink remains in ground chicken and liquid is evaporated.

Stir in next 5 ingredients. Heat, uncovered, for 10 minutes on low, stirring occasionally, until thickened. Remove from heat. Let stand to cool slightly. Stir in both cheeses.

Combine next 4 ingredients in medium bowl. Make a well in center.

Combine canola oil and first amount of milk in small bowl. Add, all at once, to dry ingredients. Stir with fork just until moistened.

Turn out and gently knead dough on floured surface, using second amount of all-purpose flour, about 8 to 10 times. Divide dough into 8 portions. Roll each out to 6 inch (15 cm) circle. Place 1/3 cup (75 mL) filling to one side of center. Moisten edge of dough with some of second amount of milk. Bring unfilled side of dough over filling and press edges together with fork tines to seal well. Cut 3 or 4 slits in top with tip of sharp knife. Place on greased baking sheet. Brush with remaining milk. Bake in 400°F (205°C) oven for 13 to 15 minutes until golden brown. Makes 8 pockets.

1 pocket: 263 Calories; 8.2 g Total Fat (1.9 g Sat., 24.2 mg Cholesterol); 464 mg Sodium; 16 g Protein; 32 g Carbohydrate; 3 g Dietary Fibre

CHOICES: 1 1/2 Grains & Starches; 1/2 Vegetables; 1 1/2 Meat & Alternatives; 1 Fats

Pineapple Pork

This flavourful, mildly sweet pork is delicious over brown rice.

Lean boneless pork loin, trimmed and thinly sliced	3/4 lb.	340 g
Canola oil	2 tsp.	10 mL
Paprika	1/2 tsp.	2 mL
Ground ginger	1/2 tsp.	2 mL
Freshly ground pepper, sprinkle		
Medium carrots, thinly sliced on diagonal	2	2
Medium green pepper, cut into large slivers	1/2	1/2
Medium red pepper, cut into large slivers	1/2	1/2
Small onion, sliced lengthwise into wedges	1	1
Can of pineapple tidbits, drained, juice reserved	14 oz.	398 mL
White vinegar	2 tbsp.	30 mL
Brown sugar, packed	1 tbsp.	15 mL
Reserved pineapple juice	1/4 cup	60 mL
Low-sodium soy sauce	1 tbsp.	15 mL
Ketchup	1 tbsp.	15 mL
Cornstarch	2 tbsp.	30 mL

Sauté pork in canola oil in large frying pan for 1 minute. Sprinkle with paprika, ginger and pepper. Sauté until no pink remains in pork.

Stir in next 4 ingredients.

Reserve 1/4 cup (60 mL) pineapple juice. Set aside. Add remaining juice and pineapple to pork mixture. Drizzle with vinegar. Sprinkle with brown sugar. Stir. Bring to a boil. Cover. Simmer for 30 minutes until carrot is tender.

Combine remaining 4 ingredients in small bowl until smooth. Stir into pork mixture. Heat and stir until boiling and thickened. Makes 5 1/4 cups (1.3 L). Serves 4.

1 serving: 274 Calories; 7.5 g Total Fat (1.9 g Sat., 49.7 mg Cholesterol); 279 mg Sodium; 20 g Protein; 32 g Carbohydrate; 3 g Dietary Fibre

CHOICES: 1 Fruits; 1 Vegetables; 3 Meat & Alternatives

Paré Pointer

When the gangsters went sky diving, they had a chute out.

Turkey Vegetable Meatloaf

Have you ever seen a pretty meatloaf? Now you have! Excellent cold in a sandwich.

Medium carrot, cut into chunks	1	1
Medium red pepper, cut into chunks	1	1
Green onions, halved	2	2
Celery rib, cut into chunks	1	1
Garlic clove (optional)	1	1
Skim evaporated milk	1/2 cup	125 mL
Egg whites (large)	3	3
Fine dry whole wheat (or white) bread crumbs (see Tip, below)	1 1/2 cups	375 mL
Seasoned salt	1 tsp.	5 mL
Pepper	1/4 tsp.	1 mL
Worcestershire sauce	1 tsp.	5 mL
Lean ground turkey breast	1 1/4 lbs.	560 g
Can of stewed tomatoes, with juice	14 oz.	398 mL
Chopped fresh parsley, for garnish		
Red pepper slices, for garnish		

Process first 7 ingredients in food processor or blender until finely chopped. Pour into large bowl.

Add next 5 ingredients. Mix very well. Form into two 8 × 5 inch (20 × 12.5 cm) loaves. Place crosswise in greased or foil-lined 9 × 13 inch (22 × 33 cm) pan.

Process tomatoes with juice until almost puréed. Pour over meatloaves. Bake, uncovered, in 325°F (160°C) oven for 1 1/2 hours. Makes 2 loaves.

Garnish with parsley and red pepper. Serves 8.

1 serving: 204 Calories; 1.6 g Total Fat (0.4 g Sat., 44.2 mg Cholesterol); 554 mg Sodium; 23 g Protein; 23 g Carbohydrate; 1 g Dietary Fibre

CHOICES: 1 Grains & Starches; 2 Vegetables; 3 Meat & Alternatives

Pictured on page 89.

 To make 1/4 cup (60 mL) dry whole wheat bread crumbs, remove the crusts from 1 slice of stale or 2-day-old whole wheat bread. Leave the bread on the counter for a day or 2 until it's dry, or, if you're in a hurry, set the bread on a baking sheet and bake in a 200°F (95°C) oven, turning occasionally, until dry. Break the bread into pieces and process until crumbs reach the desired fineness.

Curried Chicken And Bulgur

A delicious one-dish meal. Even leftovers taste good.

Canola oil	2 tsp.	10 mL
Boneless, skinless chicken breast halves	3/4 lb.	340 g
(about 3), cut into bite-size pieces		
Medium onion, chopped	1	1
Large celery rib, diced	1	1
Medium carrots, coarsely grated	2	2
Curry powder	1/2 tsp.	2 mL
Ground cumin	1/4 tsp.	1 mL
Ground cardamom	1/4 tsp.	1 mL
Can of condensed chicken broth	10 oz.	284 mL
Water	3/4 cup	175 mL
Bulgur wheat (6 oz., 170 g)	1 cup	250 mL
Light raisins	2 tbsp.	30 mL
Ground cinnamon	1/8 tsp.	0.5 mL
Salt	1/8 tsp.	0.5 mL
Finely chopped toasted pecans	2 tbsp.	30 mL
(see Tip, page 111)		

Heat canola oil in non-stick frying pan on medium-high. Sauté chicken and onion until no pink remains in chicken and onion is soft.

Stir in next 5 ingredients. Heat for about 3 minutes until fragrant and carrot is softened.

Add next 6 ingredients. Cover. Simmer for 15 to 20 minutes until bulgur is tender. Fluff with fork.

Sprinkle with pecans. Makes 5 cups (1.25 L). Serves 4.

1 1/4 cups (300 mL): 334 Calories; 7.4 g Total Fat (1.0 g Sat., 50.1 mg Cholesterol); 646 mg Sodium; 29 g Protein; 40 g Carbohydrate; 9 g Dietary Fibre

CHOICES: 2 Grains & Starches; 1 Vegetables; 3 Meat & Alternatives

Pictured on page 89.

Fruit-Stuffed Pork Loin

Definitely a company dish. The mixed fruit filling complements the pork very well.

Lean boneless pork tenderloin, trimmed (about 8 × 4 × 2 inch, 20 × 10 × 5 cm, size)	2 1/4 lbs.	1 kg
Can of unsweetened applesauce	14 oz.	398 mL
Garlic cloves, minced	3	3
Salt	1/4 tsp.	1 mL
Brown sugar, packed	2 tbsp.	30 mL
Ground cinnamon	1/8 tsp.	0.5 mL
Ground nutmeg	1/16 tsp.	0.5 mL
Boiling water	2 cups	500 mL
Mixed dried fruit (such as apricots, prunes and cranberries), diced	1 cup	250 mL
Canola oil	2 tsp.	10 mL
Dried mixed herbs	1 tbsp.	15 mL
Garlic clove, minced (optional)	1	1
Freshly ground pepper, generous sprinkle		
White wine (or apple juice), optional	1/4 cup	60 mL
SAUCE		
Cornstarch	2 tbsp.	30 mL
Sherry (or non-alcohol sherry)	1/4 cup	60 mL
Ground cinnamon	1/2 tsp.	2 mL
Pepper, sprinkle		

Butterfly tenderloin by cutting horizontally lengthwise, not quite through center. Open flat. Pound with mallet or rolling pin to an even thickness.

Combine 1/3 cup (75 mL) applesauce with garlic and salt in small bowl. Spread on cut side of pork.

Combine next 4 ingredients in medium bowl. Add dried fruit. Let stand for 10 minutes. Drain, reserving liquid. Pack fruit onto pork in even layer, leaving about 1 inch (2.5 cm) from edges on all 4 sides uncovered. Roll jelly roll fashion. Tie with butcher's string or use metal skewers to secure.

Combine next 4 ingredients and 1 tbsp. (15 mL) reserved applesauce mixture in small dish. Coat pork with herb mixture. Place on rack in small roaster or pan with sides. Add wine to bottom of roaster. Cover. Bake in 325°F (160°C) oven for about 1 1/4 hours until internal temperature reaches 160°F (75°C). Remove from oven. Tent with foil.

(continued on next page)

Sauce: Combine cornstarch and reserved liquid in small saucepan. Add remaining applesauce mixture (about 1 1/4 cups, 300 mL) and sherry. Heat and stir on medium until boiling and thickened. Makes about 2 2/3 cups (650 mL) sauce.

Remove foil from roast. Place on serving platter. Drizzle with sauce. Sprinkle with cinnamon and pepper. Serves 8.

1 serving: 288 Calories; 8.7 g Total Fat (2.7 g Sat., 74.6 mg Cholesterol); 169 mg Sodium; 29 g Protein; 22 g Carbohydrate; 3 g Dietary Fibre

CHOICES: 1 Fruits; 4 Meat & Alternatives

Pictured on page 72.

Barbecued Beef-In-A-Bun

Done in the oven, lean beef is made tender with lots of sauce.

Flank steak, trimmed	1 1/2 lbs.	680 g
Barbecue sauce	1/2 cup	125 mL
Tomato sauce	1/2 cup	125 mL
Garlic cloves, minced (optional)	2	2
Prepared mustard	1 tbsp.	15 mL
Worcestershire sauce	1 tsp.	5 mL
Chopped green pepper	1/2 cup	125 mL
Small onion, thinly sliced	1	1
Whole wheat buns, toasted	8 – 10	8 – 10

Lay steak in bottom of lightly sprayed small roaster or 3 quart (3 L) casserole.

Combine next 6 ingredients in small bowl. Pour over steak.

Top with onion. Cover. Bake in 300°F (150°C) oven for about 2 hours until meat is very tender. Remove steak. Let cool slightly. Thinly slice on diagonal. Return to roaster. Stir.

Pile about 1/3 cup (75 mL) steak and sauce onto each bun to serve. Makes 3 1/2 cups (875 mL).

1/3 cup (75 mL): 191 Calories; 5.9 g Total Fat (2.3 g Sat., 26.4 mg Cholesterol); 393 mg Sodium; 17 g Protein; 17 g Carbohydrate; 3 g Dietary Fibre

CHOICES: 1 Grains & Starches; 2 Meat & Alternatives

To Make Ahead: Fill buns and wrap in plastic wrap and foil. Label. Freeze. To serve, defrost at room temperature for 3 1/2 to 4 hours. Good cold, or wrap in paper towel and microwave on medium (50%) for 30 seconds to 1 minute until hot.

Turkey Breast With Rice Stuffing

So elegant to serve for special guests. Lots of tasty vegetables in the stuffing.

RICE STUFFING

Long grain brown rice	1/3 cup	75 mL
Wild rice	1/3 cup	75 mL
Boiling water	2 1/3 cups	575 mL
Chicken bouillon powder	1 tbsp.	15 mL
Large onion, chopped	1	1
Chopped fresh mushrooms	2 cups	500 mL
Margarine	2 tbsp.	30 mL
Coarsely grated carrot	1 cup	250 mL
Diced red pepper	2/3 cup	150 mL
Chopped fresh parsley (or 1 tbsp., 15 mL, flakes)	3 tbsp.	50 mL
Finely chopped fresh sweet basil (or 1/2 tsp., 2 mL, dried)	1 tbsp.	15 mL
Grated lemon zest (optional)	1 tsp.	5 mL
Egg white (large)	1	1
Boneless, skinless turkey breast halves (about 2 1/2 lbs., 1.1 kg), see Note	2	2
Water	1/4 cup	60 mL
White (or alcohol-free) wine	1/4 cup	60 mL
Bay leaf	1	1
Freshly ground pepper, sprinkle		
Cornstarch (optional)	1 1/2 tsp.	7 mL

Rice Stuffing: Rinse and drain both rices. Stir into boiling water and bouillon powder in medium saucepan. Cover. Simmer for 40 to 50 minutes until wild rice has popped. Set aside.

Sauté onion and mushrooms in margarine in large frying pan for about 5 minutes until mushrooms have released their juices. Add carrot and red pepper. Sauté for 4 to 5 minutes until vegetables are tender.

Stir in next 3 ingredients. Add rice mixture. Stir in egg white. Makes 4 cups (1 L) stuffing.

Butterfly each turkey breast by cutting horizontally lengthwise, not quite through thickest part. Open flat. Place, 1 at a time, inside heavy plastic bag or between 2 sheets of plastic wrap. Pound with mallet or rolling pin to an even thickness. Remove. Pack 1/2 of stuffing on center of each breast, leaving edges, about 1/2 inch (12 mm), uncovered. Starting with shortest side, roll each breast, enclosing stuffing. Tie at 2 inch (5 cm) intervals with butcher's string. Place seam side down in oval roaster.

(continued on next page)

Main Dishes

Pour water and wine on top. Add bay leaf and pepper. Cover. Bake in 350°F (175°C) oven, basting frequently, for 1 1/2 to 1 3/4 hours until internal temperature reaches 175°F (80°C). Let stand in covered roaster for 10 minutes. Remove and discard bay leaf.

Strain juices. Add enough water to equal 2/3 cup (150 mL). Combine with cornstarch in roaster. Heat and stir until boiling and thickened. Makes 2/3 cup (150 mL) sauce. Each roll cuts into 5 slices. Serves 10.

1 serving: 220 Calories; 3.6 g Total Fat (0.8 g Sat., 70.5 mg Cholesterol); 291 mg Sodium; 30 g Protein; 14 g Carbohydrate; 1 g Dietary Fibre

CHOICES: 1 Grains & Starches; 4 Meat & Alternatives

Pictured on page 89.

Note: For 1 large roll (instead of 2 smaller ones), ask the butcher to prepare a whole breast. Flatten as in method. Fill with all the stuffing.

Chicken 'N' Rice

Wholesome flavour in this time-honoured comfort dish. Only 10 minutes to put together, and then forget about it for over an hour!

Boiling water	3 cups	750 mL
Dehydrated mixed vegetables	2/3 cup	150 mL
Chicken bouillon powder	1 tbsp.	15 mL
Garlic clove, minced (optional)	1	1
Poultry seasoning	1/2 tsp.	2 mL
Ground rosemary	1/4 tsp.	1 mL
Celery salt	1/2 tsp.	2 mL
Long grain brown rice	1 1/2 cups	375 mL
Chicken parts, skin removed	1 1/2 lbs.	680 g
Paprika	1/2 tsp.	2 mL
Freshly ground pepper, sprinkle		

Lightly spray 2 quart (2 L) casserole with no-stick cooking spray. Combine first 8 ingredients in casserole.

Arrange chicken over rice mixture. Do not stir. Sprinkle with paprika and pepper. Cover tightly. Bake in 350°F (175°C) oven for 75 minutes. Stir. Cover. Bake for 15 to 20 minutes until rice is tender. Serves 6.

1 serving: 318 Calories; 3.5 g Total Fat (0.8 g Sat., 37.8 mg Cholesterol); 525 mg Sodium; 19 g Protein; 53 g Carbohydrate; 6 g Dietary Fibre

CHOICES: 4 Grains & Starches; 4 Vegetables; 2 1/2 Meat & Alternatives

Chicken And Black Bean Stir-Fry

Make the sauce a day before so you're all ready to go
for the stir-fry. Serve with brown or white rice.

BLACK BEAN SAUCE

Dried black beans (see Note)	1/3 cup	75 mL
Boiling water	3 cups	750 mL
Garlic cloves, minced	2	2
Low-sodium soy sauce	1 tbsp.	15 mL
Grated gingerroot	1 tsp.	5 mL
Water	3/4 cup	175 mL
Sherry (or alcohol-free sherry)	2 tbsp.	30 mL
Canola oil	1 tsp.	5 mL
Boneless, skinless chicken breast halves (about 3), cut into long, thin strips	3/4 lb.	340 g
Canola oil	1 tsp.	5 mL
Carrots, thinly cut on diagonal	1/2 cup	125 mL
Broccoli stems, thinly cut on diagonal	2/3 cup	150 mL
Small onion, sliced lengthwise	1	1
Sliced fresh mushrooms	2/3 cup	150 mL
Water	1 tbsp.	15 mL
Broccoli florets, cut into bite-size pieces	1 1/2 cups	375 mL
Fresh pea pods (about 4 oz., 113 g)	20	20

Black Bean Sauce: Cook beans in boiling water in small uncovered saucepan for 70 minutes. Drain. Rinse. Remove 3 tbsp. (50 mL). Freeze remainder in 3 tbsp. (50 mL) portions for future sauce.

Bring beans and next 5 ingredients to a boil in small uncovered saucepan. Boil for about 15 minutes until reduced by half. Mash beans slightly with back of spoon while cooking. Makes 1/3 cup (75 mL) sauce.

Heat first amount of canola oil in non-stick frying pan or wok. Stir-fry chicken on high for 2 to 3 minutes until no pink remains in chicken. Remove to plate.

Heat second amount of canola oil in same frying pan or wok. Stir-fry carrot and broccoli stems for 2 minutes. Add onion and mushrooms. Stir-fry for 2 minutes. Add remaining 3 ingredients. Stir. Cover. Cook for 2 to 3 minutes until broccoli is tender-crisp. Add Black Bean Sauce and chicken. Stir to coat. Makes 4 1/2 cups (1.1 L).

1 cup (250 mL): 173 Calories; 3.4 g Total Fat (0.5 g Sat., 43.8 mg Cholesterol); 134 mg Sodium; 22 g Protein; 14 g Carbohydrate; 3 g Dietary Fibre

CHOICES: 1 1/2 Vegetables; 2 1/2 Meat & Alternatives

(continued on next page)

Main Dishes

Pictured on page 89.

Note: To save time, soak beans overnight. Drain. Bring beans and water to a boil in small uncovered saucepan. Cook on medium for about 55 minutes. To save even more time, use 3 tbsp. (50 mL) rinsed and drained canned black beans. Freeze remainder in small batches for future use.

Curried Chicken And Fruit

Fast and delicious. Serve on couscous or rice.

Boneless, skinless chicken breast halves (about 3), cut into bite-size pieces	3/4 lb.	340 g
Chopped onion	1/2 cup	125 mL
Garlic cloves, minced	2	2
Canola oil	2 tsp.	10 mL
Can of stewed tomatoes, with juice, chopped	14 oz.	398 mL
Water	1/2 cup	125 mL
Diced dried apricots	1/4 cup	60 mL
Raisins	1/4 cup	60 mL
Lemon juice	2 tsp.	10 mL
Curry paste (available in Asian section of grocery store)	2 tsp.	10 mL
Chicken bouillon powder	1 tsp.	5 mL
Ground cinnamon	1/4 tsp.	1 mL
Bay leaf	1	1
Skim evaporated milk	1/2 cup	125 mL
Cornstarch	2 tsp.	10 mL

Sauté first 3 ingredients in canola oil in large frying pan for 5 minutes until onion is soft.

Stir in next 9 ingredients. Bring to a boil. Reduce heat. Cover. Simmer for 30 minutes. Remove and discard bay leaf.

Combine evaporated milk and cornstarch in small dish. Add to chicken mixture while stirring. Bring to a boil. Heat for 1 minute until slightly thickened. Makes 4 cups (1 L).

1 cup (250 mL): 244 Calories; 4.4 g Total Fat (0.6 g Sat., 50.6 mg Cholesterol); 533 mg Sodium; 24 g Protein; 28 g Carbohydrate; 3 g Dietary Fibre

CHOICES: 4 Vegetables; 3 Meat & Alternatives

Orange Codfish

This will become your favorite way to do fish! Great with Fresh Fruit Salsa, page 91.

Egg whites (large)	2	2
Frozen concentrated unsweetened orange juice, thawed	3 tbsp.	50 mL
Low-sodium soy sauce	2 tbsp.	30 mL
Fine dry bread crumbs	1/2 cup	125 mL
Parsley flakes	1 tsp.	5 mL
Seasoned salt	1/2 tsp.	2 mL
Lemon pepper	1/2 tsp.	2 mL
Fresh (or frozen, thawed) cod fillets	1 lb.	454 g
Canola oil	1 tbsp.	15 mL
Lemon juice	1 tsp.	5 mL

Beat first 3 ingredients with fork in shallow bowl. Set aside.

Combine next 4 ingredients on sheet of waxed paper.

Dip cod fillets into egg mixture. Coat completely in crumb mixture. Lay in single layer in greased shallow baking dish. Whisk canola oil and lemon juice together in small dish. Drizzle over fish fillets. Bake in 475°F (240°C) oven for 15 to 20 minutes until fish flakes easily. Serves 4.

1 serving: 217 Calories; 4.9 g Total Fat (0.6 g Sat., 49.0 mg Cholesterol); 887 mg Sodium; 25 g Protein; 17 g Carbohydrate; trace Dietary Fibre

CHOICES: 1 Grains & Starches; 3 Meat & Alternatives

Pictured on page 90.

Variation: Omit cod. Use other fish fillets, such as snapper and haddock. Cooking time will be much quicker if very thin fish, such as sole, is used.

1. Chicken And Black Bean Stir-Fry, page 86
2. Turkey Vegetable Meatloaf, page 80
3. Turkey Breast With Rice Stuffing, page 84
4. Curried Chicken And Bulgur, page 81

Fresh Fruit Salsa

A very good condiment for roast pork or grilled fish.
Will keep in the refrigerator for up to four days.

Medium mango	1	1
Large papaya	1	1
Finely chopped red onion	1/3 cup	75 mL
Small red pepper, diced	1	1
Lime juice	1/3 cup	75 mL
Diced English cucumber, with peel	3/4 cup	175 mL
Chopped fresh cilantro	1 tbsp.	15 mL
Unsweetened applesauce	2/3 cup	150 mL
Granulated sugar	1 tsp.	5 mL
Ground cinnamon	1/4 tsp.	1 mL

Fresh mint, for garnish

Peel and dice mango and papaya, with juices, into medium bowl.

Stir in next 8 ingredients. Cover. Chill for 1 hour to blend flavours.

Garnish with mint leaves if desired. Makes 3 1/2 cups (875 mL).

1/4 cup (60 mL): 30 Calories; 0.1 g Total Fat (trace Sat., 0 mg Cholesterol); 1 mg Sodium; trace Protein; 8 g Carbohydrate; 1 g Dietary Fibre

CHOICES: 1/2 Fruits

Pictured at left.

1. Tuna Casserole, page 92
2. Jambalaya, page 93
3. Fresh Fruit Salsa, above
4. Orange Codfish, page 88

Tuna Casserole

An old standby lightened up in calories and fat grams.

Finely chopped onion	2 tbsp.	30 mL
Chopped fresh mushrooms	1/2 cup	125 mL
Diced red pepper	1/2 cup	125 mL
Canola oil	2 tsp.	10 mL
All-purpose flour	2 tbsp.	30 mL
Skim evaporated milk	1 cup	250 mL
Skim milk	1 cup	250 mL
Seasoned salt	1/2 tsp.	2 mL
No-salt herb seasoning	1 tsp.	5 mL
Freshly ground pepper, generous sprinkle		
Frozen peas, thawed and drained	1 cup	250 mL
Can of white tuna, packed in water,	6 oz.	170 g
drained and broken into chunks		
Medium no-yolk egg noodles	3 cups	750 mL
Water	3 qts.	3 L
Whole wheat bread slice, processed into crumbs	1	1
Grated light sharp Cheddar cheese	1/2 cup	125 mL

Fresh dill, for garnish

Sauté first 3 ingredients in canola oil in large non-stick frying pan until onion is softened. Sprinkle with flour. Stir well. Cook for about 1 minute. Slowly add both milks, stirring constantly, until boiled and just thickened.

Stir in next 3 ingredients. Remove from heat. Stir in peas and tuna.

Cook noodles in boiling water in large uncovered pot or Dutch oven for 8 minutes until tender but firm. Drain well. Pour into greased 2 quart (2 L) casserole. Gently fold in tuna mixture.

Combine bread crumbs and cheese in small bowl. Sprinkle over casserole. Cover. Bake in 350°F (175°C) oven for 30 minutes until bubbling.

Garnish with dill if desired. Serves 6.

1 serving: 248 Calories; 4.9 g Total Fat (1.7 g Sat., 18.5 mg Cholesterol); 400 mg Sodium; 19 g Protein; 32 g Carbohydrate; 2 g Dietary Fibre

CHOICES: 1 Grains & Starches; 1 Vegetables; 1/2 Milk & Alternatives; 1 Meat & Alternatives

Pictured on page 90.

Jambalaya

Add more cayenne pepper or hot pepper sauce for some real Cajun heat!

Olive oil	1 tbsp.	15 mL
Chopped onion	1 cup	250 mL
Chopped celery	1 cup	250 mL
Garlic clove, minced	1	1
Chopped mixed bell peppers	1 cup	250 mL
Boneless, skinless chicken breast halves (about 3), cut into bite-size chunks	3/4 lb.	340 g
Uncooked long grain brown rice	1 1/4 cups	300 mL
Water	2 cups	500 mL
Chicken bouillon powder	1 tbsp.	15 mL
Can of stewed tomatoes, with juice, cut up	14 oz.	398 mL
Hot pepper sauce	1/4 – 1/2 tsp.	1 – 2 mL
Pepper	1/4 tsp.	1 mL
Dried thyme	1/4 tsp.	1 mL
Dried whole oregano	1/4 tsp.	1 mL
Cayenne pepper	1/16 – 1/8 tsp.	0.5 mL
Medium raw shrimp, peeled and deveined (4 oz., 113 g)	12	12
Diced turkey kielbasa (about 3 oz., 85 g)	1/2 cup	125 mL
Sliced green onion	1/4 cup	60 mL

Heat olive oil in large non-stick frying pan. Add next 4 ingredients. Sauté for 5 minutes on medium.

Add chicken and rice. Sauté for 5 minutes until no pink remains in chicken. Turn into lightly sprayed 3 quart (3 L) casserole.

Combine next 8 ingredients in medium saucepan. Bring to a boil. Pour over chicken mixture. Stir gently. Cover. Bake in 350°F (175°C) oven for 45 minutes.

Stir in remaining 3 ingredients. Cover. Bake for 10 minutes until rice is tender. Makes 8 cups (2 L). Serves 6.

1 serving: 331 Calories; 7.5 g Total Fat (1.7 g Sat., 76.9 mg Cholesterol); 797 mg Sodium; 24 g Protein; 42 g Carbohydrate; 4 g Dietary Fibre

CHOICES: 2 Grains & Starches; 2 Vegetables; 2 1/2 Meat & Alternatives; 1/2 Fats

Pictured on page 90.

Pad Thai

A delicious traditional stir-fry recipe from Thailand. Have the vegetables cut, noodles softened and sauce made before stir-frying.

SAUCE		
Fish sauce (available in Asian section of grocery store)	3 tbsp.	50 mL
Water	1/2 cup	125 mL
Chili sauce	1/3 cup	75 mL
Brown sugar, packed	2 tbsp.	30 mL
Low-sodium soy sauce	1/3 cup	75 mL
Cornstarch	4 tsp.	20 mL
Dried crushed chilies (optional)	1/4 tsp.	1 mL
Rice vermicelli, broken	8 oz.	225 g
Cold water, to cover		
Canola oil	2 tsp.	10 mL
Lean boneless pork loin, cut julienne (see Note)	6 oz.	170 g
Garlic cloves, minced	2	2
Shredded cabbage	2 cups	500 mL
Medium carrots, shaved into long, thin ribbons	2	2
Canola oil	1 tsp.	5 mL
Egg whites (large), fork-beaten	2	2
Canola oil	1 tsp.	5 mL
Fresh bean sprouts	1/2 cup	125 mL
Green onions, cut julienne into 4 inch (10 cm) lengths (see Note)	3	3
Chopped fresh parsley (or cilantro)	2 tbsp.	30 mL

Sauce: Combine first 7 ingredients in small bowl. Set aside. Makes about 1 1/2 cups (375 mL) sauce.

Cover vermicelli with water in large bowl. Let stand for 5 minutes. Drain well. Set aside.

Heat first amount of canola oil in large non-stick frying pan or wok on medium-high. Stir-fry pork and garlic for 1 minute. Add cabbage and carrot. Stir-fry for 4 to 5 minutes until no pink remains in pork and vegetables are tender-crisp. Remove to bowl.

Heat second amount of canola oil in same frying pan. Pour in egg white. Heat, turning once, until firm. Remove to cutting surface. Slice into long shreds. Add to pork mixture.

(continued on next page)

Main Dishes

Heat third amount of canola oil in same frying pan. Stir-fry remaining 3 ingredients on medium-high for about 1 minute. Add noodles. Toss. Stir sauce. Add to vegetable mixture. Heat and stir until boiling and slightly thickened. Add pork mixture. Toss until hot. Makes 11 cups (2.75 L). Serves 6.

1 serving: 298 Calories; 4.3 g Total Fat (0.5 g Sat., 16 mg Cholesterol); 1307 mg Sodium; 14 g Protein; 51 g Carbohydrate; 3 g Dietary Fibre

CHOICES: 2 1/2 Grains & Starches; 2 Vegetables; 1 Meat & Alternatives

Pictured on page 72.

Note: It is easier to cut pork into thin strips if slightly frozen.

Asian Chicken Packets

This recipe can easily be doubled or tripled. No dirty pans to wash up after!

Thinly sliced onion	1/2 cup	125 mL
Julienned carrot	3/4 cup	175 mL
Slivered green pepper	1/2 cup	125 mL
Fresh bean sprouts (6 oz., 170 g)	2 cups	500 mL
Couscous	6 tbsp.	100 mL
Boneless, skinless chicken breast halves (about 4 oz., 113 g, each)	2	2
Brown sugar, packed	1 tsp.	5 mL
Ground ginger	1/4 tsp.	1 mL
Garlic powder	1/4 tsp.	1 mL
Hoisin sauce	1 tbsp.	15 mL
Water	3/4 cup	175 mL
Ketchup	1 tbsp.	15 mL
Freshly ground pepper, sprinkle		

Toss first 4 ingredients in medium bowl. Divide between two 12 × 24 inch (30 × 60 cm) heavy-duty foil sheets.

Sprinkle 3 tbsp. (50 mL) couscous on each sheet. Place chicken breast half on top.

Combine next 6 ingredients in small bowl. Drizzle 1/2 (about 7 tbsp., 115 mL, each) on chicken. Sprinkle with pepper. Bring both 12 inch (30 cm) ends up and together over chicken. Fold together several times to seal. Fold sides in at an angle. Roll up to seal and create handles for removing from oven. Repeat for second packet. Cook directly on center rack in 400°F (205°C) oven for 40 minutes. Makes 2 packets.

1 packet: 371 Calories; 2.1 g Total Fat (0.5 g Sat., 65.5 mg Cholesterol); 565 mg Sodium; 35 g Protein; 53 g Carbohydrate; 5 g Dietary Fibre

CHOICES: 2 Grains & Starches; 3 Vegetables; 4 Meat & Alternatives

Indonesian Pork Dinner

Lots of colour and texture to match the variety of flavours in this dish.

Water	3 2/3 cups	900 mL
Vegetable (or chicken) bouillon powder	1 tbsp.	15 mL
Dried crushed chilies	1/4 tsp.	1 mL
Long grain brown rice	1 1/2 cups	375 mL
Chopped onion	1 cup	250 mL
Chopped celery	1 cup	250 mL
Canola oil	2 tsp.	10 mL
Garlic cloves, minced	2	2
Grated gingerroot	2 tsp.	10 mL
Boneless pork loin chops, trimmed and diced	1 lb.	454 g
Ground cumin	1/2 tsp.	2 mL
Curry powder	1 tsp.	5 mL
Diced red pepper	1/4 cup	60 mL
Diced yellow pepper	2/3 cup	150 mL
Frozen mixed vegetables, thawed	3/4 cup	175 mL
Shredded cabbage	2 cups	500 mL
Low-sodium soy sauce	1 1/2 tbsp.	25 mL

Combine first 3 ingredients in large saucepan. Bring to a boil. Stir in rice. Cover. Simmer for 60 to 65 minutes until water is absorbed and rice is tender.

Sauté onion and celery in canola oil in large non-stick frying pan or wok on medium for 2 minutes.

Add next 5 ingredients. Stir-fry for 3 to 4 minutes until no pink remains in pork.

Stir in remaining 5 ingredients. Stir-fry for 3 to 4 minutes until cabbage is softened. Add rice. Toss until rice is steaming hot. Makes 10 cups (2.5 L). Serves 6.

1 serving: 355 Calories; 8 g Total Fat (2.0 g Sat., 44.4 mg Cholesterol); 566 mg Sodium; 23 g Protein; 48 g Carbohydrate; 3 g Dietary Fibre

CHOICES: 2 1/2 Grains & Starches; 1 1/2 Vegetables; 2 Meat & Alternatives

Turkey Cutlets With Mushroom Sauce

Ready in 20 minutes. Serve with rice or noodles.

All-purpose flour	1/4 cup	60 mL
No-salt herb seasoning	1 tbsp.	15 mL
Freshly ground pepper	1/2 tsp.	2 mL
Turkey breast cutlets, cut into 4 portions	1 lb.	454 g
Canola oil	2 tsp.	10 mL
Finely chopped onion	1/4 cup	60 mL
Sliced fresh mushrooms	1 1/2 cups	375 mL
White (or alcohol-free) wine (or chicken broth)	1/2 cup	125 mL
Skim evaporated milk	1/2 cup	125 mL
Cornstarch	2 tsp.	10 mL
Chopped fresh parsley (or 1/2 tsp., 2 mL, flakes)	1 tbsp.	15 mL
Salt	1/4 tsp.	1 mL

Combine first 3 ingredients in small dish. Pour onto waxed paper. Coat both sides of cutlets.

Heat canola oil in large non-stick frying pan on medium-high. Quickly brown both sides of cutlets. Remove to plate.

Sauté onion and mushrooms in same pan on medium, stirring occasionally, until mushroom liquid has evaporated and onion and mushrooms are golden and soft. Add wine. Add cutlets and any accumulated juices from plate. Cover. Simmer for 5 minutes.

Combine remaining 4 ingredients in small dish. Add to pan. Heat and stir for 1 minute until boiling and thickened. Serves 4.

1 serving: 246 Calories; 3.4 g Total Fat (0.5 g Sat., 71.6 mg Cholesterol); 268 mg Sodium; 32 g Protein; 15 g Carbohydrate; 1 g Dietary Fibre

CHOICES: 1/2 Grains & Starches; 4 Meat & Alternatives

Turkey Pot Pie

Great way to use leftover turkey. Double filling
recipe and freeze extra for future use.

FILLING

Water	2 1/2 cups	625 mL
Chicken (or vegetable) bouillon powder	1 tbsp.	15 mL
Diced red potato, with peel	2 cups	500 mL
Chopped celery	1 cup	250 mL
Finely chopped onion	1 cup	250 mL
Dried rosemary, crushed	1/2 tsp.	2 mL
Dried thyme	1/4 tsp.	1 mL
Garlic powder (optional)	1/4 tsp.	1 mL
Freshly ground pepper, sprinkle		
Frozen mixed vegetables	3 cups	750 mL
Chopped, cooked lean turkey (about 3/4 lb., 340 g)	2 cups	500 mL
Skim evaporated milk	2/3 cup	150 mL
All-purpose flour	3 tbsp.	50 mL

CRUST

All-purpose flour	1/2 cup	125 mL
Whole wheat flour	1/2 cup	125 mL
Baking powder	1 1/2 tsp.	7 mL
Salt	1/2 tsp.	2 mL
Canola oil	2 tbsp.	30 mL
Skim milk	1/2 cup	125 mL
Skim milk	1 tbsp.	15 mL
Paprika, sprinkle		

Filling: Combine first 9 ingredients in large uncovered saucepan or Dutch oven. Bring to boil. Cover. Reduce heat. Simmer for 10 minutes.

Add vegetables and turkey. Stir. Cover. Simmer for 15 to 20 minutes until potato is tender.

Whisk evaporated milk into flour in small bowl. Add to turkey mixture. Heat and stir until boiling and thickened. Turn into ungreased 9 x 9 inch (22 x 22 cm) glass pan or 2 1/2 quart (2.5 L) shallow casserole.

Crust: Combine first 4 ingredients in medium bowl.

(continued on next page)

Main Dishes

Add canola oil and skim milk all at once. Stir just until moistened. Turn out onto floured surface. Knead gently 8 to 10 times. Roll out 2/3 of dough to 1/8 inch (3 mm) thickness. Cut into 3/4 to 1 inch (2 to 2.5 cm) wide strips. Lay strips, 1 inch (2.5 cm) apart, diagonally on casserole one way. Roll out scraps and remaining dough. Cut strips as above. Lay on casserole diagonally the other way, creating lattice top.

Brush strips with milk. Sprinkle with paprika. Bake, uncovered, in 400°F (205°C) oven for 15 to 20 minutes until bubbling and top is golden brown. Serves 6.

1 serving: 369 Calories; 7.4 g Total Fat (1.1 g Sat., 57.3 mg Cholesterol); 710 mg Sodium; 28 g Protein; 49 g Carbohydrate; 3 g Dietary Fibre

CHOICES: 2 Grains & Starches; 4 Vegetables; 2 1/2 Meat & Alternatives

Pictured on divider.

Caesar Chicken

Intense Caesar flavour.

Non-fat mayonnaise (or non-fat salad dressing)	1/4 cup	60 mL
Non-fat Caesar salad dressing	1/4 cup	60 mL
Garlic cloves, minced	2	2
Dry mustard	1/2 tsp.	2 mL
Parsley flakes	1/2 tsp.	2 mL
Freshly ground pepper, sprinkle		
Boneless, skinless chicken breast halves (about 4 oz., 113 g, each)	4	4
Fine dry bread crumbs	1/3 cup	75 mL
Grated light Parmesan cheese	2 tbsp.	30 mL
No-stick cooking spray		

Combine first 6 ingredients in small bowl. Makes 1/2 cup (125 mL) marinade. Transfer to large sealable freezer bag.

Flatten breasts slightly. Place in bag. Turn to coat. Seal. Chill for several hours or overnight.

Combine crumbs and cheese on dinner plate. Remove chicken breasts from bag one at a time, leaving as much dressing mixture on as possible. Coat well in crumb mixture. Place on greased baking sheet. Spray chicken with cooking spray. Bake, uncovered, in center of 375°F (190°C) oven for 25 minutes until no pink remains in chicken and juices run clear. Serves 4.

1 serving: 224 Calories; 4.9 g Total Fat (1.0 g Sat., 69.3 mg Cholesterol); 490 mg Sodium; 29 g Protein; 14 g Carbohydrate; trace Dietary Fibre

CHOICES: 1 Grains & Starches; 4 Meat & Alternatives

Fast-Fix Beef

Using readily available broccoli slaw makes this very quick.

SAUCE		
Water	1 cup	250 mL
Low-sodium soy sauce	1/4 cup	60 mL
Hoisin sauce	1 tbsp.	15 mL
Cornstarch	2 tbsp.	30 mL
Canola oil	2 tsp.	10 mL
Sirloin steak, trimmed and cut crosswise into very thin slices	3/4 lb.	340 g
Garlic cloves, minced	2	2
Packaged broccoli slaw	3 cups	750 mL
Green onions, sliced	3	3
Fresh (or 10 oz., 285 g, frozen, thawed and drained) pea pods	1 1/4 cups	300 mL
Instant Chinese-style noodles (2 squares), broken up	4 oz.	113 g

Sauce: Combine all 4 ingredients in small bowl. Set aside. Makes about 1 1/2 cups (375 mL) sauce.

Heat canola oil in large frying pan or wok on medium-high. Add beef and garlic. Stir-fry for 1 minute. Add slaw, onion and pea pods. Stir-fry for 3 minutes.

Stir sauce. Add to beef mixture. Stir in noodles. Heat and stir for 3 minutes until boiling and thickened. Makes 6 cups (1.5 L).

1 cup (250 mL): 227 Calories; 6.8 g Total Fat (2.1 g Sat., 41.0 mg Cholesterol); 805 mg Sodium; 19 g Protein; 23 g Carbohydrate; 3 g Dietary Fibre

CHOICES: 1 Grains & Starches; 1 Vegetables; 2 Meat & Alternatives

Mexican Enchiladas

Just a slight bite. Use hot salsa for more spice.

Extra-lean ground beef	1/2 lb.	225 g
Chopped onion	1/2 cup	125 mL
Can of diced green chilies, drained	4 oz.	113 g
Envelope of taco seasoning mix	1/2	1/2
(1 1/4 oz., 35 g)		
Can of pinto beans, drained and rinsed	14 oz.	398 mL
Salsa	1/2 cup	125 mL
Frozen kernel corn	1/3 cup	75 mL
Corn tortillas (6 inch, 15 cm, size)	12	12
Salsa	1/2 cup	125 mL
Grated light sharp Cheddar cheese	1/2 cup	125 mL

Scramble-fry ground beef and onion in large non-stick frying pan until no pink remains in beef.

Stir in next 5 ingredients. Bring to a boil.

Heat tortillas, 6 at a time, wrapped in wet paper towels in microwave on high (100%) for 45 seconds. Place scant 1/3 cup (75 mL) filling on tortilla down center. Fold both sides over filling. Place, folded side down, in lightly greased 9 x 13 inch (22 x 33 cm) pan. Repeat with remaining tortillas. Keep tortillas under damp tea towel or paper towel to prevent cracking.

Drizzle with second amount of salsa and sprinkle with cheese. Cover. Bake in 350°F (175°C) oven for 15 to 20 minutes until hot. Makes 12 enchiladas.

1 enchilada: 201 Calories; 5.4 g Total Fat (1.7 g Sat., 15.8 mg Cholesterol); 814 mg Sodium; 11 g Protein; 28 g Carbohydrate; 3 g Dietary Fibre

CHOICES: 1 1/2 Grains & Starches; 1 Meat & Alternatives

Fish Cakes

Serve with Tzatziki, page 116, or Roasted Red Pepper Sauce, page 117.

Cod (or snapper) fillets	3/4 lb.	340 g
Skim milk	1/3 cup	75 mL
Bay leaf	1	1
Medium potatoes, peeled and cut into small chunks (about 3/4 lb., 340 g)	2	2
Water	1/2 cup	125 mL
Salt	1/2 tsp.	2 mL
Non-fat plain yogurt	3 tbsp.	50 mL
Egg whites (large), fork-beaten	2	2
Dijon mustard	1 tbsp.	15 mL
Worcestershire sauce	1 tsp.	5 mL
Green onions, finely sliced	2	2
Salt	1/4 tsp.	1 mL
Pepper	1/8 tsp.	0.5 mL
Dill weed	1/2 tsp.	2 mL
Parsley flakes	1/2 tsp.	2 mL
Fine dry bread crumbs	2/3 cup	150 mL

Put first 3 ingredients into large non-stick frying pan. Cover. Poach on medium for 3 to 4 minutes until fish is opaque and flakes easily. Drain well. Remove and discard bay leaf. Chill fish.

Put next 3 ingredients into small saucepan. Cover. Bring to a boil. Heat for 15 minutes until soft. Drain, reserving about 1/4 cup (60 mL) water. Mash until no lumps remain.

Combine next 9 ingredients in small bowl. Add to potato. Mix well. Add fish. Stir, flaking fish with fork. Form into 10 patties.

Place bread crumbs on sheet of waxed paper. Coat each patty. Place on greased baking sheet. Spray patties well with cooking spray. Bake, uncovered, in 375°F (190°C) oven for 20 minutes until firm, golden brown and crisp. Makes 10 patties.

1 patty: 92 Calories; 0.7 g Total Fat (0.2 g Sat., 14.9 mg Cholesterol); 190 mg Sodium; 9 g Protein; 12 g Carbohydrate; 1 g Dietary Fibre

CHOICES: 1 Grains & Starches; 1 Meat & Alternatives

EASY FISH CAKES: Omit cod, milk and bay leaf. Use two 7 1/2 oz. (213 g) cans of salmon, drained and skin and round bones removed. Omit potatoes and first amount of salt. Use 1 1/2 cups (375 mL) leftover mashed potatoes.

Vegetable Chili

Tastes even better the next day or after being frozen.
Keep small portions in the freezer to take for lunch.

Medium onion, chopped	1	1
Garlic cloves, minced (optional)	2	2
Chopped celery	1 cup	250 mL
Canola oil	2 tsp.	10 mL
Large red pepper, chopped	1/2	1/2
Large yellow pepper, chopped	1/2	1/2
Medium carrots, diced	2	2
Sliced fresh mushrooms	2 cups	500 mL
Diced medium zucchini, with peel	2 cups	500 mL
Can of diced tomatoes, with juice	14 oz.	398 mL
Can of red kidney beans, drained and rinsed	19 oz.	540 mL
Can of chick peas (garbanzo beans), drained and rinsed	19 oz.	540 mL
Can of beans in tomato sauce	14 oz.	398 mL
Chopped fresh parsley	1/4 cup	60 mL
Chili powder	2 tsp.	10 mL
Ground cumin (optional)	1/2 tsp.	2 mL
Dried whole oregano	1/2 tsp.	2 mL
Freshly ground pepper, sprinkle		
Dried crushed chilies (optional)	1/8 tsp.	0.5 mL
Bay leaf	1	1

Freshly ground pepper, for garnish

Sauté first 3 ingredients in canola oil in heavy-bottomed Dutch oven, stirring occasionally, until very soft.

Add next 16 ingredients. Cover. Simmer for about 1 1/2 hours until carrot is tender. Stir occasionally to prevent scorching.

Remove and discard bay leaf. Sprinkle with pepper. Makes 10 cups (2.5 L).

1 cup (250 mL): 179 Calories; 2.2 g Total Fat (0.2 g Sat., 0 mg Cholesterol); 484 mg Sodium; 9 g Protein; 34 g Carbohydrate; 9 g Dietary Fibre

CHOICES: 1 1/2 Grains & Starches; 1 Vegetables; 1 Meat & Alternatives

Pictured on page 107.

Bean Dumplings In Tomato Sauce

These dumplings provide a filling, nutritious meal with a different taste.

Chopped onion	1/2 cup	125 mL
Garlic cloves, minced	2	2
Chopped green pepper	1/2 cup	125 mL
Olive oil	2 tsp.	10 mL
Can of diced tomatoes, with juice	28 oz.	796 mL
Can of tomato juice	10 oz.	284 mL
Granulated sugar	1 1/2 tsp.	7 mL
Chili powder	1/2 tsp.	2 mL
Hot pepper sauce	1/4 tsp.	1 mL
All-purpose flour	2/3 cup	150 mL
Whole wheat flour	2/3 cup	150 mL
Baking powder	1 tbsp.	15 mL
Salt	1/4 tsp.	1 mL
Freshly ground pepper	1/8 tsp.	0.5 mL
Water	1/2 cup	125 mL
Can of white kidney beans, drained and rinsed	19 oz.	540 mL
Canola oil	2 tbsp.	30 mL
Egg whites (large)	2	2
Chopped green onion	1/2 cup	125 mL
Canola oil	1 tsp.	5 mL

Sauté first 3 ingredients in olive oil in large non-stick frying pan until onion is soft. Add next 5 ingredients. Bring to a boil. Simmer, uncovered, on medium for 30 minutes, stirring several times, until thickened.

Combine next 5 ingredients in medium bowl.

Process next 4 ingredients in food processor until almost smooth. Stir in green onion. Add to flour mixture. Stir just until moistened.

Divide and roll dough into about 50 balls (1/2 tbsp., 7 mL, each). Brown in canola oil in large non-stick frying pan. Add to sauce. Heat for 5 minutes until hot. Serves 6.

1 serving: 277 Calories; 8 g Total Fat (0.8 g Sat., 0 mg Cholesterol); 636 mg Sodium; 10 g Protein; 44 g Carbohydrate; 5 g Dietary Fibre

CHOICES: 2 Grains & Starches; 2 Vegetables; 1/2 Meat & Alternatives; 1 Fats

Pictured on page 107.

Spicy Rice And Beans

Quick and easy! Leave out the jalapeño pepper to tame the spicy heat.

Chopped onion	1 cup	250 mL
Garlic cloves, minced	3	3
Chopped celery	1/2 cup	125 mL
Jalapeño pepper, ribs and seeds	1	1
removed, finely diced (see Tip, below)		
Canola oil	1 tbsp.	15 mL
Ground cumin	1 tsp.	5 mL
Ground coriander	1 tsp.	5 mL
Chili powder	2 tsp.	10 mL
Long grain brown rice, uncooked	1 1/2 cups	375 mL
Grated carrot	1/2 cup	125 mL
Water	2 3/4 cups	675 mL
Vegetable bouillon powder	1 tbsp.	15 mL
Bay leaf	1	1
Can of red kidney beans, drained and rinsed	14 oz.	398 mL
Chopped tomato	1 cup	250 mL
Kernel corn, fresh or frozen	1/2 cup	125 mL
Chopped fresh cilantro (optional)	1 tbsp.	15 mL
Chopped fresh parsley	2 tbsp.	30 mL
(or 2 tsp., 10 mL, flakes)		

Sauté first 4 ingredients in canola oil in large non-stick frying pan for 3 minutes, stirring occasionally. Add next 4 ingredients. Cook on medium, stirring occasionally, until golden.

Stir in next 4 ingredients. Cover. Simmer on medium-low for 20 minutes.

Stir in next 3 ingredients. Cover. Heat for 15 to 20 minutes until liquid is absorbed. Remove and discard bay leaf.

Stir in cilantro and 1 tbsp. (15 mL) parsley. Garnish with remaining parsley. Makes 7 cups (1.75 L).

1 cup (250 mL): 253 Calories; 4 g Total Fat (0.5 g Sat., 0.2 mg Cholesterol); 356 mg Sodium; 8 g Protein; 48 g Carbohydrate; 5 g Dietary Fibre

CHOICES: 2 1/2 Grains & Starches; 1 Vegetables; 1/2 Fats

Pictured on page 107.

 Hot peppers contain capsaicin in the seeds and ribs. Removing the seeds and ribs will lower the heat but wear rubber gloves when handling the peppers and avoid touching your eyes. Wash your hands well afterwards.

Chicken Supreme

Lots of sauce to flavour rice or noodles.

SAUCE

Cold water	1 cup	250 mL
Cornstarch	2 tbsp.	30 mL
Low-sodium soy sauce	3 tbsp.	50 mL
Hoisin sauce	2 tbsp.	30 mL
Dried crushed chilies	1/2 tsp.	2 mL
Onion powder	1/2 tsp.	2 mL
Canola oil	2 tsp.	10 mL
Boneless, skinless chicken breast halves (about 3), cut into bite-size pieces	3/4 lb.	340 g
Canola oil	1 tsp.	5 mL
Thinly sliced mixed vegetables (such as carrots, celery, broccoli, cauliflower and green peppers)	6 cups	1.5 L
Medium onion, peeled and cut lengthwise into wedges	1	1
Garlic cloves, minced	2	2

Sauce: Combine first 6 ingredients in small bowl. Set aside. Makes about 1 1/2 cups (375 mL) sauce.

Heat first amount of canola oil in non-stick frying pan or wok on medium-high. Add chicken. Stir-fry for about 4 minutes until no pink remains in chicken. Remove to bowl.

Heat second amount of canola oil in same frying pan or wok. Stir-fry next 3 ingredients for about 8 minutes until tender-crisp. Add chicken. Stir sauce. Add to chicken mixture. Heat and stir until boiling and thickened. Makes 6 cups (1.5 L).

1 cup (250 mL): 147 Calories; 3.4 g Total Fat (0.4 g Sat., 32.9 mg Cholesterol); 889 mg Sodium; 16 g Protein; 14 g Carbohydrate; 3 g Dietary Fibre

CHOICES: 3 Vegetables; 2 Meat & Alternatives

1. Bean Dumplings In Tomato Sauce, page 104
2. Vegetable Chili, page 103
3. Spicy Rice And Beans, page 105

Main Dishes

Grilled Hoisin Flank Steak

Marinade is reduced and doubles as a flavourful baste.

Low-sodium soy sauce	3 tbsp.	50 mL
Hoisin sauce	3 tbsp.	50 mL
Water	1/2 cup	125 mL
Green onion	1	1
Hot chili paste	1/2 tsp.	2 mL
Garlic cloves	3	3
Slice of peeled gingerroot (1/4 inch 6 mm, length)	1/2	1/2
Dry red (or alcohol-free) wine	1/4 cup	60 mL
Lemon juice	2 tbsp.	30 mL
Flank steak, trimmed and scored on both sides	1 1/2 lbs.	680 g

Put first 9 ingredients into blender. Blend until smooth. Pour into large sealable freezer bag. Add steak. Seal. Chill for several hours or overnight, turning several times. Drain marinade into small saucepan. Bring to a boil. Heat until reduced by half and slightly thickened. Makes 1/2 cup (125 mL) sauce. Grill steak over medium-high heat on barbecue for about 5 minutes per side, basting several times with sauce, until desired doneness. Thinly slice across grain at slight angle. Discard any remaining sauce. Serves 6.

1 serving: 219 Calories; 8.4 g Total Fat (3.6 g Sat., 46.1 mg Cholesterol); 747 mg Sodium; 26 g Protein; 7 g Carbohydrate; trace Dietary Fibre

CHOICES: 3 1/2 Meat & Alternatives

Pictured on page 72.

Variation: Grill steak on medium-high in indoor double-sided grill. Heat for about 10 minutes, basting several times, until desired doneness.

1. Creamy Garlic Penne, page 110
2. Roasted Pepper And Tomato Pasta, page 113
3. Red Chard And Garlic Pasta, page 111

Creamy Garlic Penne

For garlic lovers only! Nice bite from the cayenne pepper.

Can of skim evaporated milk	13 1/2 oz.	385 mL
Skim milk	1 1/3 cups	325 mL
All-purpose flour	3 tbsp.	50 mL
Garlic cloves, minced	2 – 4	2 – 4
Vegetable bouillon powder	2 tsp.	10 mL
Boneless, skinless chicken breast halves (about 3), cut into bite-size pieces	3/4 lb.	340 g
Olive oil	2 tsp.	10 mL
Cayenne pepper	1/2 tsp.	2 mL
Coarsely ground pepper	1/4 tsp.	1 mL
Chopped fresh tomato	1 cup	250 mL
Imitation crabmeat (about 6 oz., 170 g)	1 1/2 cups	375 mL
Penne pasta (10 oz., 285 g)	3 cups	750 mL
Boiling water	2 qts.	2 L
Salt (optional)	1 tbsp.	15 mL
Grated light Parmesan cheese (optional)	2 tbsp.	30 mL
Chopped fresh parsley (optional)		

Whisk both milks into flour in large non-stick frying pan until smooth. Add garlic and bouillon powder. Heat and stir on medium-low until boiling and thickened. Keep warm on low, stirring occasionally.

Sauté chicken in olive oil in non-stick frying pan for 5 minutes until slightly browned. Sprinkle with cayenne and pepper. Add tomato and crabmeat. Toss well until hot. Add to milk mixture. Stir. Keep warm.

Cook pasta in boiling water and salt in large pot or Dutch oven for 10 to 12 minutes until just tender. Drain.

Turn pasta into serving dish. Pour sauce over top. Toss to coat. Sprinkle with Parmesan cheese and parsley. Makes 7 1/2 cups (1.9 L). Serves 6.

1 serving: 379 Calories; 3.9 g Total Fat (0.8 g Sat., 46.7 mg Cholesterol); 549 mg Sodium; 31 g Protein; 54 g Carbohydrate; 2 g Dietary Fibre

CHOICES: 2 1/2 Grains & Starches; 1 Milk & Alternatives; 2 Meat & Alternatives

Pictured on page 108 and on back cover.

Red Chard And Garlic Pasta

A very different combination of flavours, and they go together so well.

Finely chopped onion	1 cup	250 mL
Garlic cloves, minced	5	5
Olive oil	2 tsp.	10 mL
Red chard (1 bunch)	1 lb.	454 g
Water	1/4 cup	60 mL
Vegetable bouillon powder	1 tsp.	5 mL
Finely diced non-fat, low-sodium ham	1/2 cup	125 mL
Balsamic vinegar	2 tbsp.	30 mL
Seedless red grapes, halved	30	30
Fettuccine	12 oz.	340 g
Boiling water	3 qts.	3 L
Salt	1 tbsp.	15 mL
Chopped walnuts, toasted (see Tip, below)	1/3 cup	75 mL
Chopped fresh parsley	1/4 cup	60 mL

Sauté onion and garlic in olive oil in large non-stick frying pan until onion is soft.

Fold each chard leaf lengthwise along the rib. Cut ribs out. Slice ribs crosswise. Coarsely chop leaves and set aside. Add ribs and next 3 ingredients to onion and garlic. Cover. Heat for 5 minutes until chard ribs are tender. Stir in vinegar and grapes. Keep warm.

Cook pasta in boiling water and salt in large uncovered pot or Dutch oven for 10 minutes. Stir in chard leaves. Cook for 2 to 3 minutes until pasta is tender but firm. Drain. Return to pot.

Add chard ribs mixture. Toss. Garnish with walnuts and parsley. Makes 8 cups (2 L). Serves 6.

1 1/2 cups (375 mL): 321 Calories; 7.3 g Total Fat (0.8 g Sat., 0.1 mg Cholesterol); 424 mg Sodium; 12 g Protein; 53 g Carbohydrate; 4 g Dietary Fibre

CHOICES: 3 Grains & Starches; 1 Vegetables; 1 Fats

Pictured on page 108.

 tip To toast nuts or coconut, place in shallow pan. Bake in 350°F (175°C) oven for 5 to 10 minutes, stirring often, until desired doneness.

Salmon Rice Mélange

Make rice the night before, and this casserole goes together in minutes.

Package of long grain and wild rice mix	6 1/4 oz.	180 g
Chopped onion	1/2 cup	125 mL
Chopped celery	1/2 cup	125 mL
Canola oil	2 tsp.	10 mL
All-purpose flour	2 tbsp.	30 mL
No-salt herb seasoning	1/2 tsp.	2 mL
Skim evaporated milk	3/4 cup	175 mL
Skim milk	3/4 cup	175 mL
Low-sodium soy sauce	1 tbsp.	15 mL
Frozen peas	1 cup	250 mL
Can of red salmon, drained, skin and round bones removed	7 1/2 oz.	213 g
Fine dry bread crumbs	1/4 cup	60 mL
Grated light Monterey Jack cheese	1/2 cup	125 mL

Cook rice mix as per package directions without margarine.

Saute onion and celery in canola oil in non-stick frying pan for 5 minutes until soft. Sprinkle flour and herb seasoning over top. Stir for 1 minute. Slowly add both milks, stirring constantly, until smooth.

Stir in soy sauce and peas until boiling and thickened. Add rice and salmon. Stir gently. Turn into greased 1 1/2 quart (1.5 L) casserole.

Combine bread crumbs and cheese. Sprinkle over top. Bake, uncovered, in 350°F (175°C) oven for 20 to 30 minutes until edges are bubbling and casserole is hot in center. Serves 6.

1 serving: 457 Calories; 7.2 g Total Fat (2.7 g Sat., 23.6 mg Cholesterol); 633 mg Sodium; 19 g Protein; 40 g Carbohydrate; 2 g Dietary Fibre

CHOICES: 2 Grains & Starches; 1/2 Milk & Alternatives; 2 Meat & Alternatives; 1/2 Fats

Chicken Chili

Serve on brown rice or as is with salad. Uses Tomato Vegetable Sauce, page 118.

Lean ground chicken	3/4 lb.	340 g
Finely chopped celery	1/2 cup	125 mL
Container of Tomato Vegetable Sauce (3 cups, 750 mL), page 118, thawed	1	1
Chili powder	2 tsp.	10 mL
Can of red kidney beans, drained and rinsed	14 oz.	398 mL

(continued on next page)

Scramble-fry ground chicken and celery in non-stick frying pan until starting to brown. Drain. Add remaining 3 ingredients. Cover. Simmer for 30 minutes to blend flavours. Makes 5 cups (1.25 L).

1 1/4 cups (300 mL): 239 Calories; 3.1 g Total Fat (0.5 g Sat., 49.3 mg Cholesterol); 472 mg Sodium; 27 g Protein; 27 g Carbohydrate; 8 g Dietary Fibre

CHOICES: 1/2 Grains & Starches; 2 1/2 Vegetables; 3 1/2 Meat & Alternatives

---

Roasted Pepper And Tomato Pasta

You can't beat this for easy—and the flavour is sublime!

Medium red peppers, cut into 1 inch (2.5 cm) pieces (about 4 cups, 1 L)	3	3
Medium Roma (plum) tomatoes, diced (about 4 cups, 1 L)	8	8
Garlic cloves, halved	8	8
Olive oil	1 tbsp.	15 mL
Granulated sugar, pinch		
Salt	1/4 tsp.	1 mL
Freshly ground pepper, sprinkle		
Medium bow (or shell) pasta (about 10 oz., 285 g)	3 cups	750 mL
Boiling water	3 qts.	3 L
Salt	1 tbsp.	15 mL
Grated light Parmesan cheese	3 tbsp.	50 mL

Combine first 3 ingredients in large greased shallow glass casserole or enameled roaster (see Note). Drizzle with olive oil. Toss to coat. Bake in 425°F (220°C) oven for 30 minutes. Mix. Bake for 40 minutes until pepper is soft. Sprinkle with next 3 ingredients. Mash slightly with fork.

Cook pasta in water and salt in large uncovered pot or Dutch oven for 10 minutes until tender but firm. Drain.

Toss pasta, tomato mixture and Parmesan cheese. Serves 4.

1 serving: 384 Calories; 6.2 g Total Fat (1.2 g Sat., 1.9 mg Cholesterol); 283 mg Sodium; 14 g Protein; 70 g Carbohydrate; 6 g Dietary Fibre

CHOICES: 3 1/2 Grains & Starches; 3 Vegetables; 1/2 Meat & Alternatives; 1 Fats

Pictured on page 108 and on back cover.

Note: Don't cook tomatoes in a metal pan as taste can be altered by a reaction of the acid and metal.

Beef And Sprout Stir-Fry

Crunchy with lots of sauce to serve on noodles or rice.

SAUCE		
Water	1/2 cup	125 mL
Cornstarch	1 tbsp.	15 mL
Low-sodium soy sauce	1/4 cup	60 mL
Garlic powder (optional)	1/8 tsp.	0.5 mL
Canola oil	2 tsp.	10 mL
Lean sirloin steak, trimmed and cut crosswise into very thin slices	3/4 lb.	340 g
Garlic cloves, minced	2	2
Sliced fresh mushrooms	1 cup	250 mL
Thinly sliced celery	1/2 cup	125 mL
Coarsely shredded carrot	1/2 cup	125 mL
Chopped green onion	1/2 cup	125 mL
Fresh bean sprouts	3 cups	750 mL

Sauce: Stir first 4 ingredients in small bowl. Set aside. Makes about 7/8 cup (200 mL) sauce.

Heat canola oil in non-stick frying pan or wok on medium-high. Add beef and garlic. Stir-fry for 3 minutes. Add next 3 ingredients. Stir-fry for 4 minutes.

Stir sauce. Add to beef mixture. Add green onion and bean sprouts. Heat and stir for 2 minutes until boiling and thickened. Makes 4 cups (1 L).

1 cup (250 mL): 213 Calories; 8.9 g Total Fat (2.9 g Sat., 34.6 mg Cholesterol); 736 mg Sodium; 23 g Protein; 11 g Carbohydrate; 2 g Dietary Fibre

CHOICES: 2 Vegetables; 3 Meat & Alternatives; 1/2 Fats

Green Pepper Beef Loaf

A delicious dinner that's also great for sandwiches the next day.

Medium green pepper, cut into chunks	1	1
Skim evaporated milk	1/2 cup	125 mL
Large egg	1	1
Chopped onion	1/4 cup	60 mL
Onion salt	1 tsp.	5 mL
Freshly ground pepper, sprinkle		
Parsley flakes	1 tsp.	5 mL
Extra lean ground beef	1 1/2 lbs.	680 g
Fine dry bread crumbs	1/2 cup	125 mL

(continued on next page)

114   Main Dishes

Process first 7 ingredients in blender until pepper and onion are quite finely chopped. Pour into medium bowl.

Add ground beef and bread crumbs. Mix very well. Pack into foil-lined, greased 9 x 5 x 3 inch (22 x 12.5 x 7.5 cm) loaf pan. Bake, uncovered, in 350°F (175°C) oven for 1 1/2 to 2 hours until no pink remains in beef. Drain off liquid. Turn out onto plate. Peel off foil. Cuts into 10 slices.

1 slice: 212 Calories; 10.2 g Total Fat (3.9 g Sat., 76.9 mg Cholesterol); 256 mg Sodium; 22 g Protein; 7 g Carbohydrate; trace Dietary Fibre

CHOICES: 1/2 Grains & Starches; 3 Meat & Alternatives

Vegetable Gravy

This versatile sauce can be used as a stroganoff sauce for beef or chicken just by adding a little non-fat or light sour cream. Also good as a sauce for meatballs. Make a double batch of base and freeze to always have on hand.

Water	3 cups	750 mL
Vegetable bouillon powder	1 tbsp.	15 mL
Garlic cloves, peeled	8	8
Large carrot, cut into 1 inch (2.5 cm) pieces	1	1
Large celery rib, cut into 1 inch (2.5 cm) pieces	1	1
Large onion, chopped	1	1
Cornstarch (see Note)	2 tbsp.	30 mL
Water	1/4 cup	60 mL
Light sour cream (optional)	1/4 cup	60 mL

Bring water to a boil in large saucepan. Add next 5 ingredients. Cover. Simmer for about 40 minutes until vegetables are very soft. Blend in saucepan with hand blender. Freeze at this point if desired.

Stir water into cornstarch in small dish. Stir into vegetable mixture. Heat and stir on medium, until boiling and slightly thickened. Stir in sour cream. Makes 4 cups (1 L).

1/2 cup (125 mL): 29 Calories; 0.2 g Total Fat (0.1 g Sat., 0.1 mg Cholesterol); 234 mg Sodium; 1 g Protein; 6 g Carbohydrate; 1 g Dietary Fibre

CHOICES: 1 Vegetables

Note: To freeze, omit cornstarch and water. Freeze in 2 cup (500 mL) portions. After thawing, thicken with 1 tbsp. (15 mL) cornstarch and 2 tbsp. (30 mL) water.

Creamy Pasta Sauce

Serve this garlicky sauce on your favourite pasta.

Garlic cloves, minced	4	4
Olive oil	2 tsp.	10 mL
Can of skim evaporated milk	13 1/2 oz.	385 mL
All-purpose flour	2 tbsp.	30 mL
Container of Tomato Vegetable Sauce (3 cups, 750 mL), page 118, thawed	1	1
Dried sweet basil	1/2 tsp.	2 mL
Dried whole oregano	1/2 tsp.	2 mL
Salt	1/4 tsp.	1 mL
Pepper	1/8 tsp.	0.5 mL

Sauté garlic in olive oil in medium saucepan until soft.

Whisk evaporated milk into flour in small bowl. Add to saucepan. Heat, stirring constantly, until boiling and thickened.

Add next 3 ingredients. Heat and stir until heated through. Add salt and pepper. Stir. Makes 4 cups (1 L).

1/2 cup (125 mL): 95 Calories; 2.1 g Total Fat (0.3 g Sat., 1.9 mg Cholesterol); 273 mg Sodium; 6 g Protein; 14 g Carbohydrate; 2 g Dietary Fibre

CHOICES: 1 Vegetables; 1/2 Milk & Alternatives; 1/2 Fats

Variation: For a smooth sauce, purée in blender to desired consistency.

Tzatziki

Always a favourite and so healthy when using non-fat Yogurt Cheese, page 75. Serve on warmed and torn pita bread or with Fish Cakes, page 102.

Grated English cucumber, with peel	1 cup	250 mL
Salt	1 1/2 tsp.	7 mL
Yogurt Cheese, page 75	1 cup	250 mL
Granulated sugar	1/4 tsp.	1 mL
Garlic clove(s), minced	1 – 2	1 – 2
Salt	1/4 tsp.	1 mL
Freshly ground pepper, sprinkle		

(continued on next page)

Place cucumber in colander over small bowl. Sprinkle with salt. Let stand in refrigerator for 2 hours. Squeeze out excess moisture. Discard liquid. Empty cucumber into medium bowl.

Stir in remaining 5 ingredients. Cover. Chill for 1 to 2 hours to blend flavours. Makes 1 1/2 cups (375 mL).

1 tbsp. (15 mL): *12 Calories; 0.3 g Total Fat (0.2 g Sat., 1.1 mg Cholesterol); 121 mg Sodium; 1 g Protein; 1 g Carbohydrate; trace Dietary Fibre*

CHOICES: None

Roasted Red Pepper Sauce

Try this on Fish Cakes, page 102, poached fish fillets or in a sandwich wrap.
Will keep covered in refrigerator for up to one week.

Frozen egg product, thawed (see Note)	1/2 cup	125 mL
Garlic cloves	2	2
Non-fat mayonnaise (not salad dressing)	1/2 cup	125 mL
Lemon juice	2 tsp.	10 mL
Salt	1/8 tsp.	0.5 mL
Cayenne pepper, sprinkle		
Olive oil, heated to 250° – 300°F (120° – 150°C)	1/3 cup	75 mL
Can of roasted red peppers, drained and blotted dry, cut into strips	14 oz.	398 mL

Process egg substitute and garlic in blender until garlic is finely chopped. Add next 4 ingredients. Process, scraping down sides if necessary, until smooth.

With blender running, slowly and carefully add hot olive oil in steady stream through hole in lid.

With blender running, add red pepper strips, 1 at a time, allowing each piece to completely blend before adding another, periodically scraping down sides. Makes 2 cups (500 mL).

2 tbsp. (30 mL): *52 Calories; 4.6 g Total Fat (0.6 g Sat., 0 mg Cholesterol); 82 mg Sodium; 1 g Protein; 2 g Carbohydrate; trace Dietary Fibre*

CHOICES: 1 Fats

Note: 3 tbsp. (50 mL) = 1 large egg

Tomato Vegetable Sauce

Serve on pasta as is or freeze in batches and then use in
Chicken Chili, page 112, Creamy Pasta Sauce, page 116,
Cheese Spirals, page 131, or Minestrone Soup, page 153.

Chopped onion	2 cups	500 mL
Garlic cloves, minced	6	6
Olive oil	1 tbsp.	15 mL
Cans of diced tomatoes (28 oz., 796 mL, each), with juice	3	3
Can of tomato paste	5 1/2 oz.	156 mL
Zucchini, quartered lengthwise and sliced	4 cups	1 L
Medium green, red or yellow peppers, chopped	3	3
Dried sweet basil	2 tsp.	10 mL
Dried whole oregano	2 tsp.	10 mL
Parsley flakes	2 tsp.	10 mL
Coarsely ground pepper	1/2 tsp.	2 mL
Bay leaf	1	1
Granulated sugar	1 tsp.	5 mL

Sauté onion and garlic in olive oil in large non-stick frying pan, stirring frequently, until onion is golden. Turn into 4 quart (4 L) casserole or small roaster.

Stir in remaining 10 ingredients. Bake, uncovered, in 350°F (175°C) oven for 3 hours, stirring occasionally, until slightly thickened. Remove and discard bay leaf. Mash mixture slightly. Makes 12 cups (3 L). Divide into four 3 cup (750 mL) freezer containers. Label. Freeze.

1/2 cup (125 mL): 45 Calories; 1 g Total Fat (0.1 g Sat., 0 mg Cholesterol); 171 mg Sodium; 2 g Protein; 9 g Carbohydrate; 2 g Dietary Fibre

CHOICES: 1 1/2 Vegetables

Paré Pointer

They threw eggs at the actor because ham and eggs go together.

Mediterranean Garbanzo Salad

All the flavours come together in a full and rich taste once salad has chilled.

Can of garbanzo beans (chick peas), drained and rinsed	19 oz.	540 g
Diced English cucumber, with peel	1 cup	250 mL
Medium Roma (plum) tomatoes, seeded and diced (about 1 1/3 cups, 325 mL)	3	3
Finely chopped red onion	1/4 cup	60 mL
Diced green pepper	1/2 cup	125 mL
Sliced ripe olives	1/4 cup	60 mL
FETA CHEESE DRESSING		
1% buttermilk	2 tbsp.	30 mL
Olive oil	1 tsp.	5 mL
Chopped fresh oregano leaves (or 1 tsp., 5 mL, dried)	2 tsp.	10 mL
Chopped fresh parsley (or 2 tsp., 10 mL, flakes)	1 tbsp.	15 mL
Light feta cheese, crumbled	1/2 cup	125 mL
Freshly ground pepper, sprinkle		
Grated lemon peel (or juice)	1 tsp.	5 mL
Garlic clove(s), minced (or 1/4 tsp., 1 mL, powder)	1	1

Combine first 6 ingredients in large bowl. Makes 6 cups (1.5 L) vegetables.

Feta Cheese Dressing: Process all 8 ingredients in blender until quite smooth. Makes 2/3 cup (150 mL) dressing. Add to vegetables. Toss to coat. Chill for at least 1 to 2 hours to blend flavours. Serves 8.

1 serving: 99 Calories; 3.8 g Total Fat (1.6 g Sat., 8.3 mg Cholesterol); 208 mg Sodium; 5 g Protein; 13 g Carbohydrate; 2 g Dietary Fibre

CHOICES: 1/2 Grains & Starches; 1/2 Vegetables; 1/2 Meat & Alternatives; 1/2 Fats

Pictured on page 125.

Quick Pasta Salad

Using canned peppers and enhancing bottled dressing makes this fast to prepare.

Rotini pasta	2 cups	500 mL
Boiling water	2 qts.	2 L
Salt	2 tsp.	10 mL
Can of roasted red peppers, drained and cut into 2 inch (5 cm) slivers	14 oz.	398 mL
Paper-thin sliced red onion	1 cup	250 mL
Non-fat French dressing	1/2 cup	125 mL
Garlic clove(s), minced	1 – 2	1 – 2
Dried whole oregano, crushed	1/4 tsp.	1 mL
Freshly ground pepper, sprinkle		

Cook pasta in boiling water and salt in large uncovered saucepan for 10 to 12 minutes until tender but firm. Drain. Rinse well with cold water. Drain.

Combine pasta with red pepper and onion in medium bowl.

Combine remaining 4 ingredients in small bowl. Pour over salad. Mix well. Cover. Chill. Serves 4.

1 serving: 248 Calories; 0.9 g Total Fat (0.1 g Sat., 0 mg Cholesterol); 444 mg Sodium; 8 g Protein; 52 g Carbohydrate; 4 g Dietary Fibre

CHOICES: 2 Grains & Starches; 2 Vegetables

Cheese And Artichoke Salad

The perfect recipe for a time crunch—only 15 minutes preparation time!

DRESSING		
Non-fat Italian dressing	1/2 cup	125 mL
White (or alcohol-free) wine	2 tbsp.	30 mL
Small garlic clove, minced	1	1
Dried rosemary (or pinch of ground rosemary)	1/2 tsp.	2 mL
Large shell pasta (not jumbo), about 5 oz. (140 g)	1 3/4 cups	425 mL
Boiling water	6 cups	1.5 L
Salt	1 1/2 tsp.	7 mL
Can of artichoke hearts, drained and chopped	14 oz.	398 mL
Part-skim mozzarella cheese, cut into 1/2 inch (12 mm) cubes	4 oz.	113 g
Diced red pepper	1/4 cup	60 mL

(continued on next page)

Dressing: Combine first 4 ingredients in small bowl. Let stand at room temperature for at least 15 minutes. Makes about 2/3 cup (150 mL) dressing.

Cook pasta in boiling water and salt in large saucepan for about 8 minutes until tender but firm. Drain. Rinse with cold water. Drain. Place in medium bowl.

Add remaining 3 ingredients. Add dressing. Toss to coat. Cover. Chill. Makes 5 cups (1.25 L).

1 cup (250 mL): 200 Calories; 4.3 g Total Fat (2.4 g Sat., 13.5 mg Cholesterol); 536 mg Sodium; 11 g Protein; 29 g Carbohydrate; 3 g Dietary Fibre

CHOICES: 1 1/2 Grains & Starches; 1 Meat & Alternatives

Marinated Salad

*You'll love the refreshing combination of the vegetables and marinade.
So easy to make ahead. The bulgur makes it chewy.*

Bulgur wheat	1/2 cup	125 mL
Boiling water	1 1/2 cups	375 mL
Seeded, diced tomato	2 cups	500 mL
Diced English cucumber, with peel	2 cups	500 mL
Diced green pepper	1 cup	250 mL
Sliced ripe olives	1/2 cup	125 mL
Thinly sliced green onion	1/4 cup	60 mL
Feta cheese, crumbled into small pieces, (optional)	3/4 cup	175 mL
Olive oil	2 tbsp.	30 mL
Lemon juice	2 tbsp.	30 mL
Dried whole oregano, crushed	1/4 tsp.	1 mL
Salt	1/4 tsp.	1 mL
Freshly ground pepper, to taste		
Torn romaine lettuce	6 cups	1.5 L

Soak bulgur in boiling water in small saucepan for 10 minutes. Drain. Set aside.

Combine next 11 ingredients in large bowl. Cover. Let stand at room temperature for 30 minutes. Drain and discard liquid. Add bulgur.

Add lettuce. Toss gently. Serve immediately. Serves 8.

1 serving: 70 Calories; 1.9 g Total Fat (0.3 g Sat., 0 mg Cholesterol); 142 mg Sodium; 3 g Protein; 12 g Carbohydrate; 4 g Dietary Fibre

CHOICES: 1/2 Grains & Starches; 1 Vegetables; 1/2 Fats

Pictured on divider.

Vinaigrette Potato Salad

Double or triple the recipe to serve a crowd.

Unpeeled baby potatoes	1 lb.	454 g
Water		
Medium carrot, coarsely grated	1	1
Coarsely chopped red pepper	1 cup	250 mL
Green onions, sliced	2	2
DRESSING		
Vegetable bouillon powder	1 tsp.	5 mL
Hot water	1/4 cup	60 mL
Olive oil	2 tbsp.	30 mL
Balsamic vinegar	1 tbsp.	15 mL
Lemon juice	1 tbsp.	15 mL
Garlic clove	1	1
Chopped fresh parsley (or 1 tsp., 5 mL, flakes)	1 tbsp.	15 mL
Chopped fresh marjoram leaves (or 1 tsp., 5 mL, dried)	1 tbsp.	15 mL
Dijon mustard	1 tsp.	5 mL
Salt	1/2 tsp.	2 mL
Freshly ground pepper, sprinkle		

Cook potatoes in water in small saucepan until tender. Drain. Cool. Cut into quarters, or in halves if very small. Place in medium bowl.

Add next 3 ingredients to bowl.

Dressing: Dissolve bouillon powder in hot water in blender. Add remaining 9 ingredients. Process. Pour over salad. Toss. Chill. Toss before serving. Makes 4 cups (1 L).

1 cup (250 mL): 169 Calories; 7.3 g Total Fat (1.0 g Sat., 0.1 mg Cholesterol); 524 mg Sodium; 3 g Protein; 24 g Carbohydrate; 3 g Dietary Fibre

CHOICES: 1 Grains & Starches; 2 Vegetables; 1 1/2 Fats

Pictured on page 125.

 tip There is no need to cover potatoes with water while boiling. To cook potatoes without losing their nutrients, add 1/2 to 1 inch (1.2 to 2.5 cm) water to the pot. Cover. Bring to a boil. Reduce heat. Simmer until desired doneness.

Couscous Seafood Salad

Slightly chewy with just enough dressing to flavour.

Couscous	1/2 cup	125 mL
Boiling water	2/3 cup	150 mL
Finely diced green pepper	1/2 cup	125 mL
Finely diced celery	1/4 cup	60 mL
Thinly sliced green onion	2 tbsp.	30 mL
Chopped imitation crabmeat	3/4 cup	175 mL
(about 3 oz., 85 g)		
Frozen tiny peas, thawed	1/2 cup	125 mL
Shredded fresh spinach leaves	3/4 cup	175 mL
Toasted sesame seeds (see Tip, page 111)	2 tsp.	10 mL
DRESSING		
Rice vinegar	2 tbsp.	30 mL
Ketchup	2 tsp.	10 mL
Granulated sugar	1/2 tsp.	2 mL
Garlic powder	1/8 tsp.	0.5 mL
Ground coriander	1/16 tsp.	0.5 mL
Ground oregano	1/16 tsp.	0.5 mL
Canola oil	1 tsp.	5 mL

Stir couscous into boiling water. Cover. Let stand for 5 minutes. Fluff with fork. Turn into medium bowl. Cool.

Add next 7 ingredients. Toss.

Dressing: Whisk all 7 ingredients in small bowl. Pour over spinach mixture. Toss lightly. Makes 4 cups (1 L). Serves 4.

1 cup (250 mL): 161 Calories; 2.5 g Total Fat (0.4 g Sat., 7.7 mg Cholesterol); 225 mg Sodium; 8 g Protein; 27 g Carbohydrate; 3 g Dietary Fibre

CHOICES: 1 Grains & Starches; 2 Vegetables; 1/2 Meat & Alternatives

Artichoke Salad

A delicious and nutritious salad with a colourful presentation.

Medium tomato, cut into 8 wedges	1	1
English cucumber slices, with peel	8	8
Medium ripe olives, cut in half	8	8
Can of artichoke hearts, drained and cut into quarters	14 oz.	398 mL
Medium green pepper, thinly sliced	1/2	1/2
Small red onion, thinly sliced	1/2	1/2
Olive oil	2 tbsp.	30 mL
Lemon juice	1 tbsp.	15 mL
White wine vinegar	1 1/2 tsp.	7 mL
Liquid honey	1 1/2 tsp.	7 mL
Garlic clove, minced	1	1
Dried whole oregano	1/4 tsp.	1 mL
Freshly ground pepper, sprinkle		
Mixed salad greens	6 cups	1.5 L
Crumbled feta cheese, optional	1/4 cup	60 mL

Combine first 6 ingredients in medium bowl.

Whisk next 7 ingredients together in small bowl. Pour onto vegetable mixture. Gently toss. Chill for at least 1 hour to blend flavours.

Arrange on bed of salad greens. Sprinkle with cheese. Serves 4.

1 serving: 138 Calories; 8.3 g Total Fat (1.1 g Sat., 0 mg Cholesterol); 280 mg Sodium; 4 g Protein; 15 g Carbohydrate; 5 g Dietary Fibre

CHOICES: 2 Vegetables; 1/2 Meat & Alternatives; 1 1/2 Fats

Pictured at right.

1. Mediterranean Garbanzo Salad, page 119
2. Fresh Strawberry Dressing, page 128
3. Creamy Orange Dressing, page 128
4. Artichoke Salad, above
5. Vinaigrette Potato Salad, page 122

Props courtesy of: Winners Stores

Caesar Salad Dressing

You'll never miss the eggs and oil in this tasty substitute for high-fat Caesar dressing.

Garlic clove(s)	1 – 2	1 – 2
Water	1 tbsp.	15 mL
Lemon juice	1 tbsp.	15 mL
Red wine vinegar	1 tbsp.	15 mL
Dry mustard	1/4 tsp.	1 mL
Silken (or soft) tofu	3/4 cup	175 mL
Anchovy paste	1 tbsp.	15 mL
Salt	1/8 tsp.	0.5 mL
Freshly ground pepper, sprinkle		
Grated light Parmesan cheese	1 tbsp.	15 mL

Process all 10 ingredients in blender until smooth. Makes 1 cup (250 mL).

2 tbsp. (30 mL): 27 Calories; 1.5 g Total Fat (0.3 g Sat., 2.4 mg Cholesterol); 150 mg Sodium; 3 g Protein; 1 g Carbohydrate; trace Dietary Fibre

CHOICES: 1/2 Meat & Alternatives

1. Bulgur Curry, page 145
2. Spicy Potato Bumps, page 130
3. Cheese Spirals, page 131

Creamy Orange Dressing

Serve this refreshing dressing with spinach or mixed salad greens.

Frozen concentrated orange juice, thawed (half of 12 1/2 oz., 355 mL, can)	3/4 cup	175 mL
White wine vinegar	2 tbsp.	30 mL
Non-fat plain yogurt	1/2 cup	125 mL
Liquid honey (or sugar substitute, such as Sugar Twin, to taste)	1 tbsp.	15 mL
Ground cinnamon	1/4 tsp.	1 mL

Whisk all 5 ingredients in small bowl until smooth. Makes 1 1/2 cups (375 mL).

2 tbsp. (30 mL): 40 Calories; 0.1 g Total Fat (trace Sat., 0.2 mg Cholesterol); 8 mg Sodium; 1 g Protein; 9 g Carbohydrate; trace Dietary Fibre

CHOICES: 1/2 Fruits

Pictured on page 125.

Fresh Strawberry Dressing

Wonderful strawberry flavour with a nice peppery aftertaste.

Chopped fresh strawberries	1 cup	250 mL
White wine vinegar	1 tbsp.	15 mL
Balsamic vinegar	1 1/2 tsp.	7 mL
Liquid honey (optional)	1 tsp.	5 mL
Freshly ground pepper	1 tsp.	5 mL

Process all 5 ingredients in blender until smooth. Makes 1 cup (250 mL).

2 tbsp. (30 mL): 6 Calories; 0.1 g Total Fat (trace Sat., 0 mg Cholesterol); trace Sodium; trace Protein; 2 g Carbohydrate; trace Dietary Fibre

CHOICES: None

Pictured on page 125.

Vegetable Medley

Put these in with a roast, and everything will be ready at the same time.

Red baby potatoes, halved	1 lb.	454 g
Medium sweet potatoes, cut bite size	2	2
(about 1 lb., 454 g)		
Parsnips, cut bite size	3	3
(about 2 cups, 500 mL)		
Carrots, cut bite size	5	5
(about 2 1/2 cups, 625 mL)		
Chopped onion	2/3 cup	150 mL
Boiling water	3 tbsp.	50 mL
Margarine	1 tsp.	5 mL
Chicken bouillon powder	1/2 tsp.	2 mL
Garlic clove(s), minced (optional)	1 – 2	1 – 2
Parsley flakes	1/2 tsp.	2 mL
Seasoned salt	1/2 tsp.	2 mL
Pepper	1/8 tsp.	0.5 mL

Place first 4 ingredients in greased 9 x 13 inch (22 x 33 cm) baking pan or shallow 2 quart (2 L) casserole. Add onion. Stir.

Pour boiling water over margarine and bouillon powder in small bowl. Stir to dissolve. Stir in remaining 4 ingredients. Pour bouillon mixture over vegetables. Toss gently. Cover tightly with foil or lid. Bake in 350°F (175°C) oven for 1 1/2 hours until vegetables are tender. Uncover for last 10 to 15 minutes to evaporate liquid in pan. Serves 6.

1 serving: 210 Calories; 1.3 g Total Fat (0.3 g Sat., trace Cholesterol); 218 mg Sodium; 4 g Protein; 47 g Carbohydrate; 7 g Dietary Fibre

CHOICES: 2 Grains & Starches; 3 Vegetables

Paré Pointer
The children of invisible parents wouldn't be much to look at.

Spicy Potato Bumps

Any combination of spices could be used for these, and they would still be as delicious!

Unpeeled medium baking potatoes	6	6
Olive oil	1 tbsp.	15 mL
Parsley flakes	2 tsp.	10 mL
Salt	1 1/2 tsp.	7 mL
Chili powder	1 tsp.	5 mL
Paprika	1 tsp.	5 mL
Dried thyme, crushed	1/2 tsp.	2 mL
Garlic powder	1/4 tsp.	1 mL
Cayenne pepper	1/8 tsp.	0.5 mL
Ground rosemary	1/16 tsp.	0.5 mL

Cut each potato in quarters lengthwise. Cut each quarter crosswise into 3 pieces. Toss potato with olive oil in large bowl.

Combine remaining 8 ingredients in small cup. Sprinkle over potato. Toss to coat. Spread on large greased baking sheet with sides. Bake, uncovered, in center of 425°F (220°C) oven. Cook for about 45 minutes, stirring twice, until browned and tender. Serves 6.

1 serving: 134 Calories; 2.6 g Total Fat (0.4 g Sat., 0 mg Cholesterol); 694 mg Sodium; 3 g Protein; 25 g Carbohydrate; 3 g Dietary Fibre

CHOICES: 1 1/2 Grains & Starches; 1/2 Fats

Pictured on page 126.

Crumbed Broccoli

Serve this spicy salad immediately after adding the crumbs.

Olive oil	2 tsp.	10 mL
Finely chopped jalapeño pepper, ribs and seeds removed (see Tip, page 105)	1 tbsp.	15 mL
Dry whole wheat bread crumbs (see Tip, page 80)	1/3 cup	75 mL
Garlic cloves, minced	3	3
Olive oil	2 tsp.	10 mL
Water	1/4 cup	60 mL
Head of broccoli, stems thinly sliced and florets cut bite size	1 1/2 lbs.	680 g

(continued on next page)

Heat first amount of olive oil in small non-stick frying pan on medium. Sauté jalapeño for 30 seconds to 1 minute until slightly soft. Add bread crumbs. Sauté until crumbs are toasted and golden brown. Set aside.

Sauté garlic in second amount of olive oil until sizzling but not brown. Add water. Bring to a boil. Add broccoli stems on bottom of frying pan and florets on top. Cover. Heat on low for 5 to 6 minutes until broccoli is bright green and tender-crisp. Drain. Toss broccoli with crumb mixture in medium bowl. Makes 3 1/2 cups (875 mL).

2/3 cup (150 mL): 86 Calories; 3.7 g Total Fat (0.5 g Sat., 0.1 mg Cholesterol); 78 mg Sodium; 4 g Protein; 11 g Carbohydrate; 3 g Dietary Fibre

CHOICES: 1 Vegetables; 1/2 Fats

Cheese Spirals

Uses a container of Tomato Vegetable Sauce, page 118.

Lasagna noodles	8	8
Boiling water	3 qts.	3 L
Salt	1 tbsp.	15 mL
Grated part-skim mozzarella cheese	1/2 cup	125 mL
Light ricotta cheese	1/2 cup	125 mL
Grated light Parmesan cheese	2 tbsp.	30 mL
Dried marjoram, crushed	1/2 tsp.	2 mL
Dried sweet basil	1 tsp.	5 mL
Egg white (large), fork-beaten	1	1
Container of Tomato Vegetable Sauce (3 cups, 750 mL), page 118, thawed	1	1

Cook noodles in boiling water and salt in large uncovered pot or Dutch oven for 12 to 14 minutes until tender but firm. Drain. Rinse in cold water. Drain.

Combine next 3 ingredients in small bowl. Add next 3 ingredients. Mix. Spread cheese mixture along lengths of 8 cooked noodles. Roll up each, jelly roll style. Place seam side down in shallow baking dish.

Pour Tomato Vegetable Sauce over rolls. Cover. Bake in 350°F (175°C) oven for 30 to 40 minutes until bubbling and hot. Makes 8 rolls. Serves 4.

1 serving: 315 Calories; 7.7 g Total Fat (3.8 g Sat., 20.1 mg Cholesterol); 440 mg Sodium; 17 g Protein; 46 g Carbohydrate; 4 g Dietary Fibre

CHOICES: 2 Grains & Starches; 2 Vegetables; 1 Meat & Alternatives; 1/2 Fats

Pictured on page 126.

Creamy Garlic Spaghetti

A great side dish with just about any meat.

Box of whole wheat spaghetti	13 oz.	375 g
Boiling water	4 qts.	4 L
Salt	4 tsp.	20 mL
Chopped onion	1 1/2 cups	375 mL
Garlic cloves, minced	6	6
Olive oil	1 tbsp.	15 mL
All-purpose flour	1 tbsp.	15 mL
Vegetable (or chicken) bouillon powder	1 tsp.	5 mL
Water	3/4 cup	175 mL
Skim evaporated milk	1/4 cup	60 mL
Grated light Parmesan cheese	1/4 cup	60 mL
Chopped fresh parsley, for garnish		

Cook pasta in boiling water and salt in large uncovered pot or Dutch oven for 8 to 10 minutes until tender but firm. Drain well.

Sauté onion and garlic in olive oil in large non-stick frying pan for about 5 minutes until onion is golden and very soft. Sprinkle with flour and bouillon powder. Mix well. Gradually stir in water and milk. Heat and stir until bubbling. Cover. Simmer for about 30 minutes until thickened. Purée in blender (see Safety Tip). Makes 1 1/4 cups (300 mL).

Turn pasta into large bowl. Add garlic mixture and Parmesan cheese. Toss. Garnish with parsley. Makes 6 cups (1.5 L).

1 cup (250 mL): 287 Calories; 4 g Total Fat (0.9 g Sat., 2.2 mg Cholesterol); 206 mg Sodium; 13 g Protein; 54 g Carbohydrate; 8 g Dietary Fibre

CHOICES: 3 Grains & Starches; 1/2 Vegetables; 1/2 Fats

Safety Tip: Follow manufacturer's instructions for processing hot liquids.

Paré Pointer

No wonder she dresses funny. She buys all her clothing when she's down in the dumps.

Caramelized Onion Strata

Good onion taste complements the tomatoes and crispy rye top.

Thinly sliced onion	2 cups	500 mL
Canola oil	1 tsp.	5 mL
Brown sugar, packed	1 tsp.	5 mL
Apple cider vinegar	1 tbsp.	15 mL
Rye bread cubes	6 cups	1.5 L
Medium Roma (plum) tomatoes, seeded and diced	4	4
Salt	1/2 tsp.	2 mL
Freshly ground pepper, sprinkle		
Dried whole oregano	1/2 tsp.	2 mL
No-salt herb seasoning	1 tsp.	5 mL
Grated light Swiss cheese	3/4 cup	175 mL
Frozen egg product, thawed (see Note)	1 cup	250 mL
Skim evaporated milk	3/4 cup	175 mL
Skim milk	3/4 cup	175 mL
Dry mustard	1/2 tsp.	2 mL
Grated light Swiss cheese	3/4 cup	175 mL

Sauté onion in canola oil on medium in large non-stick frying pan for about 5 minutes until softened. Stir in brown sugar and vinegar. Sauté for 4 to 5 minutes until deep golden.

Arrange 1/2 of bread cubes in greased 3 quart (3 L) shallow casserole. Layer with onion mixture and next 5 ingredients, in order. Sprinkle with first amount of cheese. Top with remaining bread cubes.

Beat next 4 ingredients in medium bowl. Pour evenly over bread cubes. Cover. Chill for several hours or overnight.

Bake, uncovered, in 325°F (160°C) oven for 1 hour. Sprinkle with second amount of cheese. Bake for about 15 minutes until set in center. Serves 6.

1 serving: 268 Calories; 6.5 g Total Fat (0.2 g Sat., 1.8 mg Cholesterol); 613 mg Sodium; 22 g Protein; 33 g Carbohydrate; 3 g Dietary Fibre

CHOICES: 1 Grains & Starches; 1 1/2 Vegetables; 1/2 Milk & Alternatives; 2 Meat & Alternatives

Note: 3 tbsp. (50 mL) = 1 large egg

Stuffed Tomatoes

Fresh flavour with a hint of tangy feta.

Large tomatoes	6	6
Chopped onion	1 cup	250 mL
Garlic cloves, minced	2	2
Olive oil	2 tsp.	10 mL
Chopped fresh mushrooms	1 cup	250 mL
Diced zucchini, with peel	1 1/2 cups	375 mL
Salt	1/2 tsp.	2 mL
Chopped fresh sweet basil (or 1 tsp., 5 mL, dried)	1 tbsp.	15 mL
Chopped fresh oregano leaves (or 1 tsp., 5 mL, dried)	1 tbsp.	15 mL
Whole wheat cracker crumbs	1/3 cup	75 mL
Crumbled feta cheese (about 4 oz., 113 g)	2/3 cup	150 g
Margarine	2 tsp.	10 mL
Whole wheat cracker crumbs	1/4 cup	60 mL
Finely chopped fresh parsley (or 1 tsp., 5 mL, flakes)	1 tbsp.	15 mL

Cut 1/4 inch (6 mm) slice from stem end of tomatoes. Scoop out pulp. Chop pulp finely. Set aside. Turn hollowed tomatoes upside down on paper towels to drain.

Sauté onion and garlic in olive oil in large non-stick frying pan on medium-high until onion is soft. Stir in mushrooms and zucchini. Sauté until soft.

Stir in next 4 ingredients. Add cheese. Add reserved tomato pulp. Stir. Makes 5 1/4 cups (1.3 L) filling. Fill tomato cavities.

Melt margarine in small saucepan. Stir in second amount of cracker crumbs and parsley. Sprinkle about 2 1/2 tsp. (12 mL) over each tomato. Place tomatoes in 9 x 13 inch (22 x 33 cm) baking pan. Pour in about 1/2 inch (12 mm) water. Bake, uncovered, in 350°F (175°C) oven for about 30 minutes until heated through. Makes 6 stuffed tomatoes.

1 stuffed tomato: 187 Calories; 10.3 g Total Fat (4.8 g Sat., 23.0 mg Cholesterol); 594 mg Sodium; 7 g Protein; 20 g Carbohydrate; 4 g Dietary Fibre

CHOICES: 2 Vegetables; 1/2 Meat & Alternatives; 2 Fats

Pictured on page 72.

Creamy Mushroom Risotto

Contains threads of spinach throughout. The continuous stirring is what makes it creamy.

Olive oil	2 tsp.	10 mL
Sliced fresh mushrooms	3 cups	750 mL
Garlic clove, minced	1	1
Dried sweet basil	1 1/2 tsp.	7 mL
Freshly ground pepper, sprinkle		
Water	1 1/2 cups	375 mL
Vegetable bouillon powder	1 tbsp.	15 mL
Short grain white (or arborio) rice	1 1/2 cups	375 mL
Water	1 1/4 cups	300 mL
White (or alcohol-free) wine	1/4 cup	60 mL
Skim milk	1/4 cup	60 mL
Fresh spinach leaves, lightly packed, cut chiffonade (see Tip, below)	3 cups	750 mL
Chopped toasted pine nuts (see Tip, page 111)	1/3 cup	75 mL
Freshly grated Parmesan cheese	1/4 cup	60 mL

Heat olive oil in large non-stick frying pan. Add next 4 ingredients. Heat and stir on medium-high for about 10 minutes until liquid is evaporated and mushrooms are browned.

Add next 3 ingredients. Bring to a boil. Heat and stir until almost all of water is absorbed.

Add second amount of water, 1/4 cup (60 mL) at a time, while stirring. Allow water to absorb with each addition.

Add wine. Heat and stir until absorbed. Stir in milk and spinach. Heat and stir until milk is absorbed and spinach is soft. Turn into warm serving bowl. Sprinkle with nuts and cheese. Makes 5 cups (1.25 L). Serves 6.

1 serving: 304 Calories; 8.4 g Total Fat (2.0 g Sat., 3.9 mg Cholesterol); 412 mg Sodium; 10 g Protein; 47 g Carbohydrate; 3 g Dietary Fibre

CHOICES: 3 Grains & Starches; 1 Fats

 To cut chiffonade: stack leaves, roll tightly lengthwise and then thinly slice crosswise.

Roasted Veggies

Love that sweet roasted flavour. Make use of the many different salt-free herb preparations to change the flavour to suit your tastes.

Red baby potatoes (about 10), halved	1 lb.	454 g
Baby carrots (about 8 oz., 225 g)	1 3/4 cups	425 mL
Large cauliflower florets (about 10 oz., 285 g)	2 1/4 cups	550 mL
Parsnips, cut into 1 inch (2.5 cm) thick slices (about 8 oz., 225 g)	4	4
Olive oil	1 tbsp.	15 mL
Water	1 tbsp.	15 mL
Garlic clove, minced (optional)	1	1
No-salt Italian herb seasoning	1 tbsp.	15 mL
Salt	1/2 tsp.	2 mL
Freshly ground pepper, sprinkle		

Combine first 4 ingredients in lightly greased 9 x 13 inch (22 x 33 cm) pan.

Combine remaining 6 ingredients in small dish. Pour over vegetable mixture. Toss well. Bake, covered, in 450°F (230°C) oven for 30 minutes. Stir. Bake, uncovered, for 30 minutes until vegetables are tender and starting to turn brown. Serves 4.

1 serving: 210 Calories; 4 g Total Fat (0.6 g Sat., 0 mg Cholesterol); 384 mg Sodium; 5 g Protein; 41 g Carbohydrate; 7 g Dietary Fibre

CHOICES: 1 1/2 Grains & Starches; 4 Vegetables; 1/2 Fats

Paré Pointer

Fish hate tennis because they don't want to be around the net.

Tomatoes Provençale

Make this dish when tomatoes are fresh out of your garden.

Whole wheat bread slices, torn up	2	2
Garlic clove, minced	1	1
Ground rosemary	1/8 tsp.	0.5 mL
Salt	1/8 tsp.	0.5 mL
Freshly ground pepper, generous sprinkle		
Medium tomatoes	4	4
Olive oil	2 tsp.	10 mL

Process first 5 ingredients in blender or food processor until crumbled.

Cut tomatoes into thick slices. Place in rows, slightly overlapping, in 9 x 13 inch (22 x 33 cm) pan or shallow 2 quart (2 L) baking dish. Brush surface with olive oil. Sprinkle with crumb mixture. Bake, uncovered, in 400°F (205°C) oven for 10 minutes until crumbs are browned and slightly crisp. Serves 6.

1 serving: 54 Calories; 2 g Total Fat (0.3 g Sat., 0.3 mg Cholesterol); 116 mg Sodium; 2 g Protein; 9 g Carbohydrate; 2 g Dietary Fibre

CHOICES: 1/2 Grains & Starches

Mashed Garlic Potatoes

Boost the flavour of ordinary mashed potatoes in one easy step!

Potatoes, peeled and cut into large chunks	1 1/2 lbs.	680 g
Garlic cloves, cut in half	6	6
Salt	1 tsp.	5 mL
Boiling water		
Skim evaporated milk	1/3 cup	75 mL
Freshly ground pepper, sprinkle		

Cook potatoes with garlic and salt in boiling water in medium saucepan for 12 minutes until tender. Drain, reserving 1/4 cup (60 mL) potato water.

Mash potato, reserved potato water, evaporated milk and pepper until smooth and fluffy. Makes 3 1/2 cups (875 mL). Serves 6.

1 serving: 106 Calories; 0.2 g Total Fat (0.1 g Sat., 0.5 mg Cholesterol); 25 mg Sodium; 4 g Protein; 23 g Carbohydrate; 2 g Dietary Fibre

CHOICES: 1 1/2 Grains & Starches

Rice Pilaf

Nice toasted grain flavour. Try the variation for even more fibre.

Chopped onion	1/2 cup	125 mL
Sliced fresh mushrooms	1 cup	250 mL
Canola oil	2 tsp.	10 mL
Long grain white rice	1/2 cup	125 mL
Bulgur wheat	1/2 cup	125 mL
Can of condensed chicken broth	10 oz.	284 mL
Water	3/4 cup	175 mL
Chopped fresh parsley (optional)	1 tbsp.	15 mL

Sauté onion and mushrooms in canola oil in large frying pan until soft. Add rice and bulgur. Sauté for about 10 minutes until rice is toasted. Turn into medium saucepan.

Stir in broth and water. Bring to a boil. Reduce heat. Cover. Simmer for 20 minutes until liquid is absorbed.

Stir in parsley. Makes 3 cups (750 mL).

1/2 cup (125 mL): 139 Calories; 2.4 g Total Fat (0.3 g Sat., 0.5 mg Cholesterol); 318 mg Sodium; 5 g Protein; 25 g Carbohydrate; 3 g Dietary Fibre

CHOICES: 1 1/2 Grains & Starches; 1/2 Fats

Variation: For more colour and fibre, stir in 1 cup (250 mL) hot cooked peas just before serving.

Barley Side Dish

Wonderful barley flavour and chewy texture.

Chopped onion	1/2 cup	125 mL
Chopped celery	1/2 cup	125 mL
Canola oil	2 tsp.	10 mL
Pearl barley	1 cup	250 mL
Boiling water	3 1/2 cups	875 mL
Beef bouillon powder	1 tbsp.	15 mL
Medium carrot, grated	1	1
Chopped green onion (or chives)	2 tbsp.	30 mL

(continued on next page)

Sauté onion and celery in canola oil in large frying pan until soft. Add barley. Sauté for about 10 minutes until barley is toasted. Turn into medium saucepan.

Stir in next 3 ingredients. Bring to a boil. Reduce heat. Cover. Simmer for 30 to 35 minutes until liquid is absorbed. Stir in green onion. Makes 4 cups (1 L).

3/4 cup (175 mL): 146 Calories; 2.5 g Total Fat (0.4 g Sat., 0.2 mg Cholesterol); 316 mg Sodium; 5 g Protein; 27 g Carbohydrate; 6 g Dietary Fibre

CHOICES: 1 1/2 Grains & Starches; 1/2 Vegetables; 1/2 Meat & Alternatives; 1/2 Fats

Lentil Rice

Exotic Middle Eastern influences in this tasty dish.
Makes a big batch and rewarms wonderfully for lunches at work.

Water	12 cups	3 L
Green lentils	2 cups	500 mL
Bay leaves	5	5
Dried crushed chilies	1/4 tsp.	1 mL
Salt	1 tsp.	5 mL
Freshly ground pepper	1 tsp.	5 mL
Long grain white rice	1 cup	250 mL
Pickled hot peppers, chopped (optional)	1/2 cup	125 mL

Combine first 6 ingredients in large pot or Dutch oven. Cover. Simmer for 40 minutes until lentils are tender but firm.

Stir in rice. Bring to a boil. Cover. Simmer for 15 to 20 minutes until rice is tender. Drain any remaining liquid. Stir in hot pepper. Makes 8 cups (2 L).

1/2 cup (125 mL): 131 Calories; 0.3 g Total Fat (0.1 g Sat., 0 mg Cholesterol); 173 mg Sodium; 8 g Protein; 24 g Carbohydrate; 3 g Dietary Fibre

CHOICES: 1 Grains & Starches; 1 Meat & Alternatives

Pictured on page 72.

 Investing in good non-stick cookware makes it easier to use less oil to keep food from sticking when cooking. Olive and canola oils add taste and are low in saturated fats.

Italian Potato Casserole

Moist and tender with herb and pepper aftertaste.

Medium onion, sliced	1	1
Garlic clove, minced	1	1
Olive oil	1 tsp.	5 mL
Skim evaporated milk	1 cup	250 mL
All-purpose flour	3 tbsp.	50 mL
Prepared mustard	2 tsp.	10 mL
Salt	1/2 tsp.	2 mL
Dried sweet basil	1/2 tsp.	2 mL
Granulated sugar	1/4 tsp.	1 mL
Dried whole oregano	1/8 tsp.	0.5 mL
Unpeeled medium new potatoes, thinly sliced (about 4 cups, 1 L)	4	4
Freshly ground pepper	1/8 tsp.	0.5 mL
Medium Roma (plum) tomatoes, sliced 1/4 inch (6 mm) thick	4	4
Grated light Parmesan cheese	1 tbsp.	15 mL

Sauté onion and garlic in olive oil in medium non-stick frying pan until onion is soft.

Combine evaporated milk and flour in small bowl until smooth. Slowly add to onion, stirring constantly, until boiling and thickened. Stir in next 5 ingredients.

Arrange 1/2 of potato in greased 2 quart (2 L) casserole. Sprinkle with pepper. Layer with 1/2 of tomato. Cover with 1/2 of onion mixture. Repeat layers. Sprinkle with Parmesan cheese. Cover. Bake in 375°F (190°C) oven for 45 minutes. Remove cover. Bake for 20 to 30 minutes until golden brown and potato is soft. Makes 5 cups (1.25 L).

3/4 cup (175 mL): 161 Calories; 1.6 g Total Fat (0.3 g Sat., 2.0 mg Cholesterol); 337 mg Sodium; 8 g Protein; 31 g Carbohydrate; 3 g Dietary Fibre

CHOICES: 1 Grains & Starches; 1 Vegetables; 1/2 Milk & Alternatives

Pictured on page 143.

Barley And Rice Pilaf

The barley makes it slightly chewy. Good blend of flavours, but you can add up to a teaspoon (5 mL) of your favourite no-salt herb seasoning for more of a flavour burst.

Pearl barley	3/4 cup	175 mL
Long grain brown rice	3/4 cup	175 mL
Canola oil	1 tbsp.	15 mL
Chopped onion	1 cup	250 mL
Chopped celery, with leaves	1 cup	250 mL
Water	3 1/2 cups	875 mL
Vegetable bouillon powder	1 tbsp.	15 mL
Coarsely grated carrot	1/2 cup	125 mL
Diced green pepper	1/2 cup	125 mL
Diced red pepper	1/2 cup	125 mL
Diced yellow or orange pepper	1/2 cup	125 mL
Garlic powder	1/4 tsp.	1 mL
Chopped fresh parsley (or 2 tsp., 10 mL, flakes)	3 tbsp.	50 mL
Salt	1 1/2 tsp.	7 mL
Pepper	1/2 tsp.	2 mL

Sauté barley and rice in canola oil in large heavy-bottomed saucepan for about 8 minutes until starting to turn golden brown.

Add onion and celery. Sauté for 3 to 4 minutes until celery is tender-crisp. Add next 3 ingredients. Bring to a boil. Reduce heat. Cover. Simmer for 40 minutes.

Stir in remaining 7 ingredients. Cover. Simmer for 20 to 30 minutes until water is absorbed and barley is tender. Makes 6 cups (1.5 L).

1/2 cup (125 mL): 115 Calories; 2 g Total Fat (0.3 g Sat., 0.1 mg Cholesterol); 502 mg Sodium; 3 g Protein; 22 g Carbohydrate; 3 g Dietary Fibre

CHOICES: 1 Grains & Starches; 1/2 Vegetables

Pictured on page 143.

Cold Dressed Asparagus

This is a great make-ahead recipe. It suits an elegant dinner party, an outdoor barbecue or a potluck.

Medium tomato, quartered	1	1
Green onion, cut into 1 inch (2.5 cm) pieces	1	1
Garlic cloves	2	2
Red wine vinegar	3 tbsp.	50 mL
Liquid honey	1 tbsp.	15 mL
Chopped fresh parsley	1 tbsp.	15 mL
Olive oil	1 tbsp.	15 mL
Anchovy paste	2 tsp.	10 mL
Paprika	1 tsp.	5 mL
Salt	1/2 tsp.	2 mL
Fresh asparagus, trimmed of tough ends	1 lb.	454 g
Very thinly sliced red onion	1 1/2 cups	375 mL
Chopped pitted ripe olives (optional)	2 tbsp.	30 mL

Process first 10 ingredients in blender for about 1 minute until smooth. Chill for 1 hour to blend flavours. Makes 1 1/4 cups (300 mL) dressing.

Steam asparagus for 4 to 5 minutes until tender-crisp. Drain. Rinse in cold water until completely cool. Drain well.

Arrange asparagus and onion on small platter. Scatter with olives. Drizzle dressing over top. Serve chilled or at room temperature. Serves 8.

1 serving: 59 Calories; 2.2 g Total Fat (0.3 g Sat., 1.5 mg Cholesterol); 238 mg Sodium; 3 g Protein; 9 g Carbohydrate; 2 g Dietary Fibre

CHOICES: 1 Vegetables, 1/2 Meat & Alternatives

Pictured at right.

1. Barley And Rice Pilaf, page 141
2. Italian Potato Casserole, page 140
3. Cold Dressed Asparagus, above

Side Dishes

Bulgur Curry

Such a warm, pretty colour—and it tastes good too. Makes an impressive buffet dish.

Large onion, chopped	1	1
Chopped fresh mushrooms	1 cup	250 mL
Diced red or green pepper	1 cup	250 mL
Olive oil	2 tsp.	10 mL
Curry paste (available in Asian section of grocery store)	1 tsp.	5 mL
Dark raisins	1/3 cup	75 mL
Water	3 cups	750 mL
Chicken bouillon powder	1 tbsp.	15 mL
Bulgur wheat	1 1/4 cups	300 mL
Chopped fresh parsley (or 1 tbsp., 15 mL, flakes)	1/4 cup	60 mL

Sauté first 3 ingredients in olive oil in large saucepan on medium for about 10 minutes until onion is soft and liquid is evaporated.

Stir in curry paste and raisins. Add next 3 ingredients. Bring to a boil. Reduce heat. Cover. Simmer for about 20 minutes until liquid is absorbed.

Stir in parsley before serving. Makes 5 cups (1.25 L).

1/2 cup (125 mL): 99 Calories; 1.5 g Total Fat (0.2 g Sat., 0.1 mg Cholesterol); 200 mg Sodium; 3 g Protein; 20 g Carbohydrate; 4 g Dietary Fibre

CHOICES: 1 Grains & Starches; 1/2 Vegetables

Pictured on page 126.

1. Lentil Soup, page 148
2. White Bean Soup, page 146
3. Curried Zucchini Chowder, page 147

White Bean Soup

The list of ingredients might seem lengthy, but you can be eating hot soup in an hour from start to finish.

Sliced leeks (halved lengthwise and rinsed well)	1 cup	250 mL
Chopped celery heart and leaves	1 cup	250 mL
Garlic cloves, minced	2	2
Olive oil	2 tsp.	10 mL
Diced carrot	1 cup	250 mL
Diced potato	1 cup	250 mL
Can of Italian-spiced diced tomatoes, with juice, puréed	14 oz.	398 mL
Water	4 cups	1 L
Chicken bouillon powder	1 tbsp.	15 mL
Hot pepper sauce	1/2 tsp.	2 mL
Celery seed	1/2 tsp.	2 mL
Salt	1/2 tsp.	2 mL
Freshly ground pepper	1/8 tsp.	0.5 mL
Dried sweet basil (optional)	1/2 tsp.	2 mL
Fennel seed, crushed (optional)	1/4 tsp.	1 mL
Can of white kidney beans, drained and rinsed	19 oz.	540 mL
Shredded fresh spinach leaves, packed	1 cup	250 mL
Finely chopped fresh parsley (or 1 tsp., 5 mL, flakes)	1 tbsp.	15 mL

Sauté first 3 ingredients in olive oil in large uncovered pot or Dutch oven until softened.

Add next 9 ingredients. Bring to a boil. Reduce heat. Simmer, partially covered, for 10 to 15 minutes until carrot and potato are tender.

Stir in remaining 5 ingredients. Cover. Simmer for 5 minutes until spinach is softened. Makes 8 cups (2 L).

1 cup (250 mL): 104 Calories; 1.7 g Total Fat (0.3 g Sat., 0.2 mg Cholesterol); 655 mg Sodium; 5 g Protein; 19 g Carbohydrate; 2 g Dietary Fibre

CHOICES: 1 1/2 Vegetables

Pictured on page 144.

Curried Zucchini Chowder

The curry flavour is mild but a swirl of yogurt, sour cream or cream in the soup at serving time will mellow the flavour even more.

Chopped onion	1 cup	250 mL
Garlic clove, minced	1	1
Margarine	2 tsp.	10 mL
Curry paste (available in Asian section of grocery store)	1/2 tsp.	2 mL
Grated zucchini (about 3 medium), with peel	4 cups	1 L
Diced potato	3 cups	750 mL
Water	3 1/4 cups	800 mL
Vegetable bouillon powder	2 tbsp.	30 mL
Bay leaf	1	1
Freshly ground pepper	1/4 tsp.	1 mL
Ground cumin	1/16 tsp.	0.5 mL

Sauté onion and garlic in margarine in large uncovered pot or Dutch oven until onion is very soft and turning golden brown. Stir in curry paste. Sauté for 1 minute.

Stir in remaining 7 ingredients. Heat on medium, partially covered, for 1 hour. Remove and discard bay leaf. Remove and reserve 2 cups (500 mL) vegetable mixture. Process remaining vegetable mixture with hand blender or in batches in blender until smooth (see Safety Tip). Combine reserved and puréed vegetable mixture in same pot. Makes 7 cups (1.75 L).

1 cup (250 mL): 92 Calories; 1.6 g Total Fat (0.4 g Sat., 0.3 mg Cholesterol); 530 mg Sodium; 3 g Protein; 18 g Carbohydrate; 3 g Dietary Fibre

CHOICES: 1 Grains & Starches; 1 Vegetables

Safety Tip: Follow manufacturer's instructions for processing hot liquids.

Pictured on page 144.

Paré Pointer
In the aftenoons, kings and queens drink royal-tea.

Lentil Soup

This thick, hearty soup is a meal in itself. Serve with crusty bread or buns.

Lean ground chicken	8 oz.	225 g
Chopped onion	1/2 cup	125 mL
Sliced fresh mushrooms	1 cup	250 mL
Canola oil	2 tsp.	10 mL
Water	5 cups	1.25 L
Can of diced tomatoes, with juice	28 oz.	796 mL
Chopped cabbage	2 cups	500 mL
Sliced celery	1 cup	250 mL
Diced carrot	1 cup	250 mL
Diced green (or other) pepper	1/2 cup	125 mL
Bay leaves	2	2
Vegetable bouillon powder	2 tsp.	10 mL
Worcestershire sauce	1/2 tsp.	2 mL
Dried thyme leaves	1/2 tsp.	2 mL
Green lentils	3/4 cup	175 mL

Sauté first 3 ingredients in canola oil in large uncovered pot or Dutch oven until starting to brown. Drain.

Add remaining 11 ingredients to ground chicken mixture. Bring to a boil. Reduce heat. Partially cover. Simmer for 45 minutes until lentils and vegetables are tender. Makes 10 cups (2.5 L).

1 cup (250 mL): 120 Calories; 1.7 g Total Fat (0.2 g Sat., 13.1 mg Cholesterol); 288 mg Sodium; 11 g Protein; 16 g Carbohydrate; 4 g Dietary Fibre

CHOICES: 1 1/2 Vegetables; 1 Meat & Alternatives

Pictured on page 144.

Paré Pointer

Saturday and Sunday are very strong days.
The other five are weekdays.

Chilled Vegetable Soup

A refreshing soup that uses up those bits of fresh herbs and vegetables in the refrigerator!

Vegetable cocktail juice	2 1/2 cups	625 mL
Diced fresh tomato	2 cups	500 mL
Water	1 cup	250 mL
Diced red or green pepper	1 cup	250 mL
Diced cucumber, with peel	1 cup	250 mL
Chopped green onion	1/2 cup	125 mL
Chopped fresh chives (or 1 tsp., 5 mL, dried)	1 tbsp.	15 mL
Chopped fresh oregano leaves (or 1/2 tsp., 2 mL, dried)	1 tbsp.	15 mL
Chopped fresh sweet basil (or 2 tsp., 10 mL, dried)	2 tbsp.	30 mL
Lemon juice	2 tbsp.	30 mL

Light sour cream, for garnish
Hot pepper sauce, for garnish

Combine first 10 ingredients in large bowl. Chill for several hours or overnight.

Purée 1/2 in blender or food processor. Return to bowl. Stir. Spoon into individual serving bowls. Add dollop of sour cream and dash of pepper sauce if desired. Makes 7 3/4 cups (1.9 L).

1 cup (250 mL): 34 Calories; 0.3 g Total Fat (trace Sat., 0 mg Cholesterol); 306 mg Sodium; 1 g Protein; 8 g Carbohydrate; 1 g Dietary Fibre

CHOICES: 1 1/2 Vegetables

Generally, when substituting dried for fresh herbs, use about 1/4 of the amount requested. For example, you would use 3/4 tsp. (4 mL) dried where the recipe called for 1 tbsp. (15 mL) of fresh herbs.

Turtle Bean Soup

Gentle heat from the chili powder and the hot pepper sauce.

Chopped onion	1 cup	250 mL
Canola oil	2 tsp.	10 mL
Garlic cloves, minced	2	2
Medium red pepper, diced	1	1
Water	4 cups	1 L
Vegetable bouillon powder	2 tbsp.	30 mL
Can of black beans, drained and rinsed	19 oz.	540 mL
Chili powder	1 1/2 tsp.	7 mL
Bay leaf	1	1
Dried whole marjoram (or oregano), crushed	1/2 tsp.	2 mL
Dried sweet basil	1 tsp.	5 mL
Kernel corn, fresh or frozen	1/2 cup	125 mL
Lime juice	2 tsp.	10 mL
Hot pepper sauce	1/2 tsp.	2 mL
Cooked mashed potato	1 cup	250 mL
Chopped fresh parsley	1/4 cup	60 mL
Chopped fresh cilantro (optional)	1 tbsp.	15 mL
Non-fat plain yogurt (or light sour cream), optional		
Sliced green onion (optional)		

Sauté onion in canola oil in large uncovered pot or Dutch oven until soft. Add garlic and red pepper. Sauté for about 2 minutes until pepper is soft.

Stir in next 11 ingredients. Cover. Simmer on medium-low for 40 minutes.

Remove and discard bay leaf. Stir in parsley and cilantro (see Note). Spoon into individual serving bowls. Top with a dollop of yogurt and sprinkle of green onion. Makes 6 cups (1.5 L).

1 cup (250 mL): 148 Calories; 2.5 g Total Fat (0.4 g Sat., 0.4 mg Cholesterol); 711 mg Sodium; 6 g Protein; 27 g Carbohydrate; 4 g Dietary Fibre

CHOICES: 1 Grains & Starches; 1 1/2 Vegetables; 1/2 Meat & Alternatives

Note: To make a thicker soup, purée 3 cups (750 mL) soup in blender. Return to pot. Heat through.

Barley Vegetable Soup

Thick, hearty soup warms the insides on a cold winter day.

Water	2 qts.	2 L
Pearl barley	1 cup	250 mL
Chopped onion	1 cup	250 mL
Chopped celery	1 cup	250 mL
Diced carrot	1 cup	250 mL
Vegetable bouillon powder	2 tbsp.	30 mL
Medium potatoes, peeled and diced	2	2
Worcestershire sauce	1 1/2 tsp.	7 mL
Dried sweet basil	1 1/2 tsp.	7 mL
Parsley flakes	1 tsp.	5 mL
Freshly ground pepper, sprinkle		
Vegetable cocktail juice	1 cup	250 mL
All-purpose flour	2 tbsp.	30 mL

Put first 6 ingredients into large uncovered pot or Dutch oven. Cover. Simmer for 30 minutes.

Add next 5 ingredients. Cover. Simmer for 15 minutes until potato is tender.

Whisk vegetable juice into flour in small bowl until smooth. Stir into soup. Simmer for 1 minute until slightly thickened. Makes 10 1/2 cups (2.6 L).

1 cup (250 mL): 117 Calories; 0.6 g Total Fat (0.2 g Sat., 0.2 mg Cholesterol); 456 mg Sodium; 4 g Protein; 26 g Carbohydrate; 4 g Dietary Fibre

CHOICES: 1 Grains & Starches; 1 Vegetables

 If your homemade soup is too salty, drop a peeled potato into the pot and remove just before serving.

Roasted Garlic Soup

*Roast some garlic the next time you have your oven on to make
this special soup. Serve small amounts for an elegant first course.*

Large heads of garlic (not individual cloves)	4	4
Olive oil	2 tsp.	10 mL
Water	1/4 cup	60 mL
Chopped onion	2/3 cup	150 mL
Olive oil	2 tsp.	10 mL
Peeled and diced potato	3 cups	750 mL
Can of condensed chicken broth	10 oz.	284 mL
Water	2/3 cup	150 mL
Dried tarragon	1 tsp.	5 mL
Granulated sugar	1 tsp.	5 mL
Salt	1/2 tsp.	2 mL
Cayenne pepper	1/8 tsp.	0.5 mL
Can of skim evaporated milk	13 1/2 oz.	385 mL
All-purpose flour	2 tbsp.	30 mL
White (or alcohol-free) wine	1/2 cup	125 mL

Remove loose papery skin from garlic heads, being careful not separate or peel
individual cloves. Cut tops off garlic heads to barely expose tops of some cloves.
Place in garlic baker or small pie plate. Drizzle 1/2 tsp. (2 mL) of first amount
of olive oil over each garlic head. Drizzle first amount of water into baking dish.
Cover tightly with lid or foil. Bake in 350°F (175°C) oven for about 45 minutes
until garlic cloves are soft and golden. Cool enough to handle. Squeeze out cloves
into small bowl.

Sauté onion in second amount of olive oil in large saucepan until soft. Add next
3 ingredients. Cover. Simmer for about 15 minutes until potato is very tender.

Stir in roasted garlic. Add next 4 ingredients. Purée in blender or food processor until
smooth. Return to saucepan. Bring to a boil.

Stir evaporated milk into flour in small bowl until smooth. Add to soup. Heat and
stir on medium until slightly thickened. Add wine. Stir. Makes 6 cups (1.5 L).

*1 cup (250 mL): 238 Calories; 4 g Total Fat (0.7 g Sat., 3.0 mg Cholesterol); 632 mg Sodium;
12 g Protein; 37 g Carbohydrate; 2 g Dietary Fibre*

CHOICES: 1 Grains & Starches; 2 Vegetables; 1/2 Milk & Alternatives; 1/2 Fats

Minestrone Soup

Thick and chunky with a rich-tasting broth. A hearty meal with some bread or buns.

Container of Tomato Vegetable Sauce (3 cups, 750 mL), page 118, thawed	1	1
Water	4 cups	1 L
Sliced celery	1/2 cup	125 mL
Finely diced carrot	1/2 cup	125 mL
Chopped cabbage	1 cup	250 mL
Beef bouillon powder	2 tsp.	10 mL
Granulated sugar	1 tsp.	5 mL
No-salt garlic and herb seasoning	1 tsp.	5 mL
Dried crushed chilies	1/8 tsp.	0.5 mL
Can of kidney beans, drained and rinsed	14 oz.	398 mL
Whole wheat elbow macaroni	1/2 cup	125 mL

Grated Parmesan cheese (optional)

Combine Tomato Vegetable Sauce and water in large saucepan. Bring to a boil. Add next 7 ingredients. Cover. Simmer for 30 minutes.

Stir in beans and pasta. Cover. Bring to a boil. Cook for 10 minutes, stirring twice, until pasta is tender.

Sprinkle individual servings with Parmesan cheese. Makes 7 cups (1.75 L).

1 cup (250 mL): 120 Calories; 1.3 g Total Fat (0.2 g Sat., 0.1 mg Cholesterol); 406 mg Sodium; 6 g Protein; 24 g Carbohydrate; 6 g Dietary Fibre

CHOICES: 1/2 Grains & Starches; 2 Vegetables

 tip To keep garlic bulbs from sprouting, softening and drying out, store in a container in the freezer. To easily peel a clove at a time, heat on high (100%) for 30 seconds in microwave.

Bean And Bacon Soup

Rich, warm flavour from bacon. Hearty comfort food.

Chopped onion	2/3 cup	150 mL
Chopped celery	2/3 cup	150 mL
Garlic cloves, minced	2	2
Canola oil	2 tsp.	10 mL
Canadian back bacon, diced	2 oz.	57 g
Water	5 cups	1.25 L
Vegetable bouillon powder	1 tbsp.	15 mL
Sliced carrot	1 cup	250 mL
Peeled, diced potato	2 cups	500 mL
Bay leaves	2	2
Can of mixed beans, drained and rinsed	19 oz.	540 mL
Can of baked beans in tomato sauce	14 oz.	398 mL

Sauté first 3 ingredients in canola oil in large uncovered pot or Dutch oven until very soft. Add bacon. Sauté until starting to brown.

Add next 5 ingredients. Bring to a boil. Cover. Simmer for 25 minutes until potato is very tender and breaking up.

Stir in both beans. Heat, uncovered, for about 10 minutes until soup is thickened. Remove and discard bay leaves. Makes 8 cups (2 L).

1 cup (250 mL): 160 Calories; 2.4 g Total Fat (0.4 g Sat., 3.7 mg Cholesterol); 626 mg Sodium; 8 g Protein; 29 g Carbohydrate; 8 g Dietary Fibre

CHOICES: 1 1/2 Grains & Starches; 1/2 Vegetables; 1 Meat & Alternatives

Measurement Tables

Throughout this book measurements are given in Conventional and Metric measure. To compensate for differences between the two measurements due to rounding, a full metric measure is not always used. The cup used is the standard 8 fluid ounce. Temperature is given in degrees Fahrenheit and Celsius. Baking pan measurements are in inches and centimetres as well as quarts and litres. An exact metric conversion is given below as well as the working equivalent (Metric Standard Measure).

Spoons

Conventional Measure	Metric Exact Conversion Millilitre (mL)	Metric Standard Measure Millilitre (mL)
1/8 teaspoon (tsp.)	0.6 mL	0.5 mL
1/4 teaspoon (tsp.)	1.2 mL	1 mL
1/2 teaspoon (tsp.)	2.4 mL	2 mL
1 teaspoon (tsp.)	4.7 mL	5 mL
2 teaspoons (tsp.)	9.4 mL	10 mL
1 tablespoon (tbsp.)	14.2 mL	15 mL

Cups

Conventional Measure	Metric Exact Conversion Millilitre (mL)	Metric Standard Measure Millilitre (mL)
1/4 cup (4 tbsp.)	56.8 mL	60 mL
1/3 cup (5 1/3 tbsp.)	75.6 mL	75 mL
1/2 cup (8 tbsp.)	113.7 mL	125 mL
2/3 cup (10 2/3 tbsp.)	151.2 mL	150 mL
3/4 cup (12 tbsp.)	170.5 mL	175 mL
1 cup (16 tbsp.)	227.3 mL	250 mL
4 1/2 cups	1022.9 mL	1000 mL (1 L)

Dry Measurements

Conventional Measure Ounces (oz.)	Metric Exact Conversion Grams (g)	Metric Standard Measure Grams (g)
1 oz.	28.3 g	28 g
2 oz.	56.7 g	57 g
3 oz.	85.0 g	85 g
4 oz.	113.4 g	125 g
5 oz.	141.7 g	140 g
6 oz.	170.1 g	170 g
7 oz.	198.4 g	200 g
8 oz.	226.8 g	250 g
16 oz.	453.6 g	500 g
32 oz.	907.2 g	1000 g (1 kg)

Oven Temperatures

Fahrenheit (°F)	Celsius (°C)
175°	80°
200°	95°
225°	110°
250°	120°
275°	140°
300°	150°
325°	160°
350°	175°
375°	190°
400°	205°
425°	220°
450°	230°
475°	240°
500°	260°

Pans

Conventional Inches	Metric Centimetres
8x8 inch	20x20 cm
9x9 inch	22x22 cm
9x13 inch	22x33 cm
10x15 inch	25x38 cm
11x17 inch	28x43 cm
8x2 inch round	20x5 cm
9x2 inch round	22x5 cm
10x4 1/2 inch tube	25x11 cm
8x4x3 inch loaf	20x10x7.5 cm
9x5x3 inch loaf	22x12.5x7.5 cm

Casseroles

CANADA & BRITAIN		UNITED STATES	
Standard Size Casserole	Exact Metric Measure	Standard Size Casserole	Exact Metric Measure
1 qt. (5 cups)	1.13 L	1 qt. (4 cups)	900 mL
1 1/2 qts. (7 1/2 cups)	1.69 L	1 1/2 qts. (6 cups)	1.35 L
2 qts. (10 cups)	2.25 L	2 qts. (8 cups)	1.8 L
2 1/2 qts. (12 1/2 cups)	2.81 L	2 1/2 qts. (10 cups)	2.25 L
3 qts. (15 cups)	3.38 L	3 qts. (12 cups)	2.7 L
4 qts. (20 cups)	4.5 L	4 qts. (16 cups)	3.6 L
5 qts. (25 cups)	5.63 L	5 qts. (20 cups)	4.5 L

Tip Index

156

Recipe Index

157

159

Recipe Notes

30-Minute
Diabetic Cooking

Jean Paré

www.companyscoming.com
visit our website

Divider Photo

1. Feta Ruby Chard,
   page 138
2. Raspberry Steak,
   page 68

Props courtesy of: Casa
                     Bugatti

*We gratefully acknowledge the following suppliers for their generous
support of our Test and Photography Kitchens:*

Broil King Barbecues
Hamilton Beach ® Canada
Proctor Silex ® Canada
Corelle ®
Lagostina ®
Tupperware ®

Company's Coming Cookbooks

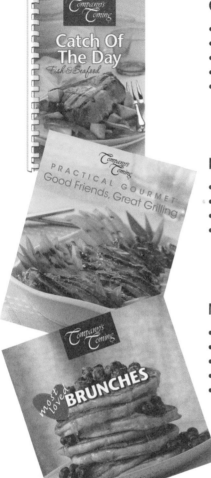

Original Series

- Softcover, 160 pages
- 6" x 9" (15 cm x 23 cm) format
- Lay-flat plastic comb binding
- Full-colour photos
- Nutrition information

Quick & easy recipes! Everyday ingredients!

Practical Gourmet Series

- Hardcover, 224 pages
- 8" x 10" (21 cm x 26 cm) format
- Full-colour throughout
- Nutrition information

Most Loved Recipe Collection

- Hardcover, 128 pages
- 8 3/4" x 8 3/4" (22 cm x 22 cm) format
- Durable sewn binding
- Full-colour throughout
- Nutrition information

Special Occasion Series

- Softcover, 176 pages
- 8 1/2" x 11" (22 cm x 28 cm) format
- Full-colour throughout
- Nutrition information

See page 157 for more cookbooks.
For a complete listing, visit
www.companyscoming.com

Table of Contents

The Company's Coming Story

Jean Paré (pronounced "jeen PAIR-ee") grew up understanding that the combination of family, friends and home cooking is the best recipe for a good life. From her mother, she learned to appreciate good cooking, while her father praised even her earliest attempts in the kitchen. When Jean left home, she took with her a love of cooking, many family recipes and an intriguing desire to read cookbooks as if they were novels!

"Never share a recipe you wouldn't use yourself."

When her four children had all reached school age, Jean volunteered to cater the 50th anniversary celebration of the Vermilion School of Agriculture, now Lakeland College, in Alberta, Canada. Working out of her home, Jean prepared a dinner for more than 1,000 people, launching a flourishing catering operation that continued for over 18 years. During that time, she had countless opportunities to test new ideas with immediate feedback—resulting in empty plates and contented customers! Whether preparing cocktail sandwiches for a house party or serving a hot meal for 1,500 people, Jean Paré earned a reputation for great food, courteous service and reasonable prices.

As requests for her recipes increased, Jean was often asked the question, "Why don't you write a cookbook?" Jean responded by teaming up with her son, Grant Lovig, in the fall of 1980 to form Company's Coming Publishing Limited. The publication of *150 Delicious Squares* on April 14, 1981 marked the debut of what would soon become one of the world's most popular cookbook series.

The company has grown since those early days when Jean worked from a spare bedroom in her home. Today, she continues to write recipes while working closely with the staff of the Recipe Factory, as the Company's Coming test kitchen is affectionately known.

There she fills the role of mentor, assisting with the development of recipes people most want to use for everyday cooking and easy entertaining. Every Company's Coming recipe is kitchen-tested before it is approved for publication.

Jean's daughter, Gail Lovig, is responsible for marketing and distribution, leading a team that includes sales personnel located in major cities across Canada. Company's Coming cookbooks are distributed in Canada, the United States, Australia and other world markets. Bestsellers many times over in English, Company's Coming cookbooks have also been published in French and Spanish.

Familiar and trusted in home kitchens around the world, Company's Coming cookbooks are offered in a variety of formats. Highly regarded as kitchen workbooks, the softcover Original Series, with its lay-flat plastic comb binding, is still a favourite among readers.

Jean Paré's approach to cooking has always called for quick and easy recipes using everyday ingredients. That view has served her well. The recipient of many awards, including the Queen Elizabeth Golden Jubilee Medal, Jean was appointed Member of the Order of Canada, her country's highest lifetime achievement honour.

Jean continues to gain new supporters by adhering to what she calls The Golden Rule of Cooking: *Never share a recipe you wouldn't use yourself.* It's an approach that has worked—millions of times over!

6

Foreword

It's a fact—diet is a key factor in managing diabetes. But these days, healthy eating is something that everyone should be concerned with. Properly portioning meals and monitoring intake of fat, salt and sugar are part of how many people live. Diabetic cooking isn't just for those with diabetes or their families; it's a healthy, balanced way to eat that all people can benefit from.

Before we started developing *30-Minute Diabetic Cooking*, we met with a focus group to find out what would be most helpful in a diabetic cookbook. The group talked about ingredients to avoid, the kinds of recipes that best suit their requirements and the need for adequate information to help them in portioning meals. But what was the most universally agreed upon request? Recipes that can be prepared quickly!

What we have created is a cookbook suitable for those with diabetes and their families. We've given you great-tasting recipes for breakfasts, lunches, dinners, desserts and snacks. The recipes were written for a busy lifestyle, so they're practical and quick to put together—ready in 30 minutes or less! We've also given you tips for diabetic eating and hints for quick and easy cooking.

Whether you're looking for a portable lunch like Toasted Chicken Caesar Sandwiches, a satisfying snack like the Tropical Tango Tofu Smoothie or a hearty serving of the Pork Apple Skillet as a main course, you're sure to find plenty of nutritious options. And because everyone needs to have at least a little chocolate to keep things fun, be sure to try the Triple-Chocolate Shortcakes in our Desserts section.

So if you're cooking for yourself or a family member with diabetes, or just wanting to eat healthier, you'll be sure to find great-tasting, nutritious meal options that are super-speedy to prepare in *30-Minute Diabetic Cooking!*

Jean Paré

Nutrition Information Guidelines

Each recipe is analyzed using the most current version of the Canadian Nutrient File from Health Canada, which is based on the United States Department of Agriculture (USDA) Nutrient Database.

- If more than one ingredient is listed (such as "butter or hard margarine"), or if a range is given (1 – 2 tsp., 5 – 10 mL), only the first ingredient or first amount is analyzed.

- For meat, poultry and fish, the serving size per person is based on the recommended 4 oz. (113 g) uncooked weight (without bone), which is 2 – 3 oz. (57 – 85 g) cooked weight (without bone)—approximately the size of a deck of playing cards.

- Milk used is 1% M.F. (milk fat), unless otherwise stated.

- Cooking oil used is canola oil, unless otherwise stated.

- Ingredients indicating "sprinkle," "optional," or "for garnish" are not included in the nutrition information.

- The fat in recipes and combination foods can vary greatly depending on the sources and types of fats used in each specific ingredient. For these reasons, the amount of saturated, monounsaturated and polyunsaturated fats may not add up to the total fat content.

Vera C. Mazurak, Ph.D.
Nutritionist

About Diabetes

Diabetes, in the most general terms, is caused when people have too much glucose in their blood because their bodies aren't processing it properly. This glucose comes from the food we consume, specifically from the digestion of carbohydrates like grains, fruits and vegetables. For most people, the pancreas produces enough insulin to break down glucose, which enables the body to use it as energy.

For individuals with Type 1 diabetes, insulin injections are required to break down glucose. This is because their bodies are producing very little insulin, or perhaps none at all. For those with Type 2 diabetes, insulin injections are generally not required as these people's bodies are able to produce some insulin. These individuals may be able to mange their diabetes with diet alone, or by using a combination of diet and medication.

Diabetic eating

Managing diabetes with a proper diet is imperative. Every person with diabetes needs to consult with a doctor or dietitian to determine an appropriate eating plan, but here are a few tips to consider:

Choosing ingredients wisely

The world is a changing place. People are becoming more and more aware of health issues and are making smarter choices about what they eat. Using ingredients with lower levels of fat, sugar and salt will help you to achieve your dietary goals.

Choosing leaner cuts of meat and lower-fat dairy products are just a few examples of ways you can make your cooking more nutritious. Also, it can be helpful to choose fats that have some nutritional benefit. Try using tub margarines that contain no trans-fats, or choose canola oil or cooking spray for frying.

Of course, how you cook your meals also makes a difference. Trim fat from your meat before cooking and use cooking methods such as grilling, poaching, baking and stir-frying to limit the amount of unwanted fat you are adding to your food.

Making smarter choices

Although ingredients like salt, fat, alcohol and sugar can make food taste better, the benefit doesn't necessarily justify the effects on your health. The same can be said about convenience foods. Although convenience foods often save on time, they are often so high in fat, salt and sugar that they just aren't worth it. Of course, this doesn't mean that you'll have to suffer through a boring diet of flavourless food or meals that take forever to prepare. It just means making smarter choices about what you are going to eat.

Choose fresh fruits and vegetables that are in season to help limit the expense. Using recipes that are quick and easy helps to reduce the amount of time you'll spend in the kitchen. Try making larger batches of foods that can be portioned and reheated later so you don't have to turn to unhealthy convenience foods when you're in a rush.

Stock up on snacks

Eating smaller quantities of food more often helps to prevent blood sugar spikes. Having lots of convenient little snacks on hand will help to fill the gaps between meals. Ensure these snacks are nutritious and low in fat. Be sure to keep some portable snacks on hand, too—this way you will always have something you can grab on your way out the door or pack in your lunch.

Everything in moderation

The best carbohydrates are the complex carbs found in unprocessed foods, like vegetables or whole grains. They're a great source of energy and they contain lots of fibre and nutrients, too. However, there are no forbidden foods in a diabetic diet. Everyone needs a special treat once in awhile, so allowing yourself a small piece of chocolate or candy will keep you from feeling like you're giving up the foods you enjoy most. Moderating your intake of sweets and starchy carbohydrates will help you to keep your blood sugar manageable.

Diabetic Choices (Beyond the Basics)

Tracking what you're eating is imperative for a diabetic diet. Each recipe in *30-Minute Diabetic Cooking* includes a basic breakdown of nutritional information, as well as diabetic choice values for the Beyond the Basics meal-planning guide. Beyond the Basics groups together foods that are similar in carbohydrate content. The names of the categories have been changed to better reflect the foods in the group. For example, Starches has become Grains and Starches, whereas Sugars has become Other Choices to better reflect the sweets and snack foods within this group. Although the serving size of each food within a particular group may vary, one serving of each food in that group will have the same approximate composition of carbohydrates, protein, fat and calories. If no choices are listed, it means that the serving size suggested for that recipe does not contain enough carbohydrates to constitute a choice in any category.

For people on insulin who require precise carbohydrate counting, the nutritional information provides a useful guideline for total grams of carbohydrate and dietary fibre.

Tips for Timely Cooking

Sure, everyone wants to eat better, but who has the time to do all that cooking? Here are a few tips that will help you to make the most of your time in the kitchen:

Planning ahead

It's a lot easier to attain a goal if you plan for it. This is also true of managing your eating. Making a weekly meal plan helps you save time in so many ways. You will have an easier time with grocery shopping if you know ahead of time what you're going to need and make a list. And you'll come home from work every evening knowing what's on the menu, so you won't have to waste time looking around your kitchen for inspiration.

Keeping high-demand items in stock

Keeping the essentials on hand is always helpful. Keep a ready supply of ingredients you use often. This can include pantry items like flour, tomato sauce or dried lentils and freezer items like frozen veggies or lean meat. When your stock starts to dwindle, just add the item to your grocery list and replenish the supply on your next shopping trip. Keeping your kitchen well-stocked is a great time saver and helps to eliminate emergency trips to the grocery store.

Doubling up

Make your freezer your best friend. You can cook larger amounts of grains in advance and freeze them in smaller portions for recipes that use them. This is especially handy for those grains that take a long time to cook, such as wild rice. You can also pre-cook and freeze chicken, ground beef or beans to cut the cooking time later. Making big batches of recipes that freeze well, then portioning and storing them for busier days, is also a great way to make sure a nutritious meal is never out of reach, even when time is a precious commodity.

Oven Pancake

Make one big pancake in the oven as a convenient alternative to frying several smaller ones. Sandwich wedges of this dense cake with yogurt, cheese or peanut butter.

Canola oil	1/2 tsp.	2 mL
All-purpose flour	1/2 cup	125 mL
Quick-cooking rolled oats	3 tbsp.	50 mL
Brown sugar, packed	2 tbsp.	30 mL
Baking powder	1 tsp.	5 mL
Ground cinnamon	1/2 tsp.	2 mL
Salt, just a pinch		
Large egg	1	1
Milk	3/4 cup	175 mL
Canola oil	1 tsp.	5 mL
Vanilla extract	1/2 tsp.	2 mL
Dried cranberries	1/4 cup	60 mL

Preheat oven to 450°F (230°C). Heat first amount of canola oil in large frying pan on medium.

Combine next 6 ingredients in medium bowl. Make a well in centre.

Whisk next 4 ingredients in small bowl. Add to well. Stir until just combined.

Scatter cranberries on bottom of frying pan. Pour batter over top. Immediately swirl batter to coat bottom, lifting and tilting pan to ensure entire bottom is covered. Bake on bottom rack in oven (see Tip, page 26) for 15 to 20 minutes until golden and centre springs back when pressed. Gently loosen sides and bottom of pancake with spatula. Carefully transfer to cutting board or plate. Cuts into 4 wedges. Serves 2.

1 serving: 343 Calories; 7.4 g Total Fat (3.5 g Mono, 1.4 g Poly, 1.6 g Sat); 99 mg Cholesterol; 60 g Carbohydrate; 2 g Fibre; 11 g Protein; 214 mg Sodium

CHOICES: 2 Grains & Starches; 1 Other Choices; 1/2 Meat & Alternatives; 1/2 Fats

Apple Barley Porridge

When it comes to nutritious breakfasts, oatmeal's always been the top choice—until now! This hearty porridge includes the goodness of flaxseed and barley with the classic, comforting flavours of apple and cinnamon.

Water	2 1/2 cups	625 mL
Large flake rolled oats	1 1/2 cups	375 mL
Cooked pot barley (about 1 cup, 250 mL, uncooked)	2 cups	500 mL
Flaxseed	1 tbsp.	15 mL
Ground cinnamon	1/2 tsp.	2 mL
Salt	1/4 tsp.	1 mL
Unsweetened applesauce	1 cup	250 mL
Brown sugar, packed	1 tbsp.	15 mL

Bring water to a boil in medium saucepan. Reduce heat to medium-low. Add oats. Stir.

Add next 4 ingredients. Stir. Simmer, covered, for about 10 minutes, stirring occasionally, until oats are tender.

Add applesauce and brown sugar. Cook and stir for about 1 minute until heated through. Makes about 6 cups (1.5 L). Serves 6.

1 serving: 182 Calories; 2.5 g Total Fat (trace Mono, 0.1 g Poly, 0.1 g Sat); 0 mg Cholesterol; 35 g Carbohydrate; 5 g Fibre; 5 g Protein; 101 mg Sodium

CHOICES: 1 1/2 Grains & Starches

Paré Pointer

After tasting his cough medicine, he said he would rather have the cough.

Orzo Sausage Bake

For cold-weather comfort food, look no further! This spicy, hearty casserole is perfect for lunch or brunch and has a texture that's halfway between stuffing and savoury bread pudding.

Water	8 cups	2 L
Salt	1 tsp.	5 mL
Orzo	1 cup	250 mL
Canola oil	1 tsp.	5 mL
Hot Italian sausage, casing removed	3/4 lb.	340 g
Chopped onion	1 cup	250 mL
Grated part-skim mozzarella cheese	1 1/2 cups	375 mL
Light ricotta cheese	1 cup	250 mL
Fine dry bread crumbs	1/2 cup	125 mL
Italian seasoning	1 tsp.	5 mL
Paprika	1/2 tsp.	2 mL

Preheat oven to 425°F (220°C). Combine water and salt in large saucepan. Bring to a boil. Add pasta. Boil, uncovered, for 8 to 10 minutes, stirring occasionally, until tender but firm. Drain. Return to same pot. Cover to keep warm.

Meanwhile, heat canola oil in large frying pan on medium-high. Add sausage and onion. Scramble-fry for about 5 minutes until sausage is browned. Drain. Add to pasta. Stir.

Add next 4 ingredients. Stir. Transfer to greased 2 quart (2 L) baking dish.

Sprinkle with paprika. Bake, uncovered, for about 15 minutes until browned and heated through. Makes about 6 cups (1.5 L). Serves 6.

1 serving: 383 Calories; 16.7 g Total Fat (5.7 g Mono, 1.5 g Poly, 7.5 g Sat); 46 mg Cholesterol; 35 g Carbohydrate; 2 g Fibre; 22 g Protein; 625 mg Sodium

CHOICES: 1 1/2 Grains & Starches; 2 Meat & Alternatives

Bacon Bean Bowl

Eating healthy doesn't have to be unpleasant—sometimes it's okay to compromise. This hearty stew includes a little bacon for flavour and a lot of spinach and beans for added fibre and protein.

Bacon slices, chopped	4	4
Chopped onion	1 cup	250 mL
Garlic cloves, minced	2	2
(or 1/2 tsp., 2 mL, powder)		
Sliced fresh white mushrooms	1 cup	250 mL
Can of white kidney beans, rinsed and drained	14 oz.	398 mL
Tiny bow pasta	1 cup	250 mL
Prepared vegetable broth	2 1/2 cups	625 mL
Fresh spinach leaves, lightly packed	6 cups	1.5 L
Grated lemon zest	1 tbsp.	15 mL
Pepper	1/4 tsp.	1 mL

Combine first 4 ingredients in large frying pan on medium-high. Cook for about 5 minutes, stirring often, until onion is softened and starting to brown.

Add next 3 ingredients. Stir. Bring to a boil. Reduce heat to medium-low. Simmer, covered, for about 10 minutes, stirring often, until pasta is tender but firm.

Add remaining 3 ingredients. Heat and stir for about 2 minutes until spinach is wilted. Makes about 5 cups (1.25 L). Serves 4.

1 serving: 440 Calories; 12.3 g Total Fat (4.6 g Mono, 1.2 g Poly, 3.7 g Sat); 15 mg Cholesterol; 66 g Carbohydrate; 8 g Fibre; 18 g Protein; 548 mg Sodium

CHOICES: 3 Grains & Starches; 1 Vegetables; 1 Meat & Alternatives

Pictured on page 18.

Mexican Egg Wraps

Taste buds still asleep? Wake them up with this combination of spicy salsa, Cheddar cheese and eggs nestled in a soft flour tortilla. This is just about the easiest and most delicious breakfast you could make.

Tub margarine	2 tsp.	10 mL
Large eggs	4	4
Salt, sprinkle		
Pepper, sprinkle		
Salsa	1/2 cup	125 mL
Whole-wheat flour tortillas	4	4
(6 inch, 15 cm, diameter)		
Grated light sharp Cheddar cheese	1/4 cup	60 mL
Finely chopped fresh cilantro	1 tsp.	5 mL

Melt margarine in large frying pan on medium. Break eggs, one at a time, into pan. Pierce yolks with fork. Sprinkle with salt and pepper. Cook, covered, for about 3 minutes until set.

Spread 2 tbsp. (30 mL) salsa on each tortilla, leaving 1 inch (2.5 cm) border. Place 1 egg over salsa on each tortilla. Sprinkle with cheese and cilantro. Fold sides over filling. Roll up from bottom to enclose filling. Makes 4 wraps.

1 wrap: 212 Calories; 9.1 g Total Fat (2.9 g Mono, 2.6 g Poly, 2.6 g Sat); 190 mg Cholesterol; 22 g Carbohydrate; 2 g Fibre; 11 g Protein; 486 mg Sodium

CHOICES: 1 Grains & Starches; 1 Meat & Alternatives

Pictured at right.

1. Creamy Couscous Parfaits, page 24
2. Waffles With Peanut Butter Spread, page 28
3. Mexican Egg Wraps, above

Props courtesy of: Danesco Inc.

Stylish Steak Sandwiches

A chic twist on a steak and cheese sandwich. Super simple to make at home, but tastes just like it came from a trendy bistro.

Flank steak	3/4 lb.	340 g
Montreal steak spice	1/4 tsp.	1 mL
Chopped roasted red pepper, blotted dry	1/2 cup	125 mL
Light herb and garlic cream cheese	1/3 cup	75 mL
Crusty whole-grain rolls, split	4	4
Montreal steak spice	1/4 tsp.	1 mL
Fresh spinach leaves, lightly packed	2 cups	500 mL

Preheat broiler. Sprinkle both sides of steak with first amount of steak spice. Place on greased baking sheet. Broil on top rack in oven for about 3 minutes per side until desired doneness. Transfer to cutting board. Cover with foil. Let stand for 10 minutes.

Meanwhile, combine red pepper and cream cheese in small bowl. Spread on bun halves.

Thinly slice steak diagonally across the grain. Sprinkle with second amount of steak spice. Arrange beef over cream cheese mixture on each bun. Top with spinach. Set bun tops over spinach. Makes 4 sandwiches.

1 sandwich: 319 Calories; 12.9 g Total Fat (3.6 g Mono, 1.2 g Poly, 5.6 g Sat); 49 mg Cholesterol; 27 g Carbohydrate; 5 g Fibre; 24 g Protein; 557 mg Sodium

CHOICES: 1 Grains & Starches; 2 1/2 Meat & Alternatives

Pictured at left.

1. Bacon Bean Bowl, page 15
2. Stylish Steak Sandwiches, above

Chipotle Turkey Joes

We're not sure who the famous sloppy joe was named after, but we're sure he'd be proud to have his name attached to this sweet and spicy update to the classic sandwich. Chipotle peppers (pronounced chih-POHT-lay) add some smoky heat.

Canola oil	1 tsp.	5 mL
Ground turkey	3/4 lb.	340 g
Chopped onion	1 cup	250 mL
Chopped roasted red pepper	1/4 cup	60 mL
Garlic cloves, minced	2	2
(or 1/2 tsp., 2 mL, powder)		
Finely chopped chipotle pepper in	1 tsp.	5 mL
adobo sauce (see Tip, page 40)		
Granulated sugar	1 tsp.	5 mL
Ground cumin	1/2 tsp.	2 mL
Ground ginger	1/2 tsp.	2 mL
Salt	1/2 tsp.	2 mL
Pepper	1/4 tsp.	1 mL
All-purpose flour	1 tbsp.	15 mL
Can of diced tomatoes (with juice)	14 oz.	398 mL
Frozen concentrated orange juice	1/4 cup	60 mL
Whole-wheat English muffins, split	4	4

Heat canola oil in large frying pan on medium-high. Add next 10 ingredients. Scramble-fry for about 6 minutes until turkey is no longer pink.

Sprinkle flour over turkey mixture. Heat and stir for 1 minute. Add tomatoes and concentrated orange juice. Stir. Bring to a boil. Reduce heat to medium-low. Simmer, covered, for 5 minutes to blend flavours.

Meanwhile, toast English muffin halves. Place 2 halves on each plate. Spoon turkey mixture over muffin halves. Serves 4.

1 serving: 328 Calories; 3.8 g Total Fat (1.0 g Mono, 0.9 g Poly, 0.3 g Sat); 34 mg Cholesterol; 47 g Carbohydrate; 5 g Fibre; 29 g Protein; 1182 mg Sodium

CHOICES: 1 1/2 Grains & Starches; 1/2 Fruits; 2 Vegetables; 3 Meat & Alternatives

Mandarin Turkey Wraps

Juicy mandarin oranges are truly outstanding in this wholesome wrap of turkey, apple, pecans and cranberries.

Canned mandarin orange segments, drained	1/2 cup	125 mL
Chopped unpeeled tart apple (such as Granny Smith)	1/4 cup	60 mL
Chopped pecans, toasted (see Tip, page 114)	2 tbsp.	30 mL
Dried cranberries	2 tbsp.	30 mL
Non-fat plain yogurt	2 tbsp.	30 mL
Light mayonnaise	1 tbsp.	15 mL
Whole-wheat tortillas (9 inch, 22 cm diameter)	4	4
Lettuce leaves	4	4
Grated part-skim mozzarella cheese	1/2 cup	125 mL
Deli turkey breast slices (about 1/2 lb., 225 g)	8	8

Combine first 6 ingredients in small bowl.

Arrange tortillas on work surface. Layer remaining 3 ingredients, in order given, on each tortilla. Spoon orange mixture along centre of turkey. Fold bottom ends of tortillas over filling. Fold in sides, slightly overlapping, leaving top ends open. Secure with wooden picks. Makes 4 wraps.

1 wrap: 246 Calories; 8.2 g Total Fat (2.9 g Mono, 2.3 g Poly, 2.0 g Sat); 31 mg Cholesterol; 29 g Carbohydrate; 3 g Fibre; 17 g Protein; 819 mg Sodium

CHOICES: 1/2 Grains & Starches; 1/2 Fruits; 2 Meat & Alternatives; 1/2 Fats

Oven Omelette

Can't seem to get the hang of making omelettes in a frying pan?
Try this oven method for quick and tasty results. All of the flavour
with none of the fuss!

Low-cholesterol egg product	1 1/2 cups	375 mL
Finely chopped green onion	2 tbsp.	30 mL
Skim milk	2 tbsp.	30 mL
Salt	1/4 tsp.	1 mL
Pepper	1/8 tsp.	0.5 mL
Cooking spray		
Grated Swiss cheese	1/2 cup	125 mL
Deli turkey breast slices, cut into thin strips	2 oz.	57 g

Preheat oven to 400°F (205°C). Heat 9 x 13 inch (22 x 33 cm) baking dish in oven for 3 minutes. Meanwhile, combine first 5 ingredients in small bowl.

Spray hot baking dish with cooking spray. Pour egg mixture into dish. Bake, uncovered, for about 8 minutes until eggs start to set but are still moist on surface. Cut into 4 pieces.

Sprinkle cheese and turkey onto half of each piece. Bake, uncovered, for about 2 minutes until cheese is melted. Fold omelettes over turkey and cheese. Makes 4 omelettes.

1 omelette: 132 Calories; 5.9 g Total Fat (0 g Mono, 0 g Poly, 2.5 g Sat); 95 mg Cholesterol; 3 g Carbohydrate; trace Fibre; 15 g Protein; 456 mg Sodium

CHOICES: 2 Meat & Alternatives

Paré Pointer

Weather is so colourful—the sun rose and the wind blue.

Thai Beef Lettuce Wraps

Add a taste of Asia to your next lunch. A bold, nutty beef filling is nestled in delicate lettuce leaves for delicious flavour and texture contrasts.

Cooking spray		
Extra-lean ground beef	1 lb.	454 g
Finely grated gingerroot (or 1/4 tsp., 1 mL, ground ginger)	1 tsp.	5 mL
Garlic clove, minced (or 1/4 tsp., 1 mL, powder)	1	1
Diced English cucumber (with peel)	1 1/2 cups	375 mL
Grated carrot	1/2 cup	125 mL
Coarsely chopped fresh basil (or mint), lightly packed	1/4 cup	60 mL
Sweet chili sauce	2 tbsp.	30 mL
Peanut sauce	1/3 cup	75 mL
Hoisin sauce	1 tbsp.	15 mL
Butter lettuce leaves	24	24

Heat large frying pan on medium. Spray with cooking spray. Add beef. Scramble-fry for about 5 minutes until beef is no longer pink.

Add ginger and garlic. Cook for about 3 minutes, stirring occasionally, until beef is browned. Remove from heat.

Add next 6 ingredients. Stir well. Transfer to small bowl. Makes about 3 1/2 cups (875 mL) filling.

Serve beef mixture on lettuce leaves. Serves 4.

1 serving: 239 Calories; 10.2 g Total Fat (4.6 g Mono, 2.1 g Poly, 2.6 g Sat); 60 mg Cholesterol; 12 g Carbohydrate; 2 g Fibre; 26 g Protein; 263 mg Sodium

CHOICES: 3 Meat & Alternatives

Creamy Couscous Parfaits

This blend of fruit, yogurt and whole grains makes for a hearty breakfast and is also good as a healthy dessert.

Skim milk	2/3 cup	150 mL
Salt, just a pinch		
Whole-wheat couscous	1/3 cup	75 mL
Can of pineapple tidbits, drained and juice reserved	14 oz.	398 mL
Coarsely chopped kiwifruit	1 cup	250 mL
Coarsely chopped strawberries	1 cup	250 mL
Reserved pineapple juice	1/4 cup	60 mL
Chopped fresh mint	2 tbsp.	30 mL
Light sour cream	1/2 cup	125 mL
Non-fat peach yogurt	1/2 cup	125 mL
Liquid honey	1 tbsp.	15 mL
Minced crystallized ginger	1 tsp.	5 mL
Grated orange zest	1/2 tsp.	2 mL

Combine milk and salt in small saucepan. Bring to a boil. Add couscous. Stir. Remove from heat. Let stand, covered, for about 5 minutes until tender. Fluff with fork. Spread on baking sheet with sides. Freeze for 5 minutes.

Meanwhile, combine next 5 ingredients in medium bowl. Let stand for 15 minutes, stirring occasionally.

Combine remaining 5 ingredients in separate medium bowl. Add chilled couscous. Stir. Spoon half of fruit mixture into 4 parfait glasses or small bowls. Spoon couscous mixture over fruit. Top with remaining fruit mixture. Makes 4 parfaits.

1 parfait: 223 Calories; 3.1 g Total Fat (trace Mono, 0.1 Poly, 1.6 g Sat); 11 mg Cholesterol; 43 g Carbohydrate; 5 g Fibre; 6 g Protein; 67 mg Sodium

CHOICES: 1/2 Grains & Starches; 1 1/2 Fruits; 1/2 Milk & Alternatives; 1/2 Fats

Pictured on page 17.

Instant Apple Cream Oatmeal

Make this deliciously satisfying oatmeal for your family any day of the week. Boil the water, stir in the oatmeal and fruit, and it will be ready to eat by the time everyone is up and dressed.

Water	3 cups	750 mL
Quick-cooking rolled oats	1/2 cup	125 mL
Quick-cooking rolled oats	1 cup	250 mL
Chopped dried apples	1/2 cup	125 mL
Skim milk powder	1/4 cup	60 mL
Brown sugar, packed	2 tbsp.	30 mL
Ground cinnamon	3/4 tsp.	4 mL
Salt	1/2 tsp.	2 mL

Bring water to a boil in medium saucepan.

Meanwhile, process first amount of oats in blender or food processor until powdery. Transfer to medium bowl.

Add remaining 6 ingredients. Stir. Slowly add to boiling water, stirring constantly. Remove from heat. Let stand, uncovered, for about 5 minutes until thickened (see Note). Makes about 3 1/2 cups (875 mL). Serves 4.

1 serving: 234 Calories; 2.3 g Total Fat (trace Mono, 0 g Poly, trace Sat); 1 mg Cholesterol; 46 g Carbohydrate; 5 g Fibre; 8 g Protein; 470 mg Sodium

CHOICES: 1 Grains & Starches; 1 Fruits; 1/2 Other Choices

Note: You can adjust the consistency of the oatmeal by adding more water.

Paré Pointer

Fast food restaurants stop thieves with a burger alarm.

Ham And Asparagus Frittata

Because frittatas are easier to make, they are sometimes thought of as shortcuts for omelets. Ham, asparagus and peppery eggs ensure there's no shortcut on flavour in this brunch favourite.

Low-cholesterol egg product	2 cups	500 mL
Grated light sharp Cheddar cheese	1/4 cup	60 mL
Skim milk	1/4 cup	60 mL
Pepper	1/2 tsp.	2 mL
Tub margarine	4 tsp.	20 mL
Chopped fresh asparagus	2 cups	500 mL
Chopped no-fat deli ham	3/4 cup	175 mL
Chopped green onion	2 tbsp.	30 mL
Grated light sharp Cheddar cheese	1/4 cup	60 mL

Preheat broiler. Whisk first 4 ingredients in medium bowl.

Melt margarine in large non-stick frying pan on medium-high. Add next 3 ingredients. Stir-fry for about 3 minutes until asparagus is tender-crisp. Pour egg mixture over asparagus mixture. Reduce heat to medium-low. Cook, covered, for about 8 minutes until almost set. Remove from heat.

Sprinkle with second amount of cheese. Broil on centre rack (see Tip, below) for about 5 minutes until cheese is melted and eggs are set. Cuts into 6 wedges.

1 wedge: 138 Calories; 6.2 g Total Fat (1.1 g Mono, 1.0 g Poly, 1.6 g Sat); 79 mg Cholesterol; 5 g Carbohydrate; 1 g Fibre; 15 g Protein; 477 mg Sodium

CHOICES: 2 Meat & Alternatives; 1/2 Fats

 tip When baking or broiling food in a frying pan with a handle that isn't ovenproof, wrap the handle in foil and keep it to the front of the oven, away from the element.

Wild Rice Apricot Pancakes

These deliciously addictive, fluffy pancakes include chewy wild rice and apricot for an interesting texture contrast. So flavourful, you could easily skip out on the butter and syrup!

Large eggs, fork-beaten	2	2
Cooked wild rice	1/2 cup	125 mL
Chopped dried apricot	1/3 cup	75 mL
Skim milk	1/3 cup	75 mL
Unsweetened applesauce	2 tbsp.	30 mL
Buttermilk pancake mix	2/3 cup	150 mL
Canola oil	2 tsp.	10 mL

Combine first 5 ingredients in small bowl. Add pancake mix. Stir until just moistened. Batter will be lumpy.

Heat 1/2 tsp. (2 mL) canola oil in large frying pan on medium. Pour batter into pan, using 1/2 cup (125 mL) for each pancake. Cook for about 2 minutes until bubbles form on top and edges appear dry. Turn pancake over. Cook for about 2 minutes until golden. Remove to plate. Cover to keep warm. Repeat with remaining batter, heating more canola oil if necessary to prevent sticking. Makes about 4 pancakes. Serves 2.

1 pancake: 198 Calories; 5.4 g Total Fat (2.7 g Mono, 1.2 g Poly, 1.0 g Sat); 93 mg Cholesterol; 31 g Carbohydrate; 2 g Fibre; 8 g Protein; 434 mg Sodium

CHOICES: 1 1/2 Grains & Starches; 1/2 Fruits; 1/2 Meat & Alternatives

Waffles With Peanut Butter Spread

Make ordinary toaster waffles extraordinary with the addition of a creamy peanut, cranberry and coconut topping.

Reduced-fat peanut butter	1/3 cup	75 mL
Light cream cheese	2 tbsp.	30 mL
Liquid honey	1 tbsp.	15 mL
Dried cranberries	2 tbsp.	30 mL
Medium unsweetened coconut	2 tbsp.	30 mL
Whole-wheat frozen waffles	8	8

Stir first 3 ingredients in small bowl until smooth.

Add cranberries and coconut. Stir. Makes about 1 cup (250 mL).

Toast waffles. Spread 2 tbsp (30 mL) peanut butter mixture over each waffle. Makes 8 waffles. Serves 4.

1 waffle: 342 Calories; 13.5 g Total Fat (1.2 g Mono, 0.6 g Poly, 4.7 g Sat); 9 mg Cholesterol; 48 g Carbohydrate; 5 g Fibre; 12 g Protein; 881 mg Sodium

CHOICES: 2 Grains & Starches; 1/2 Meat & Alternatives; 1/2 Fats

Pictured on page 17.

Chicken Salsa Wraps

The whole family will love these warm, cheesy tortillas filled with chicken and salsa. These wraps are the ultimate convenience food.

Whole-wheat flour tortillas (9 inch, 22 cm, diameter)	4	4
Salsa	1 cup	250 mL
Chopped cooked chicken (see Tip, page 38)	1 1/3 cups	325 mL
Thinly sliced red pepper	1 cup	250 mL
Grated jalapeño Monterey Jack cheese	1 cup	250 mL

(continued on next page)

Preheat oven to 400°F (205°C). Arrange tortillas on work surface. Spoon salsa down centre of each tortilla.

Layer remaining 3 ingredients over salsa. Fold bottom end of each tortilla over filling. Fold in sides. Fold over from bottom to enclose filling. Place, seam-side down, on greased baking sheet. Bake for about 15 minutes until golden. Makes 4 wraps.

1 wrap: 306 Calories; 12.1 g Total Fat (trace Mono, 1.2 g Poly, 5.0 g Sat); 64 mg Cholesterol; 26 g Carbohydrate; 4 g Fibre; 27 g Protein; 1052 mg Sodium

CHOICES: 1 Grains & Starches; 1 Vegetables; 3 Meat & Alternatives

Toasted Chicken Caesar Sandwiches

Transform your favourite meal salad into a sandwich! Makes for the perfect light lunch.

Chopped cooked chicken (see Tip, page 38)	2 cups	500 mL
Light creamy Caesar dressing	1/4 cup	60 mL
Finely chopped red onion	2 tbsp.	30 mL
Grated Romano cheese	2 tbsp.	30 mL
Real bacon bits	2 tbsp.	30 mL
Whole-wheat bread slices, toasted	4	4
Romaine lettuce leaves, torn in half	4	4
Light creamy Caesar dressing	4 tsp.	20 mL
Whole-wheat bread slices, toasted	4	4

Combine first 5 ingredients in medium bowl.

Arrange first amount of toast slices on work surface. Spread chicken mixture on toasts. Arrange lettuce over chicken mixture.

Spread second amount of Caesar dressing on remaining 4 toast slices. Place, dressing-side down, over lettuce. Press down gently. Makes 4 sandwiches.

1 sandwich: 328 Calories; 10.0 g Total Fat (3.3 g Mono, 2.1 g Poly, 2.6 g Sat); 68 mg Cholesterol; 32 g Carbohydrate; 4 g Fibre; 29 g Protein; 904 mg Sodium

CHOICES: 1 1/2 Grains & Starches; 3 Meat & Alternatives

Mango Chutney Steak Salad

Few things say summer like mango and barbecue. In this recipe, mango chutney lends its sweetness to tender grilled steak and crisp romaine. The perfect salad for a summer get-together.

Mango chutney	6 tbsp.	100 mL
Rice vinegar	3 tbsp.	50 mL
Sesame oil (for flavour)	3 tbsp.	50 mL
Soy sauce	4 tsp.	20 mL
Chili paste (sambal oelek)	3/4 tsp.	4 mL
Pepper	1/4 tsp.	1 mL
Beef strip loin steak, trimmed of fat	1 lb.	454 g
Romaine lettuce mix, lightly packed	6 cups	1.5 L
Thinly sliced yellow pepper	2 cups	500 mL

Preheat gas barbecue to medium-high. Process first 6 ingredients in blender until smooth. Transfer 1/2 cup (125 mL) chutney mixture to large bowl. Set aside.

Cook steak on greased grill for about 3 minutes per side, brushing occasionally with remaining chutney mixture, until desired doneness. Transfer to plate. Cover with foil. Let stand for 5 minutes. Cut diagonally across the grain into thin slices.

Add lettuce mix, yellow pepper and steak to reserved chutney mixture. Toss. Makes about 9 1/2 cups (2.4 L). Serves 6.

1 serving: 233 Calories; 12.8 g Total Fat (4.4 g Mono, 3.1 g Poly, 2.7 g Sat); 33 mg Cholesterol; 13 g Carbohydrate; 2 g Fibre; 18 g Protein; 382 mg Sodium

CHOICES: 1/2 Fruits; 2 Meat & Alternatives; 1 Fats

Pictured on page 35.

Greek Bread Salad

If croutons are your favourite part of the salad, then you must try this!
Soft bread cubes absorb all the great flavour of a Dijon vinaigrette in this
Greek-inspired salad.

Olive oil	1 tbsp.	15 mL
Greek seasoning	2 tsp.	10 mL
Whole-wheat bread cubes	3 cups	750 mL
(1/2 inch, 12 mm)		
Spring mix lettuce, lightly packed	4 cups	1 L
Chopped red pepper	1 cup	250 mL
Can of sliced black olives	1/2 cup	125 mL
Crumbled light feta cheese	1/2 cup	125 mL
Olive oil	1/3 cup	75 mL
Red wine vinegar	1/4 cup	60 mL
Dijon mustard	1 tsp.	5 mL
Dried oregano	1 tsp.	5 mL
Salt	1/2 tsp.	2 mL
Pepper	1/2 tsp.	2 mL

Preheat oven to 400°F (205°C). Combine olive oil and Greek seasoning in medium bowl. Add bread cubes. Toss until coated. Spread in single layer on ungreased baking sheet with sides. Bake for about 5 minutes, stirring at halftime, until starting to turn golden. Transfer to large bowl.

Add next 4 ingredients. Toss.

Combine remaining 6 ingredients in small cup. Drizzle over lettuce mixture. Toss. Makes about 8 cups (2 L). Serves 6.

1 serving: 242 Calories; 18.5 g Total Fat (11.8 g Mono, 1.6 g Poly, 3.6 g Sat); 7 mg Cholesterol; 15 g Carbohydrate; 3 g Fibre; 7 g Protein; 673 mg Sodium

CHOICES: 1/2 Grains & Starches; 3 Fats

Pictured on page 108.

Layered Turkey Taco Salad

With its stylish layers of delicious southwestern ingredients, this taco salad works as a super-quick weeknight supper, but it's also fancy enough for company!

Canola oil	1 tsp.	5 mL
Extra-lean ground turkey	3/4 lb.	340 g
Chili powder	2 tsp.	10 mL
Ground cumin	2 tsp.	10 mL
Salt	1/4 tsp.	1 mL
Can of black beans, rinsed and drained	19 oz.	540 mL
Frozen kernel corn	1/2 cup	125 mL
Water	1/4 cup	60 mL
Shredded iceberg lettuce, lightly packed	4 cups	1 L
Salsa	1 1/2 cups	375 mL
Light sour cream	3/4 cup	175 mL
Ripe medium avocado, diced (see Note)	1	1
Broken tortilla chips	3/4 cup	175 mL
Grated light sharp Cheddar cheese	1/2 cup	125 mL

Heat canola oil in large frying pan on medium-high. Add next 4 ingredients. Scramble-fry for about 5 minutes until no longer pink.

Add next 3 ingredients. Cook for about 5 minutes, stirring occasionally, until water is evaporated. Spread on baking sheet with sides. Cool for 5 minutes.

Put lettuce into large bowl. Spoon turkey mixture over. Layer next 5 ingredients, in order given, over turkey mixture. Makes about 10 1/2 cups (2.6 L). Serves 6.

1 serving: 300 Calories; 12.1 g Total Fat (1.0 g Mono, 0.7 g Poly, 3.2 g Sat); 38 mg Cholesterol; 30 g Carbohydrate; 7 g Fibre; 25 g Protein; 898 mg Sodium

CHOICES: 1 Grains & Starches; 3 Meat & Alternatives; 1 1/2 Fats

Note: Toss avocado with 1 tsp. (5 mL) lime juice to prevent browning.

Chorizo Bean Soup

A classic soup gets a spicy, smoky makeover from the addition of chorizo sausage.

Canola oil	1 tsp.	5 mL
Chorizo sausage, casing removed	3/4 lb.	340 g
Canola oil	1 tsp.	5 mL
Chopped celery	1 cup	250 mL
Chopped onion	1 cup	250 mL
Garlic cloves, minced	2	2
(or 1/2 tsp., 2 mL, powder)		
Prepared vegetable broth	4 cups	1 L
Can of white kidney beans,	19 oz.	540 mL
rinsed and drained		
Dried rosemary, crushed	1 tsp.	5 mL
Dried thyme	1/2 tsp.	2 mL

Heat first amount of canola oil in medium frying pan on medium. Add sausage. Scramble-fry for about 10 minutes until browned. Drain. Cover to keep warm.

Meanwhile, heat second amount of canola oil in large saucepan on medium-high. Add next 3 ingredients. Cook, uncovered, for about 5 minutes, stirring often, until onion is softened.

Add remaining 4 ingredients. Stir. Bring to a boil. Simmer, covered, for 10 minutes to blend flavours. Carefully process with hand blender or in blender until smooth (see Safety Tip). Add sausage. Stir. Makes about 6 1/2 cups (1.6 L). Serves 6.

1 serving: 218 Calories; 10.5 g Total Fat (4.4 g Mono, 1.4 g Poly, 2.9 g Sat); 16 mg Cholesterol; 20 g Carbohydrate; 5 g Fibre; 11 g Protein; 700 mg Sodium

CHOICES: 1/2 Grains & Starches; 1 Meat & Alternatives

Safety Tip: Follow manufacturer's instructions for processing hot liquids.

Orange Quinoa Salad

Spicy dishes don't have to be overpowering. In this citrusy quinoa,
spicy chili paste blends perfectly with the flavours of soy, maple and orange
for a nicely warming heat.

Frozen concentrated orange juice, thawed	1/4 cup	60 mL
Rice vinegar	2 tbsp.	30 mL
Low-sodium soy sauce	1 tbsp.	15 mL
Maple (or maple-flavoured) syrup	1 tbsp.	15 mL
Chili paste (sambal oelek)	1/2 tsp.	2 mL
Garlic powder	1/2 tsp.	2 mL
Ground ginger	1/2 tsp.	2 mL
Cooked quinoa	3 cups	750 mL
Diced red pepper	1 cup	250 mL
Diced yellow pepper	1 cup	250 mL
Diced zucchini (with peel)	1 cup	250 mL

Whisk first 7 ingredients in medium bowl until combined.

Add remaining 4 ingredients. Toss. Makes about 6 cups (1.5 L). Serves 6.

1 serving: 365 Calories; 5.1 g Total Fat (1.3 g Mono, 2.1 g Poly, 0.5 g Sat); 0 mg Cholesterol;
70 g Carbohydrate; 7 g Fibre; 12 g Protein; 111 mg Sodium

CHOICES: 3 1/2 Grains & Starches

Pictured at right.

1. Shrimp And Potato Salad, page 40
2. Orange Quinoa Salad, above
3. Tropical Shrimp Fruit Salad, page 37
4. Mango Chutney Steak Salad, page 30

Props courtesy of: Cherison Enterprises Inc.

Tropical Shrimp Fruit Salad

Filled with tropical flavours, this salad is the perfect lunch for a hot summer day. Cayenne adds just a touch of heat to this refreshing combination.

Reserved pineapple juice	1/4 cup	60 mL
Chopped fresh mint	2 tbsp.	30 mL
Lime juice	2 tbsp.	30 mL
Liquid honey	2 tbsp.	30 mL
Cayenne pepper	1/4 tsp.	1 mL
Can of pineapple chunks, juice reserved	14 oz.	398 mL
Bag of frozen, cooked medium shrimp (peeled and deveined), thawed	3/4 lb.	340 g
Diced avocado	1 cup	250 mL
Frozen mango pieces, thawed and larger pieces chopped	1 cup	250 mL
Chopped celery	1/2 cup	125 mL

Combine first 5 ingredients in medium bowl.

Add remaining 5 ingredients. Toss. Let stand for 20 minutes. Makes about 6 cups (1.5 L). Serves 6.

1 serving: 184 Calories; 4.8 g Total Fat (2.6 g Mono, 0.9 g Poly, 0.8 g Sat); 86 mg Cholesterol; 24 g Carbohydrate; 3 g Fibre; 13 g Protein; 95 mg Sodium

CHOICES: 1 Fruits; 1/2 Other Choices; 1 1/2 Meat & Alternatives; 1 Fats

Pictured on page 35.

1. Five-Spice Chicken Noodle Soup, page 38
2. Pumpkin Apple Soup, page 44
3. Chicken Corn Soup, page 41

Props courtesy of: Danesco Inc.
Cherison Enterprises Inc.
Casa Bugatti

Five-Spice Chicken Noodle Soup

Asian flavours are just a few minutes away when you cook this fabulous soup in your microwave. Just as fast as packaged instant noodles, but a whole lot tastier!

Low-sodium prepared chicken broth	4 cups	1 L
Low-sodium soy sauce	1 tbsp.	15 mL
Chinese five-spice powder	1/4 tsp.	1 mL
Garlic powder	1/4 tsp.	1 mL
Ground ginger	1/8 tsp.	0.5 mL
Chopped bok choy	2 cups	500 mL
Dry, thin Chinese-style instant noodles, broken up	3.25 oz.	100 g
Finely chopped red pepper	1/4 cup	60 mL
Sliced green onion	2 tbsp.	30 mL
Chopped cooked chicken (see Tip, below)	1 1/2 cups	375 mL

Combine first 5 ingredients in large microwave-safe bowl. Microwave, covered, on high (100%) for about 10 minutes until boiling.

Add next 4 ingredients. Stir. Microwave, covered, on high (100%) for about 2 minutes until noodles are tender.

Add chicken. Stir. Microwave, uncovered, on high (100%) for about 1 minute until heated through. Makes about 6 1/2 cups (1.6 L). Serves 4.

1 serving: 213 Calories; 5.3 g Total Fat (1.5 g Mono, 1.0 g Poly, 1.2 g Sat); 67 mg Cholesterol; 14 g Carbohydrate; 1 g Fibre; 26 g Protein; 1040 mg Sodium

CHOICES: 1/2 Grains & Starches; 2 Meat & Alternatives

Pictured on page 36.

 Don't have any leftover chicken? Start with 2 boneless, skinless chicken breast halves (4 – 6 oz., 113 – 170 g, each). Place in large frying pan with 1 cup (250 mL) water or chicken broth. Simmer, covered, for 12 to 14 minutes until no longer pink inside. Drain. Chop. Makes about 2 cups (500 mL) of cooked chicken.

Fennel And Grapefruit Soup

Ready to try something completely new? Caramelizing onion and fennel
brings out a natural sweetness that is brightened by tart grapefruit juice.
These flavours go surprisingly well together!

Canola oil	2 tsp.	10 mL
Chopped fennel bulb (white part only)	2 cups	500 mL
Chopped onion	1/2 cup	125 mL
Garlic clove, minced	1	1
(or 1/4 tsp., 1 mL, powder)		
Fennel seeds	1/2 tsp.	2 mL
Ground ginger	1/4 tsp.	1 mL
Brown sugar, packed	1 tsp.	5 mL
Low-sodium prepared chicken broth	2 cups	500 mL
Red grapefruit juice	1/4 cup	60 mL
Instant potato flakes	1/2 cup	125 mL
2% evaporated milk	1/2 cup	125 mL
Sliced green onion, for garnish		

Heat canola oil in large saucepan on medium. Add next 5 ingredients.
Cook for about 10 minutes, stirring often, until fennel and onion start
to brown.

Add sugar. Heat and stir for about 1 minute until fennel and onion
are golden.

Add broth and juice. Stir. Bring to a boil. Add potato flakes. Heat and
stir until boiling and thickened. Add evaporated milk. Cook and stir until
heated through. Carefully process with hand blender or in blender until
smooth (see Safety Tip).

Garnish with green onion. Makes about 4 cups (1 L). Serves 4.

1 serving: 158 Calories; 3.4 g Total Fat (1.6 g Mono, 0.7 g Poly, 0.6 g Sat); 5 mg Cholesterol;
28 g Carbohydrate; 7 g Fibre; 7 g Protein; 441 mg Sodium

CHOICES: 2 Vegetables; 1/2 Fats

Safety Tip: Follow manufacturer's instructions for processing hot liquids.

Shrimp And Potato Salad

Get your protein, carbs and greens—all together in a tasty salad! Shrimp, potatoes and crisp, fresh veggies mingle in a balsamic and Dijon vinaigrette.

Baby potatoes, quartered	1 lb.	454 g
Water	1/4 cup	60 mL
Montreal steak spice	1/2 tsp.	2 mL
Balsamic vinegar	2 tbsp.	30 mL
Olive (or canola) oil	2 tbsp.	30 mL
Dijon mustard	2 tsp.	10 mL
Salt	1/4 tsp.	1 mL
Pepper	1/4 tsp.	1 mL
Spring mix lettuce, lightly packed	4 cups	1 L
Cooked medium shrimp	1/2 lb.	225 g
(peeled and deveined)		
Thinly sliced red pepper	1/2 cup	125 mL

Put potato and water into medium microwave-safe bowl. Microwave, covered, on high (100%) for about 10 minutes, stirring every 3 minutes, until tender. Rinse with cold water. Drain. Add steak spice. Toss.

Meanwhile, combine next 5 ingredients in large bowl. Makes about 1/3 cup (75 mL) dressing.

Add remaining 3 ingredients and potato. Toss. Makes about 8 cups (2 L). Serves 8.

1 cup (250 mL): 117 Calories; 3.9 g Total Fat (2.6 g Mono, 0.5 g Poly, 0.6 g Sat); 43 mg Cholesterol; 12 g Carbohydrate; 1 g Fibre; 8 g Protein; 177 mg Sodium

CHOICES: 1/2 Grains & Starches; 1 Meat & Alternatives; 1/2 Fats

Pictured on page 35.

tip Chipotle chili peppers are smoked jalapeño peppers. Be sure to wash your hands after handling. To store any leftover chipotle chili peppers, divide into recipe-friendly portions and freeze, with sauce, in airtight containers for up to one year.

Chicken Corn Soup

Your standard chicken soup just went south of the border and came back loaded with exciting new flavours.

Canola oil	1 tsp.	5 mL
Frozen kernel corn	2 cups	500 mL
Chopped onion	1 cup	250 mL
Garlic cloves, minced (or 1/2 tsp., 2 mL, powder)	2	2
Finely chopped chipotle pepper in adobo sauce (see Tip, page 40)	1/2 tsp.	2 mL
Low-sodium prepared chicken broth	3 cups	750 mL
Can of diced tomatoes (with juice)	14 oz.	398 mL
Pepper	1/4 tsp.	1 mL
Chopped cooked chicken (see Tip, page 38)	2 cups	500 mL
Chopped fresh cilantro	1 tbsp.	15 mL
Lime juice	1 tbsp.	15 mL

Heat canola oil in large saucepan on medium-high. Add next 4 ingredients. Cook, uncovered, for about 4 minutes, stirring often, until onion is softened.

Add next 3 ingredients. Stir. Bring to a boil. Reduce heat to medium. Boil gently, covered, for 6 minutes to blend flavours.

Add chicken. Cook and stir for about 3 minutes until heated through.

Add cilantro and lime juice. Stir. Makes about 7 cups (1.75 L). Serves 6.

1 serving: 201 Calories; 5.6 g Total Fat (1.8 g Mono, 1.1 g Poly, 1.1 g Sat); 58 mg Cholesterol; 16 g Carbohydrate; 1 g Fibre; 22 g Protein; 699 mg Sodium

CHOICES: 1/2 Grains & Starches; 1/2 Vegetables; 1 1/2 Meat & Alternatives

Pictured on page 36.

Bean Medley Soup

A hearty meatless soup with the spicy flavour of chipotle pepper and the freshness of lime. Adding a garnish of sour cream and cilantro will give this flavourful soup a little extra punch.

Olive (or canola) oil	2 tsp.	10 mL
Chopped onion	1 cup	250 mL
Garlic cloves, minced	2	2
(or 1/2 tsp., 2 mL, powder)		
Ground cumin	1 tsp.	5 mL
Prepared vegetable broth	3 cups	750 mL
Can of mixed beans, rinsed and drained	19 oz.	540 mL
Can of navy beans, rinsed and drained	14 oz.	398 mL
Finely chopped chipotle peppers	2 tsp.	10 mL
in adobo sauce (see Tip, page 40)		
Lime juice	1 tbsp.	15 mL

Heat olive oil in large saucepan on medium. Add next 3 ingredients. Cook, uncovered, for about 5 minutes, stirring often, until onion is softened.

Add next 4 ingredients. Bring to a boil. Reduce heat to medium-low. Simmer, partially covered, for 10 minutes, stirring occasionally. Remove 1 cup (250 mL) of solids. Mash. Add to soup. Stir.

Add lime juice. Stir. Makes about 6 cups (1.5 L). Serves 4.

1 serving: 282 Calories; 3.8 g Total Fat (1.7 g Mono, 0.4 g Poly, 0.4 g Sat); 0 mg Cholesterol; 49 g Carbohydrate; 12 g Fibre; 16 g Protein; 958 mg Sodium

CHOICES: 2 Grains & Starches; 2 Meat & Alternatives; 1/2 Fats

Tuna Chowder

This chowder gets its thick and hearty texture from grated potato instead of rich milk or cream—what a concept!

Prepared vegetable broth	4 cups	1 L
Frozen cut green beans	2 cups	500 mL
Grated peeled potato	2 cups	500 mL
Dried basil	1/2 tsp.	2 mL
Dried thyme	1/4 tsp.	1 mL
Pepper	1/4 tsp.	1 mL
Olive oil	1 tsp.	5 mL
Chopped onion	1 cup	250 mL
Chopped green pepper	1/2 cup	125 mL
Garlic clove, minced	1	1
(or 1/4 tsp., 1 mL, powder)		
Can of chunk light tuna in water, drained	6 oz.	170 g

Bring broth to a boil in large saucepan. Add next 5 ingredients. Reduce heat to medium. Boil gently, covered, for 10 minutes, stirring occasionally.

Heat olive oil in small frying pan on medium. Add next 3 ingredients. Cook for about 5 minutes, stirring often, until onion is softened. Add to broth mixture.

Add tuna. Stir. Simmer, covered, for about 2 minutes until heated through. Makes about 7 1/2 cups (1.9 L). Serves 6.

1 serving: 130 Calories; 5 g Total Fat (2.0 g Mono, 0.6 g Poly, 1.4 g Sat); 9 mg Cholesterol; 19 g Carbohydrate; 3 g Fibre; 10 g Protein; 339 mg Sodium

CHOICES: 1/2 Grains & Starches; 1 Vegetables; 1 Meat & Alternatives

Pumpkin Apple Soup

Harvest from your pantry for the ingredients to make this light and delicious soup. It's easy enough for a quick lunch, sophisticated enough for a dinner party and easily doubled so you'll have lots left over.

Prepared chicken broth	2 cups	500 mL
Can of pure pumpkin (no spices)	14 oz.	398 mL
Unsweetened applesauce	1 cup	250 mL
Ground cinnamon	1/2 tsp.	2 mL
Ground cumin	1/4 tsp.	1 mL
Skim evaporated milk	1/2 cup	125 mL

Combine first 5 ingredients in medium saucepan. Bring to a boil, stirring occasionally.

Add evaporated milk. Heat and stir for 1 minute. Makes about 5 cups (1.25 L). Serves 4.

1 serving: 97 Calories; 1.0 g Total Fat (0.3 g Mono, 0.2 g Poly, 0.3 g Sat); 1 mg Cholesterol; 20 g Carbohydrate; 4 g Fibre; 4 g Protein; 785 mg Sodium

CHOICES: 1/2 Fruits; 1 Vegetables

Pictured on page 36.

Curly Ribbon Salad

Like presents, some meals are best when topped with ribbons! Serve this pretty salad and see for yourself.

Chopped fresh basil	3 tbsp.	50 mL
White vinegar	2 tbsp.	30 mL
Olive oil	1 tbsp.	15 mL
Granulated sugar	2 tsp.	10 mL
Salt	1/4 tsp.	1 mL
Thinly sliced English cucumber (with peel), see Note	3 cups	750 mL
Thinly sliced peeled daikon radish (see Note)	2 cups	500 mL

(continued on next page)

Whisk first 5 ingredients in large bowl until sugar is dissolved.

Add cucumber and daikon. Toss until coated. Makes about 3 1/2 cups (875 mL). Serves 4.

1 serving: 65 Calories; 4.5 g Total Fat (2.5 g Mono, 0.3 g Poly, 0.5 g Sat); 0 mg Cholesterol; 6 g Carbohydrate; trace Fibre; 2 g Protein; 148 mg Sodium

CHOICES: 1/2 Fats

Note: Use a vegetable peeler to cut long, thin, ribbon-like slices.

Chard And Hazelnut Salad

Sweet mandarin orange, salty blue cheese and toasted hazelnuts combine in a deep green salad—the flavours intermingle in the most delightful way!

Chopped or torn ruby (or Swiss) chard, lightly packed	4 cups	1 L
Can of mandarin orange segments, drained and juice reserved	10 oz.	284 mL
Coarsely chopped hazelnuts (filberts), toasted (see Tip, page 114)	1/2 cup	125 mL
Thinly sliced red onion	1/2 cup	125 mL
Crumbled blue cheese	1/4 cup	60 mL
ORANGE DRESSING		
Olive (or canola) oil	3 tbsp.	50 mL
Red wine vinegar	2 tbsp.	30 mL
Reserved mandarin orange juice	2 tbsp.	30 mL
Granulated sugar	1 tbsp.	15 mL
Salt	1/4 tsp.	1 mL

Combine first 5 ingredients in large bowl.

Orange Dressing: Combine all 5 ingredients in jar with tight-fitting lid. Shake well. Makes about 1/2 cup (125 mL) dressing. Drizzle over salad. Toss. Makes about 6 cups (1.5 L). Serves 4.

1 serving: 258 Calories; 21.0 g Total Fat (14.0 g Mono, 2.0 g Poly, 3.3 g Sat); 6 mg Cholesterol; 16 g Carbohydrate; 3 g Fibre; 5 g Protein; 322 mg Sodium

CHOICES: 1/2 Fruits; 4 Fats

White Bean Hummus
And Pita Chips

A hearty helping of hummus and pita makes for an unbeatable snack. This version uses white beans and replaces the tahini with lower-fat yogurt and sesame oil. Baked whole-wheat pita chips make the perfect dipper.

WHITE BEAN HUMMUS

Can of white kidney beans, rinsed and drained	19 oz.	540 mL
Lemon juice	2 tbsp.	30 mL
Low-fat plain yogurt	1/3 cup	75 mL
Sesame oil (for flavour)	2 tsp.	10 mL
Garlic clove, minced (or 1/4 tsp., 1 mL, powder)	1	1
Ground cumin	1/2 tsp.	2 mL
Salt	1/4 tsp.	1 mL
Pepper	1/4 tsp.	1 mL

PITA CHIPS

Whole-wheat pita breads (7 inch, 18 cm, diameter)	4	4
Cooking spray		
Salt, sprinkle		
Pepper, sprinkle		

White Bean Hummus: Preheat oven to 375°F (190°C). Process all 8 ingredients in blender or food processor until smooth. Makes about 1 1/2 cups (375 mL) hummus.

Pita Chips: Spray 1 side of each pita bread with cooking spray. Sprinkle with salt and pepper. Stack pitas. Cut stack into 8 wedges. Spread in single layer on ungreased baking sheet. Bake for about 10 minutes until crisp and golden. Serve with hummus. Makes 32 pita chips.

1/4 cup (60 mL) hummus with 5 pita chips: 207 Calories; 3.5 g Total Fat (0.7 g Mono, 1.1 g Poly, 0.5 g Sat); 1 mg Cholesterol; 37 g Carbohydrate; 7 g Fibre; 9 g Protein; 362 mg Sodium

CHOICES: 2 Grains & Starches; 1/2 Meat & Alternatives

Chocolate Chip Softies

Like a white lie—using mini-chips makes it look like there's more chocolate in these satisfying bite-sized cookies. Everyone is sure to enjoy these soft little cookies, and applesauce replaces some of the butter and sugar.

Tub margarine	1/4 cup	60 mL
Granulated sugar	1/4 cup	60 mL
Unsweetened applesauce	1/4 cup	60 mL
Skim milk	1 tbsp.	15 mL
Egg white	1	1
Vanilla extract	1 tsp.	5 mL
All-purpose flour	3/4 cup	175 mL
Mini semi-sweet chocolate chips	1/4 cup	60 mL
Baking soda	1/4 tsp.	1 mL
Salt	1/8 tsp.	0.5 mL

Preheat oven to 375°F (190°C). Cream margarine and sugar in medium bowl until fluffy. Beat in next 4 ingredients.

Add remaining 4 ingredients. Stir. Drop, using about 1 tbsp. (15 mL) for each, about 1 inch (2.5 cm) apart onto greased cookie sheet. Bake for about 10 minutes until golden. Let stand on cookie sheet for 5 minutes. Remove cookies from cookie sheet and place on wire rack to cool. Makes about 16 cookies.

1 cookie: 77 Calories; 3.9 g Total Fat (1.5 g Mono, 1.2 g Poly, 1.0 g Sat); trace Cholesterol; 10 g Carbohydrate; trace Fibre; 1 g Protein; 80 mg Sodium

CHOICES: 1/2 Other Choices; 1/2 Fats

Pictured on page 144.

Paré Pointer

If you sell mobile homes, are you a wheel estate agent?

Banana Oat Muffins

These bite-sized muffins are loaded with the goodness of oats, banana, peanut butter and whole wheat for a satisfying snack—you may just forget that they're good for you! Processing the wet ingredients ensures even distribution throughout the muffins.

Large flake rolled oats	1 cup	250 mL
All-purpose flour	1/2 cup	125 mL
Whole-wheat flour	1/2 cup	125 mL
Brown sugar, packed	1/4 cup	60 mL
Baking powder	1 tbsp.	15 mL
Ground cinnamon	1 tsp.	5 mL
Ground cardamom	1/2 tsp.	2 mL
Salt	1/4 tsp.	1 mL
Large egg	1	1
Overripe medium banana (see Tip, below)	1	1
Milk	1/2 cup	125 mL
Peanut butter	1/3 cup	75 mL
Vanilla extract	1 tsp.	5 mL

Preheat oven to 375°F (190°C). Measure first 8 ingredients into large mixing bowl. Make a well in centre.

Process remaining 5 ingredients in blender or food processor until smooth. Add to well. Stir until just moistened. Fill 24 greased mini-muffin cups. Bake for about 12 minutes until lightly browned and wooden pick inserted in centre of muffin comes out clean. Let stand in pan for 5 minutes. Remove muffins from pan and place on wire rack to cool. Makes 24 mini-muffins.

1 mini-muffin: 71 Calories; 2.4 g Total Fat (1.0 g Mono, 0.6 g Poly, 0.5 g Sat); 8 mg Cholesterol; 11 g Carbohydrate; 1 g Fibre; 3 g Protein; 64 mg Sodium

CHOICES: 1/2 Grains & Starches

 tip When your bananas get too ripe to enjoy fresh, peel and cut them into 2 inch (5 cm) chunks and freeze on a baking sheet. Once frozen, transfer to freezer bag for use in any blended beverage. Ripe bananas have superior flavour for beverages.

Berry Minty Smoothie

Fresh mint adds a refreshing coolness to this creamy blend of berries and bananas. If you don't like the seeds in blackberries, choose a berry mix without them or just pick the blackberries out before measuring.

Frozen mixed berries	1 1/2 cups	375 mL
Overripe medium banana, cut up	1	1
(see Tip, page 48)		
Soy milk	1/2 cup	125 mL
Ground flaxseed	1 tbsp.	15 mL
Fresh mint leaves	6	6

Process all 5 ingredients in blender or food processor until smooth. Makes about 1 3/4 cups (425 mL). Serves 2.

1 serving: 152 Calories; 1.9 g Total Fat (0.3 g Mono, 0.5 g Poly, 0.2 g Sat); 0 mg Cholesterol; 31 g Carbohydrate; 7 g Fibre; 5 g Protein; 34 mg Sodium

CHOICES: 1 1/2 Fruits

Peppered Popcorn

Transform ordinary microwave popcorn into a peppery, flavourful treat with the addition of a spicy secret ingredient.

Tub margarine	2 tbsp.	30 mL
Cayenne pepper	1/2 tsp.	2 mL
Bag of trans fat-free microwave popcorn	3 oz.	85 g

Combine margarine and cayenne pepper in small microwave-safe bowl. Microwave, uncovered, on high (100%) for about 30 seconds until margarine is melted. Stir.

Microwave popcorn on high (100%) for 2 to 3 minutes until popping slows to 1 second between pops. Carefully remove bag from microwave. Transfer popcorn to extra-large bowl. Drizzle with margarine mixture. Toss until coated. Makes about 11 cups (2.75 L).

1 cup (250 mL): 52 Calories; 2.8 g Total Fat (1.2 g Mono, 1.1 g Poly, 0.4 g Sat); 0 mg Cholesterol; 6 g Carbohydrate; 1 g Fibre; 1 g Protein; 66 mg Sodium

CHOICES: 1/2 Fats

Razzle-Dazzle Smoothie

The addition of chocolate makes this raspberry smoothie dazzle! Forget fat-filled milkshakes—this nutritious beverage is the best way to get your next chocolate fix.

Frozen whole raspberries	2 cups	500 mL
Non-fat raspberry yogurt	2 cups	500 mL
Light hot chocolate mix	1/2 cup	125 mL
Skim milk	1/2 cup	125 mL
Large banana, sliced	1	1
Ice cubes	8	8

Process all 6 ingredients in blender or food processor until smooth. Makes about 5 cups (1.25 L). Serves 4.

1 serving: 230 Calories; 0.7 g Total Fat (trace Mono, trace Poly, 0.1 g Sat); 3 mg Cholesterol; 43 g Carbohydrate; 7 g Fibre; 13 g Protein; 534 mg Sodium

CHOICES: 2 1/2 Fruits; 1 Milk & Alternatives

Pictured on page 54.

Blueberry Smoothie

Double the flavours, double the taste! A double-dose of blueberry flavour is rounded out by milk and vanilla for a quick and satisfying snack.

Frozen blueberries	1 1/2 cups	375 mL
Non-fat blueberry yogurt	1 cup	250 mL
Skim milk	3/4 cup	175 mL
Skim milk powder	2 tbsp.	30 mL
Vanilla extract	1 tsp.	5 mL

Process all 5 ingredients in blender or food processor until smooth. Makes about 3 cups (750 mL). Serves 2.

1 serving: 183 Calories; 1.0 g Total Fat (0.1 g Mono, trace Poly, 0.1 g Sat); 6 mg Cholesterol; 33 g Carbohydrate; 3 g Fibre; 11 g Protein; 145 mg Sodium

CHOICES: 1/2 Fruits; 1 1/2 Milk & Alternatives

Pictured on page 54.

Pumpkin Power Puffs

These fibre and protein-packed puffs are a cross between a muffin and a cookie, each topped with a big chocolate kiss!

All-purpose flour	3/4 cup	175 mL
Whole-wheat flour	3/4 cup	175 mL
Brown sugar, packed	1/2 cup	125 mL
Baking powder	1 1/2 tsp.	7 mL
Ground cinnamon	1/2 tsp.	2 mL
Salt	1/4 tsp.	1 mL
Ground nutmeg	1/8 tsp.	0.5 mL
Ground cloves, just a pinch		
Large egg	1	1
Canned navy beans, rinsed and drained	1/2 cup	125 mL
Canned pure pumpkin (no spices)	1/2 cup	125 mL
Milk	3 tbsp.	50 mL
Canola oil	2 tbsp.	30 mL
Vanilla extract	1 tsp.	5 mL
Chocolate rosette candies	27	27

Preheat oven to 375°F (190°C). Combine first 8 ingredients in large bowl. Make a well in centre.

Process next 6 ingredients in blender or food processor until smooth. Add to well. Stir until just moistened. Drop, using 1 tbsp. (15 mL) for each, about 1 inch (2.5 cm) apart onto 2 greased cookie sheets (see Note).

Press one chocolate rosette, pointed-side down, into centre of each cookie. Bake on separate racks in oven for about 12 minutes, switching position of cookie sheets at halftime, until bottoms are golden. Let stand on cookie sheets for 5 minutes. Remove cookies from cookie sheets and place on wire racks to cool. Makes about 27 puffs.

1 puff: 84 Calories; 2.8 g Total Fat (0.7 g Mono, 0.4 g Poly, 1.1 g Sat); 8 mg Cholesterol; 13 g Carbohydrate; 1 g Fibre; 2 g Protein; 63 mg Sodium

CHOICES: 1/2 Other Choices

Pictured on page 144 and on back cover.

Note: To save time, use a small self-clearing ice cream scoop to portion the cookies easily and uniformly.

Cocoa Coconut Macaroons

It's unlikely that there's a more fitting combination than chocolate and coconut. These light cookies are quick to make and so good that they'll probably disappear just as fast.

Box of angel food cake mix	15 oz.	430 g
Medium unsweetened coconut	1 cup	250 mL
Cocoa, sifted if lumpy	1/4 cup	60 mL
Water	1/3 cup	75 mL

Preheat oven to 300°F (150°C). Combine first 3 ingredients in medium bowl.

Add water. Mix well. Drop, using about 1 tbsp. (15 mL) for each, about 2 inches (5 cm) apart onto 2 greased cookie sheets. Flatten with fork. Bake on separate racks in oven for about 12 minutes, switching position of cookie sheets at halftime, until cookies are crisp. Let stand on cookie sheets for 5 minutes. Remove cookies from cookie sheets and place on wire racks to cool. Makes about 40 cookies.

1 cookie: 53 Calories; 1.3 g Total Fat (0.1 g Mono, trace Poly, 1.1 g Sat); 0 mg Cholesterol; 10 g Carbohydrate; trace Fibre; 1 g Protein; 79 mg Sodium

CHOICES: 1/2 Other Choices

Pictured on page 144.

1. Thai Spinach Dip, page 58
2. Veggie Pinwheels, page 60

Props courtesy of: Danesco Inc.

Peppermint Patty Puffs

These dense, brownie-like cupcakes pack some peppermint punch! Just as satisfying as the ever-popular mint and chocolate treat they're named for.

Semi-sweet chocolate baking squares (1 oz., 28 g, each), chopped	2	2
Granulated sugar	1 cup	250 mL
All-purpose flour	1/2 cup	125 mL
Cocoa, sifted if lumpy	1/2 cup	125 mL
Salt	1/4 tsp.	1 mL
Large eggs, fork-beaten	2	2
Unsweetened applesauce	1/2 cup	125 mL
Peppermint extract	1/2 tsp.	2 mL

Preheat oven to 350°F (175°C). Put chocolate into small microwave-safe bowl. Microwave on medium (50%) for about 90 seconds, stirring every 30 seconds, until almost melted. Stir until smooth.

Combine next 4 ingredients in medium bowl. Make a well in centre.

Whisk remaining 3 ingredients and melted chocolate in small bowl. Add to well. Stir until just moistened. Fill 24 greased mini-muffin cups 3/4 full. Bake for 12 to 15 minutes until wooden pick inserted in centre of puff comes out clean. Do not overbake. Makes 24 puffs.

1 puff: 62 Calories; 1.0 g Total Fat (0.4 g Mono, 0.1 g Poly, 0.5 g Sat); 16 mg Cholesterol; 13 g Carbohydrate; 1 g Fibre; 1 g Protein; 30 mg Sodium

CHOICES: 1/2 Other Choices

1. Blueberry Smoothie, page 50
2. Razzle-Dazzle Smoothie, page 50
3. Tropical Tango Tofu Smoothie, page 60
4. Tart Cranberry Refresher, page 58
5. Caramel Mocha Smoothie, page 61

Props courtesy of: The Bay

Chocolate Crackle Cakes

With portion sizes just large enough for a tiny treat, even white chocolate can be part of a healthy diet. We've used just enough to suggest decadence, but these crackle cakes won't send your blood sugar skyrocketing.

Large egg	1	1
Granulated sugar	1/3 cup	75 mL
Canola oil	2 tbsp.	30 mL
Vanilla extract	1 1/2 tsp.	7 mL
All-purpose flour	2/3 cup	150 mL
Baking powder	1/4 tsp.	1 mL
Salt	1/8 tsp.	0.5 mL
White chocolate baking square (1 oz., 28 g), chopped	1	1

Preheat oven to 350°F (175°C). Whisk first 4 ingredients in medium bowl until smooth.

Add next 3 ingredients. Whisk until combined.

Put chocolate into small microwave-safe bowl. Microwave, uncovered, on medium (50%) for about 45 seconds, stirring every 15 seconds, until chocolate is almost melted. Stir until smooth. Add to batter. Fill 12 greased mini-muffin cups 3/4 full. Bake for 10 to 12 minutes until wooden pick inserted in centre of cake comes out clean. Let stand in pan for 5 minutes. Remove cakes from pan and place on wire rack to cool. Makes 12 cakes.

1 cake: 83 Calories; 4.0 g Total Fat (2.0 g Mono, 0.8 g Poly, 1.1 g Sat); 16 mg Cholesterol; 11 g Carbohydrate; trace Fibre; 1 g Protein; 35 mg Sodium

CHOICES: 1/2 Fats; 1/2 Other Choices

Paré Pointer
Guess who fell down the chimney last Christmas? Santa Klutz.

Chocolate Orange Muffins

There's a secret ingredient in these muffins, and no one will ever guess what it is. Beans add lots of fibre and protein while a shiny orange glaze gives the appearance of party fare.

All-purpose flour	1 1/4 cups	300 mL
Whole-wheat flour	3/4 cup	175 mL
Cocoa, sifted if lumpy	1/4 cup	60 mL
Baking powder	2 tsp.	10 mL
Salt	1/2 tsp.	2 mL
Large eggs	2	2
Canned white kidney beans, rinsed and drained	1 cup	250 mL
Skim milk	2/3 cup	150 mL
Brown sugar, packed	1/2 cup	125 mL
Canola oil	1/4 cup	60 mL
Frozen concentrated orange juice, thawed	2 tbsp.	30 mL
Brown sugar, packed	1 tbsp.	15 mL

Preheat oven to 400°F (205°C). Measure first 5 ingredients into large bowl. Stir. Make a well in centre.

Process next 5 ingredients in blender or food processor until smooth. Add to well. Stir until just moistened. Fill 12 greased muffin cups 2/3 full. Bake for about 15 minutes until wooden pick inserted in centre of muffin comes out clean.

Meanwhile, combine concentrated orange juice and second amount of sugar in small cup. Brush over tops of hot muffins. Let stand in pan for 5 minutes. Remove muffins from pan and place on wire rack to cool. Makes 12 muffins.

1 muffin: 189 Calories; 5.9 g Total Fat (3.1 g Mono, 1.5 g Poly, 0.8 g Sat); 31 mg Cholesterol; 30 g Carbohydrate; 2 g Fibre; 5 g Protein; 169 mg Sodium

CHOICES: 1 Grains & Starches; 1/2 Other Choices; 1 Fats

Thai Spinach Dip

The fresh, light flavours of Thai cuisine shine in a rich and creamy spinach dip. Dunk in your favourite cut-up vegetables and enjoy!

Olive (or canola) oil	1 tsp.	5 mL
Chopped onion	1/2 cup	125 mL
Dried crushed chilies	1/2 tsp.	2 mL
Chopped fresh spinach leaves, lightly packed	1 cup	250 mL
Light sour cream	1/2 cup	125 mL
Non-fat plain yogurt	1/2 cup	125 mL
Light chunky peanut butter	3 tbsp.	50 mL
Chopped fresh mint	2 tbsp.	30 mL
Lime juice	1 tbsp.	15 mL
Liquid honey	1 tbsp.	15 mL
Low-sodium soy sauce	1 1/2 tsp.	7 mL

Heat olive oil in small frying pan on medium. Add onion and chilies. Cook for about 5 minutes, stirring often, until onion is softened.

Add spinach. Heat and stir for about 1 minute until wilted. Remove from heat.

Whisk remaining 7 ingredients in medium bowl. Add spinach mixture. Stir. Makes about 1 1/2 cups (375 mL).

3 tbsp. (50 mL): 85 Calories; 4.3 g Total Fat (0.4 g Mono, trace Poly, 1.5 g Sat); 6 mg Cholesterol; 8 g Carbohydrate; 1 Fibre; 3 g Protein; 96 mg Sodium

CHOICES: 1/2 Fats

Pictured on page 53.

Tart Cranberry Refresher

You'll be tickled pink by the tart flavours of cranberry and raspberry in this refreshing pink smoothie.

Non-fat raspberry yogurt	2 cups	500 mL
Frozen raspberries	1 cup	250 mL
Cranberry juice	1/2 cup	125 mL
Frozen cranberries	1/2 cup	125 mL

(continued on next page)

Process all 4 ingredients in blender or food processor until smooth. Makes about 3 1/2 cups (875 mL). Serves 2.

1 serving: 211 Calories; 0.6 g Total Fat (0 g Mono, 0 g Poly, 0 g Sat); 5 mg Cholesterol; 44 g Carbohydrate; 4 g Fibre; 9 g Protein; 117 mg Sodium

CHOICES: 1 Fruits; 1 1/2 Milk & Alternatives

Pictured on page 54.

Quick PB Cookies

If you love peanut butter cookies, you can feel free to indulge in this healthier version. Light peanut butter and applesauce provide most of the sweetness and help to reduce the fat.

Large egg, fork-beaten	1	1
Chunky light peanut butter	1 cup	250 mL
Unsweetened applesauce	1/4 cup	60 mL
Granulated sugar	3 tbsp.	50 mL
All-purpose flour	1/4 cup	60 mL
Baking powder	1/4 tsp.	1 mL

Preheat oven to 325°F (160°C). Combine first 4 ingredients in medium bowl.

Add flour and baking powder. Mix until no white streaks remain. Drop, using about 1 tbsp. (15 mL) for each, about 2 inches (5 cm) apart onto 2 ungreased cookie sheets. Bake on separate racks in oven for about 12 minutes, switching position of cookie sheets at halftime, until edges are golden. Let stand on cookie sheets for 5 minutes. Remove cookies from cookie sheets and place on wire racks to cool. Makes about 21 cookies.

1 cookie: 89 Calories; 4.8 g Total Fat (0.1 g Mono, trace Poly, 1.0 g Sat); 9 mg Cholesterol; 9 g Carbohydrate; 1 g Fibre; 3 g Protein; 90 mg Sodium

CHOICES: 1/2 Meat & Alternatives

Pictured on page 144.

Tropical Tango Tofu Smoothie

You may not think of healthy drinks as being rich, creamy and sweet—but this sunny yellow smoothie certainly is! Makes a great breakfast or snack and the tofu provides enough protein to help get you through to your next meal.

Unsweetened orange juice	2 cups	500 mL
Package of coconut dessert tofu	10 1/2 oz.	300 g
Frozen pineapple pieces	1 cup	250 mL
Frozen mango pieces	3/4 cup	175 mL

Process all 4 ingredients in blender until smooth. Makes about 4 cups (1 L). Serves 4.

1 serving: 179 Calories; 1.5 g Total Fat (0.1 g Mono, 0.1 g Poly, 0.2 g Sat); 0 mg Cholesterol; 40 g Carbohydrate; 2 g Fibre; 4 g Protein; 8 mg Sodium

CHOICES: 2 Fruits; 1/2 Meat & Alternatives

Pictured on page 54.

Veggie Pinwheels

These crisp and attractive tortilla spirals are filled with a warm filling of cream cheese and veggies. These taste just as good as they look!

Whole-wheat tortillas	2	2
(9 inch, 22 cm, diameter)		
Light garlic and herb cream cheese	1/3 cup	75 mL
Finely chopped celery	1/4 cup	60 mL
Finely chopped red pepper	1/4 cup	60 mL
Grated carrot	1/4 cup	60 mL
Pepper	1/4 tsp.	1 mL

Cooking spray

Preheat oven to 400°F (205°C). Place tortillas on work surface. Spread with cream cheese.

Sprinkle with next 4 ingredients. Roll up, jelly-roll style. Place, seam-side down, on ungreased baking sheet.

(continued on next page)

Spray with cooking spray. Bake for about 15 minutes until browned and crisp. Cut into 1 inch (2.5 cm) pieces. Makes about 14 pinwheels.

1 pinwheel: 26 Calories; 1.0 g Total Fat (0 g Mono, 0.2 g Poly, 0.6 g Sat); 4 mg Cholesterol; 4 g Carbohydrate; trace Fibre; 1 g Protein; 66 mg Sodium

CHOICES: None

Pictured on page 53.

Caramel Mocha Smoothie

You could start your morning with one of those expensive and high-calorie coffee house drinks—or you could make this healthier version yourself. A cool, sweet smoothie filled with the decadent flavours of coffee, chocolate and caramel.

Non-fat vanilla yogurt	2 cups	500 mL
Light hot chocolate mix	1/3 cup	75 mL
Cold strong prepared coffee	1/4 cup	60 mL
Caramel ice cream topping	1 tbsp.	15 mL

Process first 3 ingredients in blender or food processor until smooth. Makes about 2 1/2 cups (625 mL). Divide between 2 glasses.

Drizzle with ice cream topping. Serves 2.

1 serving: 366 Calories; trace Total Fat (trace Mono, 0 g Poly, trace Sat); 5 mg Cholesterol; 66 g Carbohydrate; 4 g Fibre; 22 g Protein; 839 mg Sodium

CHOICES: 1 1/2 Other Choices; 2 1/2 Milk & Alternatives

Pictured on page 54.

Paré Pointer

Bloodhounds are in the money. They're always picking up scents.

Orange Beef Capellini

Asian flavour takes an orange twist in this stir-fried one-dish meal.
Dress this dish up for company by adding a garnish of chopped
parsley and fresh orange segments.

Water	8 cups	2 L
Salt	1 tsp.	5 mL
Capellini pasta	8 oz.	225 g
Sesame (or canola) oil	2 tsp.	10 mL
Beef stir-fry strips	1 lb.	454 g
Fresh mixed stir-fry vegetables, larger pieces cut smaller	6 cups	1.5 L
Garlic cloves, minced (or 1/2 tsp., 2 mL, powder)	2	2
Finely grated gingerroot (or 1/2 tsp., 2 mL, ground ginger)	2 tsp.	10 mL
Prepared beef broth	1/2 cup	125 mL
Hoisin sauce	3 tbsp.	50 mL
Soy sauce	3 tbsp.	50 mL
Frozen concentrated orange juice	1/4 cup	60 mL
Cornstarch	1 tsp.	5 mL
Sesame oil (for flavour)	1 tsp.	5 mL

Combine water and salt in large saucepan or Dutch oven. Bring to a boil. Add pasta. Boil, uncovered, for 4 to 6 minutes, stirring occasionally, until tender but firm. Drain. Return to same pot. Cover to keep warm.

Meanwhile, heat first amount of sesame oil in large frying pan on medium-high. Add beef. Stir-fry for 1 minute. Add next 3 ingredients. Stir-fry for about 5 minutes until vegetables start to soften.

Combine remaining 6 ingredients in small bowl. Add to beef mixture. Cook for about 2 minutes, stirring occasionally, until sauce is boiling and slightly thickened and vegetables are tender-crisp. Add pasta. Toss until coated. Makes about 8 cups (2 L). Serves 4.

1 serving: 580 Calories; 12.7 g Total Fat (4.0 g Mono, 1.8 g Poly, 3.4 g Sat); 43 mg Cholesterol; 76 g Carbohydrate; 3 g Fibre; 38 g Protein; 1815 mg Sodium

CHOICES: 3 Grains & Starches; 1/2 Fruits; 4 Vegetables; 3 Meat & Alternatives; 1/2 Fats

Pictured on page 71.

Apricot Beef Stir-Fry

You'll have no beefs with this tasty stir-fry of beef,
broccoli and sweet dried apricots.

Cornstarch	2 tsp.	10 mL
Prepared beef broth	1 tbsp.	15 mL
Prepared beef broth	1 cup	250 mL
Garlic powder	1/2 tsp.	2 mL
Ground cumin	1/2 tsp.	2 mL
Ground ginger	1/2 tsp.	2 mL
Ground cinnamon	1/4 tsp.	1 mL
Pepper	1/4 tsp.	1 mL
Canola oil	2 tsp.	10 mL
Beef top sirloin steak, trimmed of fat and thinly sliced	1 lb.	454 mL
Broccoli florets	2 cups	500 mL
Chopped dried apricot	1/4 cup	60 mL
Grated orange zest	2 tsp.	10 mL

Stir cornstarch into first amount of broth in small cup. Set aside.

Combine next 6 ingredients in small bowl. Set aside.

Heat large frying pan or wok on medium-high until very hot. Add canola oil. Add beef. Stir-fry for about 2 minutes until no longer pink. Remove to small bowl with slotted spoon. Cover to keep warm. Reduce heat to medium.

Add broccoli and apricot to same frying pan. Stir-fry for 1 minute. Add broth mixture. Cook, covered, for about 3 minutes, stirring occasionally, until broccoli is tender-crisp. Stir cornstarch mixture. Add to broccoli mixture. Heat and stir for 1 to 2 minutes until boiling and thickened.

Add orange zest and beef. Stir. Makes about 4 cups (1 L). Serves 4.

1 serving: 238 Calories; 10.5 g Total Fat (4.7 g Mono, 1.0 g Poly, 3.3 g Sat); 60 mg Cholesterol; 10 g Carbohydrate; 2 g Fibre; 26 g Protein; 374 mg Sodium

CHOICES: 1/2 Fruits; 3 1/2 Meat & Alternatives; 1/2 Fats

Dijon Beef On Rye

Dijon mustard and caraway seed flavour a warm, creamy beef stew served on toasted rye bread. Try it on caraway rye bread for even more flavour. Serve with a crisp salad for a complete meal.

Canola oil	1 tsp.	5 mL
Beef stir-fry strips, cut into 1 inch (2.5 cm) pieces	1 lb.	454 g
Chopped fresh white mushrooms	1 1/2 cups	375 mL
Chopped onion	1/2 cup	125 mL
Diced celery	1/2 cup	125 mL
Garlic clove, minced (or 1/4 tsp., 1 mL, powder)	1	1
All-purpose flour	3 tbsp.	50 mL
Can of skim evaporated milk	13 1/2 oz.	385 mL
Frozen cut green beans, thawed	1 1/2 cups	375 mL
Dijon mustard	1 1/2 tbsp.	25 mL
Caraway seed	3/4 tsp.	4 mL
Salt	1/2 tsp.	2 mL
Pepper	1/4 tsp.	1 mL
Rye bread slices	4	4
Dijon mustard	4 tsp.	20 mL

Heat canola oil in large frying pan on medium-high. Add next 5 ingredients. Scramble-fry for about 7 minutes until celery is softened.

Sprinkle flour over beef mixture. Heat and stir for 1 minute.

Add milk. Heat and stir until boiling and thickened. Add next 5 ingredients. Cook and stir until heated through.

Toast bread slices. Spread with mustard. Transfer to 4 plates. Spoon beef mixture over toast slices. Serves 4.

1 serving: 390 Calories; 10.0 g Total Fat (4.5 g Mono, 1.0 g Poly, 3.0 g Sat); 73 mg Cholesterol; 37 g Carbohydrate; 4 g Fibre; 36 g Protein; 838 mg Sodium

CHOICES: 1 Grains & Starches; 1 Vegetables; 1/2 Milk & Alternatives; 3 Meat & Alternatives

Pictured on page 72.

Greek Beef Burritos

Opa meets olé! Try burritos with a Greek twist for dinner tonight. For even quicker prep, set bowls of the beef and toppings on the table and have everybody assemble their own burritos.

Flour tortillas (9 inch, 22 cm, diameter)	4	4
Beef top sirloin steak	1 lb.	454 g
Greek seasoning, sprinkle		
Low-fat plain yogurt	1/4 cup	60 mL
Chopped fresh basil	2 tbsp.	30 mL
Sliced red onion	1/4 cup	60 mL
Shredded lettuce, lightly packed	1 cup	250 mL
Chopped tomato	1/2 cup	125 mL
Crumbled feta cheese	1/2 cup	125 mL
Can of sliced black olives, drained	4 1/2 oz.	128 mL

Wrap tortillas in foil. Preheat gas barbecue to medium-high (see Tip, page 77). Place tortillas on ungreased grill. Turn burner under tortillas to low and leave opposite burner on medium-high. Close lid. Cook for about 10 minutes until warmed.

Meanwhile, sprinkle both sides of steak with Greek seasoning. Cook steak on greased grill for about 5 minutes per side until desired doneness. Remove to plate. Cover with foil. Let stand for 5 minutes.

Combine yogurt and basil in small cup.

Layer remaining 5 ingredients, in order given, on warmed tortillas. Thinly slice steak. Arrange over olives. Drizzle with yogurt mixture. Fold bottom ends of tortillas over filling. Fold in sides. Fold over from bottom to enclose filling. Makes 4 burritos.

1 burrito: 398 Calories; 17.9 g Total Fat (5.8 g Mono, 0.6 g Poly, 6.2 g Sat); 69 mg Cholesterol; 27 g Carbohydrate; 2 g Fibre; 31 g Protein; 787 mg Sodium

CHOICES: 1 1/2 Grains & Starches; 3 Meat & Alternatives; 1/2 Fats

Peppered Beef

This lively stir-fry is peppered with, well—peppers! Sliced bell peppers, seasoned with black and cayenne pepper. A terrific topper for rice, noodles or even mashed potatoes.

Low-sodium beef broth	1/2 cup	125 mL
Low-sodium soy sauce	1/4 cup	60 mL
Cornstarch	1 tbsp.	15 mL
Garlic powder	1/2 tsp.	2 mL
Pepper	1/2 tsp.	2 mL
Cayenne pepper	1/8 tsp.	0.5 mL
Canola oil	1 tsp.	5 mL
Thinly sliced green pepper	1 1/2 cups	375 mL
Thinly sliced red pepper	1 1/2 cups	375 mL
Sliced fresh white mushrooms	2 cups	500 mL
Canola oil	2 tsp.	10 mL
Beef stir-fry strips	3/4 lb.	340 g

Combine first 6 ingredients in small bowl. Set aside.

Heat wok or large frying pan on medium-high until very hot. Add first amount of canola oil. Add green and red peppers. Stir-fry for 1 minute. Add mushrooms. Stir-fry for about 2 minutes until peppers are tender-crisp. Remove vegetables to plate. Cover to keep warm.

Heat second amount of canola oil in same wok. Add beef. Stir-fry for about 2 minutes until starting to brown. Add broth mixture. Heat and stir for about 1 minute until sauce is boiling and thickened. Add vegetables. Stir. Makes about 4 cups (1 L). Serves 4.

1 serving: 206 Calories; 8.6 g Total Fat (4.2 g Mono, 1.4 g Poly, 2.1 g Sat); 52 mg Cholesterol; 11 g Carbohydrate; 2 g Fibre; 21 g Protein; 551 mg Sodium

CHOICES: 1 Vegetables; 2 1/2 Meat & Alternatives; 1/2 Fats

Apricot Ginger Pork

Rich, sweet apricot and ginger does double-duty as an attractive glaze and a dipping sauce for flavourful pork.

Pork tenderloin, trimmed of fat	1 lb.	454 g
Cooking spray		
Seasoned salt	1/2 tsp.	2 mL
Apricot jam	1/2 cup	125 mL
Apple cider vinegar	2 tbsp.	30 mL
Liquid honey	1 tbsp.	15 mL
Low-sodium soy sauce	1 tbsp.	15 mL
Finely grated gingerroot (or 1/2 tsp., 2 mL, ground ginger)	2 tsp.	10 mL
Garlic powder	1/4 tsp.	1 mL

Preheat oven to 475°F (240°C). Place tenderloin on greased wire rack set on foil-lined baking sheet. Spray with cooking spray. Sprinkle with seasoned salt. Bake for 20 minutes.

Meanwhile, combine remaining 6 ingredients in small saucepan. Bring to a boil. Simmer, uncovered, for about 7 minutes, stirring occasionally, until thickened. Measure 3 tbsp. (50 mL) jam mixture into small cup. Brush over pork. Reserve remaining jam mixture. Bake pork for about 5 minutes until meat thermometer inserted into thickest part of tenderloin reads 155°F (68°C). Transfer to serving dish. Cover with foil. Let stand for 5 minutes. Internal temperature should rise to at least 160°F (70°C). Serve with reserved jam mixture. Serves 4.

1 serving: 264 Calories; 4.9 g Total Fat (2.2 g Mono, 0.5 g Poly, 1.7 g Sat); 71 mg Cholesterol; 31 g Carbohydrate; trace Fibre; 24 g Protein; 370 mg Sodium

CHOICES: 2 Other Choices; 3 Meat & Alternatives

Paré Pointer

If you have a copper ore, you need a copper boat to go with it.

Raspberry Steak

Tangy-sweet raspberries and perfectly cooked steak make this a truly decadent, yet surprisingly light dinner option.

Olive (or canola) oil	1 tbsp.	15 mL
Beef top sirloin steak	1 lb.	454 g
Salt	1/4 tsp.	1 mL
Pepper	1/2 tsp.	2 mL
Fresh (or frozen whole) raspberries	3/4 cup	175 mL
Water	1/4 cup	60 mL
Liquid honey	2 tbsp.	30 mL
Tub margarine	1 tbsp.	15 mL
Ground cinnamon	1/2 tsp.	2 mL
Ground ginger	1/4 tsp.	1 mL
Balsamic vinegar	2 tsp.	10 mL

Heat olive oil in large frying pan on medium-high. Sprinkle both sides of steak with salt and pepper. Add to frying pan. Cook for 3 to 4 minutes per side until desired doneness. Transfer to cutting board. Cover with foil. Let stand for 5 minutes.

Meanwhile, reduce heat to medium. Add next 6 ingredients to same frying pan. Heat and stir until boiling. Simmer for about 4 minutes until sauce starts to thicken.

Add vinegar. Stir. Slice steak diagonally across the grain into 1/4 inch (6 mm) thick slices. Serve sauce over beef. Serves 4.

1 serving: 267 Calories; 13.9 g Total Fat (6.9 g Mono, 2.4 g Poly, 3.6 g Sat); 67 mg Cholesterol; 12 g Carbohydrate; 2 g Fibre; 22 g Protein; 238 mg Sodium

CHOICES: 1/2 Other Choices; 3 Meat & Alternatives

Pictured on divider.

Portuguese Pork Chops

A versatile Portuguese-inspired sauce of tomatoes, olives and clams served with tender pork chops. The sauce is also great over rice, pasta or green beans.

Olive (or canola) oil	2 tsp.	10 mL
Boneless pork loin chops, trimmed of fat (about 4 oz., 113 g, each)	6	6
Olive (or canola) oil	2 tsp.	10 mL
Chopped onion	1 cup	250 mL
Garlic clove, minced (or 1/4 tsp., 1 mL, powder)	1	1
Chopped red pepper	1 cup	250 mL
Can of diced tomatoes (with juice)	14 oz.	398 mL
Can of sliced black olives, drained	4 1/2 oz.	125 mL
Reserved clam liquid	1/2 cup	125 mL
Red wine vinegar	1/4 cup	60 mL
Tomato paste (see Tip, page 120)	3 tbsp.	50 mL
Paprika	1 tsp.	5 mL
Cayenne pepper	1/4 tsp.	1 mL
Pepper	1/8 tsp.	0.5 mL
Can of whole baby clams, drained and liquid reserved	5 oz.	142 g
Chopped fresh parsley	1/2 cup	125 mL

Heat first amount of olive oil in large frying pan on medium. Add pork chops. Cook for 2 to 3 minutes per side until browned. Remove to plate. Cover to keep warm.

Heat second amount of olive oil in same frying pan on medium. Add next 3 ingredients. Cook for about 5 minutes, stirring often, until softened.

Add next 8 ingredients. Stir. Bring to a boil.

Add clams and pork chops. Reduce heat to low. Cook, covered, for about 5 minutes until pork is no longer pink inside.

Add parsley. Stir. Serves 6.

1 serving: 298 Calories; 14.4 g Total Fat (7.4 g Mono, 1.6 g Poly, 3.8 g Sat); 91 mg Cholesterol; 12 g Carbohydrate; 2 g Fibre; 31 g Protein; 571 mg Sodium

CHOICES: 1 Vegetables; 4 Meat & Alternatives; 1/2 Fats

Beef & Pork

Grilled Caesar Burgers

This burger's got all the flavours of the classic salad. Try serving in your favourite crusty rolls, or add soy-based imitation bacon bits for smoky flavour without adding fat.

Garlic and herb croutons	1 cup	250 mL
Light Caesar dressing	1/2 cup	125 mL
Quick-cooking rolled oats	1/3 cup	75 mL
Lean ground beef	1 lb.	454 g
Shredded romaine lettuce, lightly packed	4 cups	1 L
Light Caesar dressing	1/4 cup	60 mL
Whole-wheat bread slices	4	4

Preheat gas barbecue to medium. Process croutons in blender or food processor until coarse crumbs form. Transfer to large bowl. Add first amount of dressing and oats. Stir. Add beef. Mix well. Divide into 4 equal portions. Shape into four 4 inch (10 cm) diameter patties. Cook on greased grill for about 7 minutes per side until fully cooked and internal temperature reaches 160°F (70°C).

Combine lettuce and second amount of dressing in medium bowl. Spoon onto bread slices. Top with patties. Makes 4 burgers.

1 burger: 438 Calories; 21.2 g Total Fat (8.9 g Mono, 2.1 g Poly, 7.3 g Sat); 69 mg Cholesterol; 34 g Carbohydrate; 4 g Fibre; 28 g Protein; 835 mg Sodium

CHOICES: 1 1/2 Grains & Starches; 3 Meat & Alternatives

1. Orange Beef Capellini, page 62
2. Herb-Rubbed Pork Tenderloin, page 77

Props courtesy of: Danesco Inc.

Curried Fruit Pork Chops

Enjoy the exotic spices of curry—without the rich and heavy sauces that usually go along with it. A fresh medley of tropical fruit adds lots of flavour to these juicy chops.

Curry powder	1 tbsp.	15 mL
Salt	1/2 tsp.	2 mL
Boneless centre-cut pork chops, trimmed of fat	4	4
Canola oil	2 tsp.	10 mL
Diced banana	1 cup	250 mL
Diced fresh pineapple	1 cup	250 mL
Diced ripe mango	1 cup	250 mL
Unsweetened applesauce	1/4 cup	60 mL

Combine curry powder and salt in small cup. Sprinkle over both sides of pork chops.

Heat canola oil in large frying pan on medium-high. Add pork chops. Cook for 1 to 2 minutes per side until browned. Reduce heat to medium-low.

Add remaining 4 ingredients. Stir. Cook, covered, for about 4 minutes, stirring at halftime, until pork is no longer pink inside. Serves 4.

1 serving: 346 Calories; 16.9 g Total Fat (7.5 g Mono, 2.4 g Poly, 5.4 g Sat); 78 mg Cholesterol; 23 g Carbohydrate; 3 g Fibre; 26 g Protein; 363 mg Sodium

CHOICES: 1 1/2 Fruits; 3 1/2 Meat & Alternatives; 1/2 Fats

1. Dijon Beef On Rye, page 64

Pork Apple Skillet

An Oktoberfest special! The traditional German flavours of sauerkraut and caraway, sweetened with apple. A perfect accompaniment to tender, golden-brown pork chops.

Canola oil	2 tsp.	10 mL
Boneless fast-fry pork chops	6	6
(about 4 oz., 113 g, each)		
Pepper	1/2 tsp.	2 mL
Sliced fresh white mushrooms	2 cups	500 mL
Sliced onion	1 1/2 cups	375 mL
Medium peeled cooking apples	2	2
(such as McIntosh), sliced		
Caraway seed	1 tsp.	5 mL
Jar of wine sauerkraut, drained	17 1/2 oz.	500 mL
Can of diced tomatoes (with juice)	14 oz.	398 mL

Heat canola oil in large frying pan on medium-high. Add pork chops to frying pan. Sprinkle with pepper. Cook for about 2 minutes per side until browned and no longer pink. Remove to plate. Cover to keep warm.

Add mushrooms to same frying pan. Cook and stir for about 1 minute until mushrooms start to release liquid. Add next 3 ingredients. Reduce heat to medium. Cook for about 3 minutes, stirring occasionally, until onion starts to soften.

Add sauerkraut and tomatoes. Cook and stir for about 2 minutes until heated through. Serve with pork chops. Serves 6.

1 serving: 247 Calories; 8.2 g Total Fat (3.8 g Mono, 1.0 g Poly, 2.5 g Sat); 65 mg Cholesterol; 18 g Carbohydrate; 4 g Fibre; 26 g Protein; 778 mg Sodium

CHOICES: 1/2 Fruits; 1 Vegetables; 3 Meat & Alternatives

Ginger Wasabi Skewers

Japanese flavours of pickled ginger, mirin and wasabi transform meatball skewers into something extraordinary. Use the leftover green onion tops for salads, soups or pasta.

WASABI MAYONNAISE		
Mayonnaise (not salad dressing)	1/2 cup	125 mL
Wasabi paste (Japanese horseradish)	2 tsp.	10 mL

MEATBALL SKEWERS		
Large egg, fork-beaten	1	1
Crushed soda crackers	1/2 cup	125 mL
Finely chopped pickled ginger slices	2 tbsp.	30 mL
Soy sauce	2 tbsp.	30 mL
Thinly sliced green onion (green part only)	2 tbsp.	30 mL
Mirin (Japanese sweet cooking seasoning)	1 tbsp.	15 mL
Lean ground beef	1 lb.	454 g
Pickled ginger slices, larger slices folded in half	24	24
Green onions (white part only), cut into 2 inch (5 cm) pieces	24	24
Bamboo skewers (8 inches, 20 cm, each), soaked in water for 10 minutes	8	8

Wasabi Mayonnaise: Combine mayonnaise and wasabi paste in small bowl. Chill. Makes about 1/2 cup (125 mL) mayonnaise.

Meatball Skewers: Preheat gas barbecue to medium (see Tip, page 77). Combine first 6 ingredients in large bowl. Add beef. Mix well. Roll into 32 balls, about 1 inch (2.5 cm) diameter each.

Thread meatballs and second amounts of ginger slices and green onion alternately onto skewers, beginning and ending with meatballs. Cook skewers on greased grill for about 14 minutes, turning occasionally, until meatballs are no longer pink inside and internal temperature reaches 160°F (71°C). Serve with Wasabi Mayonnaise. Makes 8 skewers. Serves 4.

1 serving: 556 Calories; 39.9 g Total Fat (8.1 g Mono, 0.8 g Poly, 9.8 g Sat); 124 mg Cholesterol; 19 g Carbohydrate; 3 g Fibre; 27 g Protein; 879 mg Sodium

CHOICES: 1/2 Grains & Starches; 1 Vegetables; 3 Meat & Alternatives; 4 Fats

Lemon Grass Beef

If you're looking for a ground beef recipe that's just a little different, try this lovely, light curry that goes great over rice or pasta.

Canola oil	1 tsp.	5 mL
Extra-lean ground beef	1 lb.	454 g
Chopped onion	1 cup	250 mL
Frozen sliced carrot	2 cups	500 mL
Chopped red pepper	1 cup	250 mL
Lime juice	2 tbsp.	30 mL
Soy sauce	2 tbsp.	30 mL
Brown sugar, packed	1 tbsp.	15 mL
Finely chopped lemon grass, bulb only (root and stalk removed)	1 tbsp.	15 mL
Garlic cloves, minced (or 1/2 tsp., 2 mL, powder)	2	2
Finely grated gingerroot	1 tsp.	5 mL
Red curry paste	1/4 tsp.	1 mL
All-purpose flour	1 tbsp.	15 mL
Light coconut milk	1/2 cup	125 mL
Chopped fresh cilantro	2 tsp.	10 mL

Heat canola oil in large frying pan on medium-high. Add beef and onion. Scramble-fry for 5 to 10 minutes until beef is no longer pink. Drain.

Add next 9 ingredients. Cook for about 5 minutes, stirring occasionally, until red pepper is tender-crisp.

Sprinkle with flour. Heat and stir for 1 minute.

Add coconut milk. Heat and stir for about 1 minute until boiling and thickened.

Sprinkle with cilantro. Makes about 5 cups (1.25 L). Serves 4.

1 serving: 281 Calories; 10.8 g Total Fat (3.8 g Mono, 0.6 g Poly, 4.9 g Sat); 60 mg Cholesterol; 19 g Carbohydrate; 3 g Fibre; 26 g Protein; 521 mg Sodium

CHOICES: 2 Vegetables; 3 Meat & Alternatives

Beef & Pork

Herb-Rubbed Pork Tenderloin

Grilled pork tenderloin is both lean and delicious, but the secret to cooking up juicy, tender pork on the barbecue is being careful not to overcook it! The flavourful herbs and spices make this recipe truly unforgettable.

Pork tenderloin, trimmed of fat	1 lb.	454 g
Canola oil	1 tbsp.	15 mL
Dried basil	1 tbsp.	15 mL
Dried oregano	1 tbsp.	15 mL
Dried parsley flakes	1 tbsp.	15 mL
Chili powder	2 tsp.	10 mL
Garlic powder	1 tsp.	5 mL
Salt	1/2 tsp.	2 mL
Coarsely ground pepper	1 tsp.	5 mL

Preheat gas barbecue to medium (see Tip, below). Brush tenderloin with canola oil.

Combine next 7 ingredients in small bowl. Rub over surface of tenderloin. Cook on greased grill for about 20 minutes, turning occasionally, until meat thermometer inserted into thickest part of tenderloin reads 155°F (68°C). Remove from grill and transfer to cutting board. Cover with foil. Let stand for 10 minutes. Internal temperature should rise to at least 160°F (70°C). Cut into 1/2 inch (12 mm) slices. Serves 4.

1 serving: 190 Calories; 8.5 g Total Fat (4.2 g Mono, 1.6 g Poly, 1.9 g Sat); 71 mg Cholesterol; 3 g Carbohydrate; 1 g Fibre; 25 g Protein; 365 mg Sodium

CHOICES: 3 Meat & Alternatives; 1/2 Fats

Pictured on page 71.

 tip Too cold to barbecue? Use the broiler instead! Your food should cook in about the same length of time—and remember to turn or baste as directed. Set your oven rack so that the food is about 3 to 4 inches (7.5 to 10 cm) away from the top element—for most ovens, this is the top rack.

White Chicken Chili

Chili without tomatoes? Why not? The absence of heavy tomato flavour lets your taste buds focus on the subtle taste of chili, lime and cilantro.

Canola oil	2 tsp.	10 mL
All-purpose flour	1/4 cup	60 mL
Chili powder	2 tsp.	10 mL
Garlic powder	1/2 tsp.	2 mL
Ground cumin	1/2 tsp.	2 mL
Boneless, skinless chicken thighs, cut into 1 inch (2.5 cm) pieces	1 lb.	454 g
Sliced fresh white mushrooms	2 cups	500 mL
Chopped onion	1/2 cup	125 mL
Low-sodium prepared chicken broth	1 1/2 cups	375 mL
Can of white kidney beans, rinsed and drained	19 oz.	540 mL
Chopped fresh cilantro	3 tbsp.	50 mL
Sliced green onion	2 tbsp.	30 mL
Lime juice	4 tsp.	20 mL

Heat canola oil in large saucepan on medium-high. Combine next 4 ingredients in large resealable freezer bag. Add chicken. Toss until coated. Add chicken to pan, reserving any remaining flour mixture. Cook, uncovered, for about 5 minutes, stirring occasionally, until browned on all sides. Remove to plate. Cover to keep warm.

Add mushrooms and onion to same saucepan. Cook for about 3 minutes, stirring often, until onion is softened. Add chicken and reserved flour mixture. Heat and stir for 1 minute.

Slowly add broth, stirring constantly until smooth. Heat and stir until boiling and thickened. Add beans. Stir. Reduce heat to medium-low. Cook, covered, for about 3 minutes until heated through.

Add remaining 3 ingredients. Stir. Makes about 4 3/4 cups (1.2 L). Serves 4.

1 serving: 342 Calories; 12.2 g Total Fat (4.6 g Mono, 2.7 g Poly, 2.6 g Sat); 76 mg Cholesterol; 28 g Carbohydrate; 6 g Fibre; 29 g Protein; 352 mg Sodium

CHOICES: 1 Grains & Starches; 3 1/2 Meat & Alternatives

Pictured on page 89.

Country Herb Turkey

Basil and lemon pepper lend a refreshing tanginess to this medley of turkey and fresh vegetables. Serve over pasta, rice or mashed potatoes.

Canola oil	1 tbsp.	15 mL
Turkey scaloppine	8	8
(about 2 oz., 57 g, each)		
Lemon pepper, sprinkle		
Chopped onion	1 cup	250 mL
Chopped carrot	1/2 cup	125 mL
Chopped celery	1/2 cup	125 mL
Dried thyme	1/2 tsp.	2 mL
All-purpose flour	2 tbsp.	30 mL
Low-sodium prepared chicken broth	2 cups	500 mL
Basil pesto	1 tbsp.	15 mL

Heat 1 tsp. (5 mL) canola oil in large frying pan on medium-high. Sprinkle turkey with lemon pepper. Add to frying pan. Cook, in 4 batches, for about 30 seconds per side, until no longer pink inside, adding 1 tsp. (5 mL) canola oil for each batch. Remove to plate. Cover to keep warm. Reduce heat to medium.

Add next 4 ingredients to same frying pan. Cook, covered, for about 2 minutes until vegetables start to soften.

Sprinkle with flour. Heat and stir for 1 minute. Slowly add broth, stirring constantly until boiling and thickened.

Add pesto. Stir. Cook for about 5 minutes until vegetables are tender. Add turkey. Cook for about 1 minute until turkey is heated through. Serves 4.

1 serving: 216 Calories; 7.0 g Total Fat (2.0 g Mono, 1.1 g Poly, 0.6 g Sat); 48 mg Cholesterol; 10 g Carbohydrate; 1 g Fibre; 30 g Protein; 422 mg Sodium

CHOICES: 1 Vegetables; 4 Meat & Alternatives; 1 Fats

Pictured on page 89.

Coconut Chicken Curry

This spicy coconut curry is the perfect way to jazz up your weekday dinner with a little exotic flair. Spoon the sauce over basmati or jasmine rice.

Canola oil	1 tbsp.	15 mL
Boneless, skinless chicken thighs, cut into 1 inch (2.5 cm) cubes	1 lb.	454 g
Salt, sprinkle		
Pepper, sprinkle		
Can of chickpeas (garbanzo beans), rinsed and drained	19 oz.	540 mL
Can of light coconut milk	14 oz.	398 mL
Can of stewed tomatoes	14 oz.	398 mL
Dark raisins	1/4 cup	60 mL
Hot Madras curry paste	2 tbsp.	30 mL
Garlic cloves, minced (or 3/4 tsp., 4 mL, powder)	3	3
Finely grated gingerroot	1 tbsp.	15 mL
Brown sugar, packed	2 tsp.	10 mL
Chopped fresh cilantro	2 tbsp.	30 mL

Heat canola oil in large frying pan on medium-high. Add chicken. Sprinkle with salt and pepper. Cook for about 5 minutes, stirring occasionally, until starting to brown. Drain.

Add next 8 ingredients. Stir. Bring to a boil. Reduce heat to medium. Boil gently, uncovered, for about 12 minutes, stirring often, until chicken is no longer pink inside and sauce is slightly thickened.

Sprinkle with cilantro. Makes about 5 1/2 cups (1.4 L). Serves 6.

1 serving: 312 Calories; 14.7 g Total Fat (3.9 g Mono, 2.7 g Poly, 5.4 g Sat); 50 mg Cholesterol; 25 g Carbohydrate; 4 g Fibre; 19 g Protein; 484 mg Sodium

CHOICES: 1/2 Grains & Starches; 1/2 Fruits; 2 Meat & Alternatives

Chicken Lettuce Wraps

Cut the carbs by replacing tortillas with lettuce leaves in these sweet and spicy Asian-flavoured wraps. Use the large outside leaves from a head of green leaf lettuce, or overlap two smaller leaves.

Sesame (or canola) oil	2 tsp.	10 mL
Boneless, skinless chicken breast halves, cut into 1/4 inch (6 mm) strips	1 lb.	454 g
Garlic cloves, minced (or 1/2 tsp., 2 mL, powder)	2	2
Liquid honey	2 tbsp.	30 mL
Soy sauce	2 tbsp.	30 mL
Peanut butter	1 tbsp.	15 mL
Chili paste (sambal oelek)	1/2 tsp.	2 mL
Cooked long-grain brown rice (about 3/4 cups, 175 mL, uncooked)	2 cups	500 mL
Large green leaf lettuce leaves	8	8

Heat sesame oil in medium frying pan on medium. Add chicken and garlic. Cook for about 8 minutes, stirring occasionally, until chicken is no longer pink.

Add next 4 ingredients. Heat and stir for 2 minutes.

Add rice. Cook and stir for about 2 minutes until heated through. Makes about 3 1/2 cups (875 mL) filling.

Spoon about 6 tbsp. (100 mL) chicken mixture in centre of 1 leaf. Fold sides over filling. Roll up from bottom to enclose. Repeat with remaining chicken mixture and lettuce. Makes 8 wraps. Serves 4.

1 serving: 322 Calories; 7.0 g Total Fat (2.6 g Mono, 2.2 g Poly, 1.4 g Sat); 66 mg Cholesterol; 33 g Carbohydrate; 2 g Fibre; 30 g Protein; 482 mg Sodium

CHOICES: 1 1/2 Grains & Starches; 1/2 Other Choices; 3 Meat & Alternatives

Walnut Dijon-Crusted Chicken

Tender chicken dresses for success with a coating of crunchy walnuts, tangy Dijon and mildly sweet graham crumbs.

Dijon mustard	1/4 cup	60 mL
Boneless, skinless chicken breast halves (4 – 6 oz., 113 – 170 g, each)	4	4
Graham cracker crumbs	1/2 cup	125 mL
Ground walnuts	1/2 cup	125 mL
Tub margarine, melted	2 tbsp.	30 mL
Ground coriander	1/2 tsp.	2 mL
Ground ginger	1/2 tsp.	2 mL
Salt	1/4 tsp.	1 mL

Preheat oven to 425°F (220°C). Brush mustard on both sides of each chicken breast.

Combine remaining 6 ingredients in medium shallow dish. Press both sides of each chicken breast into crumb mixture until coated. Place on greased baking sheet. Bake for about 20 minutes until golden and internal temperature reaches 170°F (77°C). Serves 4.

1 serving: 167 Calories; 5.2 g Total Fat (1.4 g Mono, 2.3 g Poly, 0.9 g Sat); 66 mg Cholesterol; 2 g Carbohydrate; trace Fibre; 26 g Protein; 328 mg Sodium

CHOICES: 4 Meat & Alternatives

Baked Italian Patties

These hearty patties may be short on ingredients, but they're long on flavour! No burger buns are required, just a tossed green salad and a side of pasta.

Large egg, fork-beaten	1	1
Fine dry bread crumbs	1/3 cup	75 mL
Sun-dried tomato pesto	2 tbsp.	30 mL
Italian seasoning	1 tsp.	5 mL
Lean ground chicken breast	1 lb.	454 g
Tomato sauce	1/4 cup	60 mL
Grated Italian cheese blend	6 tbsp.	100 mL

(continued on next page)

Preheat oven to 400°F (205°C). Combine first 4 ingredients in medium bowl. Add chicken. Mix well. Divide into 4 equal portions. Shape into 1/2 inch (12 mm) thick oval patties. Arrange on greased baking sheet. Bake for about 12 minutes until fully cooked and internal temperature reaches 175°F (80°C).

Spread tomato sauce over patties. Sprinkle with cheese. Bake for about 3 minutes until cheese is melted. Makes 4 patties.

1 patty: 240 Calories; 6.2 g Total Fat (1.2 g Mono, 0.7 g Poly, 2.7 g Sat); 120 mg Cholesterol; 12 g Carbohydrate; 1 g Fibre; 32 g Protein; 626 mg Sodium

CHOICES: 1/2 Grains & Starches; 3 1/2 Meat & Alternatives

Pineapple Chicken

A quick and delicious chicken dish with great sweet-and-sour flavour.
Best served over jasmine rice.

Sesame (or canola) oil	1 tsp.	5 mL
Boneless, skinless chicken breast halves, cut into 1/4 inch (6 mm) strips	1 lb.	454 g
Garlic clove, minced (or 1/4 tsp., 1 mL, powder)	1	1
Soy sauce	1 tbsp.	15 mL
Can of pineapple chunks, drained	14 oz.	398 mL
Unsweetened applesauce	1/2 cup	125 mL
Sweet-and-sour sauce	1/4 cup	60 mL
Chopped green onion	2 tbsp.	30 mL

Heat sesame oil in large frying pan on medium. Add chicken. Cook for 5 minutes, stirring occasionally.

Add garlic and soy sauce. Cook for about 5 minutes, stirring occasionally, until chicken is no longer pink.

Add next 3 ingredients. Heat and stir for about 2 minutes until boiling.

Add green onion. Stir. Makes about 3 cups (750 mL). Serves 4.

1 serving: 236 Calories; 3.1 g Total Fat (0.9 g Mono, 0.9 g Poly, 0.7 g Sat); 66 mg Cholesterol; 25 g Carbohydrate; 2 g Fibre; 27 g Protein; 267 mg Sodium

CHOICES: 1 Fruits; 3 1/2 Meat & Alternatives

Mushroom Turkey Scaloppine

Not all mushroom sauces are calorie-laden. These tender turkey slices are covered in a light and flavourful sauce with nary a drop of cream.

Package of dried porcini mushrooms	3/4 oz.	22 g
Boiling water	1 cup	250 mL
All-purpose flour	1/2 cup	125 mL
Salt	1/2 tsp.	2 mL
Pepper	1/2 tsp.	2 mL
Turkey scaloppine (about 2 oz., 57 g, each)	8	8
Olive (or canola) oil	4 tsp.	20 mL
Olive (or canola) oil	1 tsp.	5 mL
Finely chopped onion	1/2 cup	125 mL
Apple juice	1/4 cup	60 mL
White wine vinegar	2 tsp.	10 mL
Salt	1/4 tsp.	1 mL
Pepper	1/4 tsp.	1 mL
Chopped fresh parsley	1 tbsp.	15 mL

Put mushrooms into small heatproof bowl. Add boiling water. Stir. Let stand for about 5 minutes until softened. Drain, reserving 3/4 cup (175 mL) liquid. Chop mushrooms. Set aside.

Meanwhile, combine next 3 ingredients on a plate. Press both sides of turkey into flour mixture. Discard any remaining flour mixture.

Heat 1 tsp. (5 mL) of first amount of olive oil in large frying pan on medium-high. Cook turkey, in 4 batches, for about 30 seconds per side, until no longer pink inside, adding 1 tsp. (5 mL) olive oil for each batch. Transfer to plate. Cover to keep warm. Reduce heat to medium.

Heat second amount of olive oil in same frying pan. Add onion and mushrooms. Cook for about 3 minutes, stirring often, until onion is softened.

Add next 4 ingredients and reserved mushroom liquid. Bring to a boil. Simmer for about 2 minutes until thickened. Pour over turkey.

Sprinkle with parsley. Serves 4.

1 serving: 242 Calories; 7.4 g Total Fat (4.3 g Mono, 0.6 g Poly, 0.8 g Sat); 45 mg Cholesterol; 15 g Carbohydrate; 1 g Fibre; 31 g Protein; 434 mg Sodium

CHOICES: 1/2 Grains & Starches; 3 Meat & Alternatives; 1 Fats

Quick Kabobs

Somehow, food that's served on a stick just seems like more fun! With lots of colourful veggies, these are just as pretty as they are delicious.

Thick teriyaki basting sauce	1/4 cup	60 mL
Lemon juice	2 tbsp.	30 mL
Garlic cloves, minced	2	2
(or 1/2 tsp., 2 mL, powder)		
Pepper	1/2 tsp.	2 mL
Boneless, skinless chicken breast halves,	1 lb.	454 g
cut into 24 equal pieces		
Medium green pepper,	1	1
cut into 24 equal pieces		
Medium red pepper,	1	1
cut into 24 equal pieces		
Medium fresh whole white	16	16
mushrooms, stems removed		
Bamboo skewers (8 inches, 20 cm, each),	8	8
soaked in water for 10 minutes		

Preheat barbecue to medium (see Tip, page 77). Combine first 4 ingredients in small cup.

Thread next 4 ingredients alternately onto skewers. Brush with half of teriyaki mixture. Cook on greased grill for about 13 minutes, turning occasionally and brushing with remaining teriyaki mixture, until chicken is no longer pink inside. Makes 8 kabobs. Serves 4.

1 serving: 173 Calories; 2.1 g Total Fat (0.5 g Mono, 0.5 g Poly, 0.5 g Sat); 66 mg Cholesterol; 9 g Carbohydrate; 1 g Fibre; 29 g Protein; 759 mg Sodium

CHOICES: 3 1/2 Meat & Alternatives

Grilled Chicken Fajitas

First, grill the chicken, peppers and onions on the barbecue for a smoky flavour, then have everybody assemble their own fajita—now that's a time-saver! Be sure to lay the chicken thighs flat on the grill to speed up the cooking time.

Olive (or canola) oil	2 tbsp.	30 mL
Balsamic vinegar	1 tbsp.	15 mL
Dijon mustard	1 tsp.	5 mL
Garlic clove, minced	1	1
(or 1/4 tsp., 1 mL, powder)		
Ground cumin	1 tsp.	5 mL
Cayenne pepper	1/2 tsp.	2 mL
Boneless, skinless chicken thighs	1 lb.	454 g
Large red pepper, quartered	1	1
Large yellow pepper, quartered	1	1
Medium red onion, quartered	1	1
Whole-wheat flour tortillas	4	4
(9 inch, 22 cm, diameter)		
Light sour cream	1/2 cup	125 mL
Salsa	1/2 cup	125 mL
Chopped green onion	1/4 cup	60 mL

Preheat gas barbecue to medium-high. Combine first 6 ingredients in small bowl.

Arrange next 4 ingredients on greased grill. Brush with olive oil mixture. Cook for about 12 minutes, turning occasionally and brushing with remaining olive oil mixture, until peppers and onions are softened and internal temperature of chicken reaches 170°C (77°F). Transfer to plate. Cover with foil. Let stand for 5 minutes. Cut chicken, peppers and onions into strips. Transfer to bowl.

Arrange chicken and vegetables down center of each tortilla. Add remaining 3 ingredients. Fold up bottoms. Fold in sides, leaving top ends open. Serves 4.

1 serving: 405 Calories; 19.3 g Total Fat (8.2 g Mono, 3.7 g Poly, 4.8 g Sat); 84 mg Cholesterol; 32 g Carbohydrate; 4 g Fibre; 27 g Protein; 481 mg Sodium

CHOICES: 1 Grains & Starches; 1 Vegetables; 3 Meat & Alternatives; 1 Fats

Pictured on front cover and on page 90.

Citrus Herb Turkey Kabobs

Summery citrus and herb flavours make these kabobs a hit when it's just too hot to turn on the stove.

Orange juice	1/2 cup	125 mL
Lemon juice	3 tbsp.	50 mL
Lime juice	3 tbsp.	50 mL
Canola oil	1 tbsp.	15 mL
Liquid honey	1 tbsp.	15 mL
Italian seasoning	1 tsp.	5 mL
Chopped fresh cilantro	1 tbsp.	15 mL
Grated orange zest	1/2 tsp.	2 mL
Boneless, skinless turkey breast halves, cut into 1 inch (2.5 cm) cubes	1 lb.	454 g
Bamboo skewers (8 inches, 20 cm, each), soaked in water for 10 minutes	4	4
Salt, sprinkle		
Pepper, sprinkle		

Preheat gas barbecue to medium (see Tip, page 77). Combine first 6 ingredients in small saucepan. Bring to a boil. Boil gently, uncovered, on medium for about 12 minutes, stirring often, until reduced by half.

Add cilantro and orange zest. Stir.

Meanwhile, thread turkey onto skewers. Sprinkle with salt and pepper. Cook on greased grill for about 12 minutes, turning and brushing occasionally with orange juice mixture, until turkey is fully cooked and no longer pink inside. Makes 4 kabobs.

1 kabob: 226 Calories; 8.0 g Total Fat (4.3 g Mono, 2.3 g Poly, 0.8 g Sat); 70 mg Cholesterol; 9 g Carbohydrate; 0.1 g Fibre; 28 g Protein; 56 mg Sodium

CHOICES: 4 Meat & Alternatives; 1 Fats

Lemon Sage Turkey Patties

Want some sage advice? Add oatmeal to lean turkey burgers to eliminate dryness and sneak in some fibre, too! Sage and lemon add a fresh summery flavour.

Large flake rolled oats	1 cup	250 mL
Milk	1/3 cup	75 mL
Chopped fresh sage (or 3/4 tsp., 4 mL, dried)	1 tbsp.	15 mL
Grated lemon zest	1 tsp.	5 mL
Salt	1/2 tsp.	2 mL
Pepper	1/4 tsp.	1 mL
Extra-lean ground turkey breast	1 lb.	454 g

Combine oats and milk in large bowl. Let stand for 3 minutes.

Add next 4 ingredients. Stir. Add turkey. Mix well. Heat large frying pan on medium. Divide mixture into 4 equal portions. Shape into 4 1/2 inch (11 cm) diameter patties. Spray pan with cooking spray. Add patties. Cook for about 5 minutes per side until browned and internal temperature reaches 175°F (80°C). Makes 4 patties.

1 patty: 210 Calories; 3.0 g Total Fat (0.1 g Mono, 0 g Poly, 0.1 g Sat); 46 mg Cholesterol; 15 g Carbohydrate; 2 g Fibre; 32 g Protein; 368 mg Sodium

CHOICES: 1 Grains & Starches; 4 Meat & Alternatives

1. Rosemary Chicken Polenta, page 92
2. White Chicken Chili, page 78
3. Country Herb Turkey, page 79

Props courtesy of: Danesco Inc.
Wiltshire®

Chicken & Turkey

Mustard Dill Chicken

Tangy mustard chicken in a dill-y of a sauce! Serve with potatoes or egg noodles.

Canola oil	1 tbsp.	15 mL
Boneless, skinless chicken thighs (about 3 oz., 85 g, each)	8	8
Low-sodium prepared chicken broth	3/4 cup	175 mL
Dijon mustard (with whole seeds)	1 tbsp.	15 mL
Dried dillweed	1 tsp.	5 mL
Pepper	1/8 tsp.	0.5 mL
Milk	2 tbsp.	30 mL
Cornstarch	1 1/2 tsp.	7 mL

Heat canola oil in large frying pan on medium-high. Add chicken. Cook for 2 to 3 minutes per side until browned. Drain.

Add next 4 ingredients. Bring to a boil, stirring constantly and scraping any brown bits from bottom of pan. Reduce heat to medium. Boil gently, covered, for about 5 minutes until chicken is no longer pink inside.

Stir milk into cornstarch in small cup. Add to chicken mixture. Heat and stir for about 1 minute until boiling and thickened. Serves 4.

1 serving: 291 Calories; 16.6 g Total Fat (6.9 g Mono, 3.9 g Poly, 3.9 g Sat); 113 mg Cholesterol; 2 g Carbohydrate; trace Fibre; 31 g Protein; 297 mg Sodium

CHOICES: 4 Meat & Alternatives; 1/2 Fats

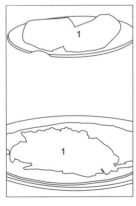

1. Grilled Chicken Fajitas, page 86

Props courtesy of: Danesco Inc.

Rosemary Chicken Polenta

This creamy chicken and mushroom medley is served over dense, firm polenta for a divinely different dinner.

Canola oil	2 tsp.	10 mL
Boneless, skinless chicken breast halves, thinly sliced	1 lb.	454 g
Canola oil	2 tsp.	10 mL
Sliced fresh white mushrooms	2 cups	500 mL
Chopped onion	1 cup	250 mL
Chopped fresh rosemary (or 1/4 tsp., 1 mL, dried, crushed)	2 tsp.	10 mL
Garlic clove, minced (or 1/4 tsp., 1 mL, powder)	1	1
Salt	1/2 tsp.	2 mL
Pepper	1/4 tsp.	1 mL
All-purpose flour	3 tbsp.	50 mL
Can of 2% evaporated milk	13 1/2 oz.	385 mL
Grated lemon zest	1 tsp.	5 mL
Slices of prepared polenta roll, about 1/2 inch (12 mm) thick	8	8
Chopped fresh parsley	1 tbsp.	15 mL

Preheat broiler. Heat canola oil in large frying pan on medium-high. Add chicken. Cook for about 5 minutes, stirring often, until no longer pink. Remove to bowl. Cover to keep warm. Reduce heat to medium.

Heat second amount of canola oil in same frying pan. Add next 6 ingredients. Cook for about 5 minutes, stirring often, until mushrooms and onion are softened.

Add flour. Heat and stir for 1 minute. Slowly add evaporated milk, stirring constantly until boiling and thickened. Add lemon zest and chicken. Stir.

Meanwhile, place polenta slices on greased baking sheet. Broil on top rack in oven for about 3 minutes until golden. Remove to plate. Spoon chicken mixture over polenta.

Sprinkle with parsley. Serves 4.

(continued on next page)

1 serving: 380 Calories; 8.4 g Total Fat (3.7 g Mono, 1.9 g Poly, 2.0 g Sat); 73 mg Cholesterol; 37 g Carbohydrate; 2 g Fibre; 37 g Protein; 817 mg Sodium

CHOICES: 1 1/2 Grains & Starches; 1 Vegetables; 1/2 Milk & Alternatives; 3 1/2 Meat & Alternatives; 1 Fats

Pictured on page 89.

Coconut Chicken

With the help of a few ingredients from your pantry, you'll have a delightful dinner with the smooth, light flavours of coconut and curry draped over tender chicken.

Boneless, skinless chicken breasts (4 – 6 oz., 113 – 170 g, each)	6	6
Cooking spray		
Can of light coconut milk	14 oz.	398 mL
All-purpose flour	2 tbsp.	30 mL
Brown sugar, packed	1 tbsp.	15 mL
Lime juice	1 tbsp.	15 mL
Soy sauce	1 tbsp.	15 mL
Thai red curry paste	1/2 tsp.	2 mL
Pepper	1/4 tsp.	1 mL

Preheat broiler. Arrange chicken in greased 9 x 9 inch (22 x 22 cm) baking dish. Spray with cooking spray. Broil on centre rack in oven for 5 minutes. Reduce heat to 450°F (230°C).

Meanwhile, whisk remaining 7 ingredients in small microwave-safe bowl until smooth. Microwave, covered, on high (100%) for about 2 minutes until hot. Carefully pour over chicken. Bake, uncovered, for about 12 minutes until chicken is fully cooked and internal temperature reaches 170°F (77°C). Serves 6.

1 serving: 196 Calories; 6.3 g Total Fat (0.5 g Mono, 0.4 g Poly, 3.8 g Sat); 66 mg Cholesterol; 6 g Carbohydrate; trace Fibre; 26 g Protein; 223 mg Sodium

CHOICES: 4 Meat & Alternatives

Basa With Mango Nut Salsa

Basa is a firm, mild fish that's definitely been gaining popularity. Its mild taste goes great with all sorts of flavours—like the freshness of mango, orange and lime.

MANGO NUT SALSA		
Finely chopped frozen mango pieces, thawed	1 cup	250 mL
Finely chopped red pepper	1/4 cup	60 mL
Chopped whole hazelnuts (filberts), toasted (see Tip, page 114)	1/4 cup	60 mL
Chili powder	1 tbsp.	15 mL
Lime juice	1 tbsp.	15 mL
Frozen concentrated orange juice, thawed	2 tsp.	10 mL
LEMON PEPPER BASA		
Canola oil	2 tsp.	10 mL
Basa fillets, cut into 4 equal portions	1 lb.	454 g
Lemon pepper	1/2 tsp.	2 mL
All-purpose flour	1/3 cup	75 mL

Mango Nut Salsa: Combine all 6 ingredients in small bowl. Makes about 1 cup (250 mL) salsa.

Lemon Pepper Basa: Heat canola oil in large frying pan on medium. Sprinkle both sides of fillets with lemon pepper. Press both sides of fillets into flour until coated. Discard any remaining flour. Add to frying pan. Cook for about 3 minutes per side until golden and fish flakes easily when tested with fork. Serve with Mango Nut Salsa. Serves 4.

1 serving: 242 Calories; 11.7 g Total Fat (4.7 g Mono, 1.4 g Poly, 2.3 g Sat); 51 mg Cholesterol; 19 g Carbohydrate; 2 g Fibre; 17 g Protein; 118 mg Sodium

CHOICES: 1/2 Grains & Starches; 1/2 Fruits; 2 Meat & Alternatives; 1 Fats

Mango Jicama Scallops

Scallops cook so quickly on the grill that you'll be rewarded with an upscale, impressive dinner in less time than it takes to make reservations! Make the salsa first and let it stand to blend the flavours while you grill the scallops.

JICAMA SALSA

Chopped frozen mango pieces, thawed	1 cup	250 mL
Grated peeled jicama	1 cup	250 mL
Finely chopped red pepper	2 tbsp.	30 mL
Chopped fresh basil	1 tbsp.	15 mL
Lime juice	1 tbsp.	15 mL
Sliced green onion	1 tbsp.	15 mL
Brown sugar, packed	1 tsp.	5 mL
Finely grated gingerroot	1 tsp.	5 mL
Cayenne pepper, just a pinch		

SCALLOPS

Large sea scallops	1 lb.	454 g
Bamboo skewers (8 inches, 20 cm, each), soaked in water for 10 minutes	8	8
Canola oil	1 tsp.	5 mL
Salt, sprinkle		
Pepper, sprinkle		

Jicama Salsa: Preheat gas barbecue to medium-high (see Tip, page 77). Combine all 9 ingredients in small bowl. Let stand for 30 minutes to blend flavours. Makes about 2 cups (500 mL) salsa.

Scallops: Thread scallops onto skewer (see Note). Brush with canola oil. Sprinkle with salt and pepper. Cook on greased grill for about 2 minutes per side until opaque. Serve with Jicama Salsa. Serves 4.

1 serving: 156 Calories; 2.2 g Total Fat (0.8 g Mono, 0.7 g Poly, 0.2 g Sat); 37 mg Cholesterol; 14 g Carbohydrate; 2 g Fibre; 20 g Protein; 185 mg Sodium

CHOICES: 1/2 Fruits; 2 1/2 Meat & Alternatives

Pictured on page 107.

Note: You can use 2 skewers for each scallop skewer for better control when turning on grill.

Jalapeño Halibut

*Try this tangy, spicy substitute for high-fat tartar sauce
tonight—just for the halibut!*

Halibut fillets, any small bones removed (about 4 – 5 oz., 113 – 140 g, each)	4	4
Salt	1/4 tsp.	1 mL
Pepper	1/4 tsp.	1 mL
Light creamy Caesar dressing	2 tbsp.	30 mL
Light mayonnaise	1 tbsp.	15 mL
Finely chopped pickled jalapeño pepper (see Tip, page 130)	1 tsp.	5 mL

Preheat oven to 425°F (220°C). Arrange fillets on greased baking sheet.
Sprinkle with salt and pepper.

Combine remaining 3 ingredients in small cup. Spread over fillets. Bake for
about 7 minutes until fish flakes easily when tested with fork. Serves 4.

*1 serving: 146 Calories; 4.2 g Total Fat (1.6 g Mono, 1.4 g Poly, 0.4 g Sat); 38 mg Cholesterol;
2 g Carbohydrate; trace Fibre; 24 g Protein; 330 mg Sodium*

CHOICES: 3 Meat & Alternatives

Saucy Seafood Grill

*Your barbecue can do more than just grill! Here, it gently cooks delicate
seafood in a sweet and spicy chili sauce. Any extra sauce goes great over
pasta, rice or veggies.*

Sweet chili sauce	1/3 cup	75 mL
Low-sodium soy sauce	2 tbsp.	30 mL
Chili paste (sambal oelek)	1/2 tsp.	2 mL
Small bay scallops	3/4 lb.	340 g
Uncooked medium shrimp (peeled and deveined)	3/4 lb.	340 g
Haddock fillet, cut into 1 inch (2.5 cm) pieces	1/2 lb.	225 g

(continued on next page)

Preheat gas barbecue to medium-high. Combine first 3 ingredients in medium bowl.

Add remaining 3 ingredients. Stir until coated. Transfer to 2 greased 9 inch (22 cm) foil pie plates. Cover with foil. Place on grill. Cook for about 6 minutes, stirring once, until scallops are opaque, shrimp turn pink and fish flakes easily when tested with fork. Makes about 5 cups (1.25 L). Serves 6.

1 serving: 169 Calories; 1.7 g Total Fat (0.2 g Mono, 0.6 g Poly, 0.3 g Sat); 126 mg Cholesterol; 8 g Carbohydrate; trace Fibre; 28 g Protein; 498 mg Sodium

CHOICES: 4 Meat & Alternatives

Saucy Shrimp And Fennel

Cook gourmet the easy way—in your microwave! This hearty combination makes lots of sauce to spoon over rice or pasta.

Chunky tomato pasta sauce	2 cups	500 mL
Thinly sliced fennel bulb (white part only)	2 cups	500 mL
Thinly sliced celery	1 cup	250 mL
Prepared vegetable broth	1/4 cup	60 mL
Pepper	1/4 tsp.	1 mL
Cooked medium shrimp (peeled and deveined)	3/4 lb.	340 g

Combine first 5 ingredients in 2 quart (2 L) casserole. Microwave, covered, on high (100%) for about 13 minutes, stirring every 3 minutes, until fennel starts to soften.

Add shrimp. Stir. Microwave, covered, on high (100%) for about 2 minutes until shrimp are heated through. Makes about 5 cups (1.25 L). Serves 4.

1 serving: 198 Calories; 1.9 g Total Fat (0.2 g Mono, 0.4 g Poly, 0.3 g Sat); 166 mg Cholesterol; 27 g Carbohydrate; 6 g Fibre; 22 g Protein; 660 mg Sodium

CHOICES: 4 Vegetables; 2 Meat & Alternatives

Thai Haddock Stir-Fry

This family-friendly stir-fry won't "Thai" you up in the kitchen for long!
Super-speedy to make and best served with brown rice.

Canola oil	2 tsp.	10 mL
Haddock fillets, any small bones removed, cut into 1 inch (2.5 cm) pieces	1 lb.	454 g
Prepared vegetable broth	1 cup	250 mL
Brown sugar, packed	1 tbsp.	15 mL
Lime juice	1 tbsp.	15 mL
Garlic powder	1/2 tsp.	2 mL
Ground ginger	1/2 tsp.	2 mL
Thai red curry paste	1/2 tsp.	2 mL
Frozen Oriental mixed vegetables	6 cups	1.5 L
Soy sauce	1 tbsp.	15 mL
Cornstarch	1 tbsp.	15 mL

Heat wok or large frying pan on medium-high until very hot. Add cooking oil. Add fish. Stir-fry for 2 to 3 minutes until fish flakes easily when tested with fork. Remove to small bowl with slotted spoon. Cover to keep warm.

Add next 6 ingredients to same frying pan. Stir. Bring to a boil. Add vegetables. Cook, covered, for about 3 minutes, stirring occasionally, until tender-crisp.

Stir soy sauce into cornstarch in small cup. Add to vegetable mixture. Heat and stir for about 1 minute until boiling and thickened. Add fish. Stir gently. Makes about 4 1/2 cups (1.1 L). Serves 4.

1 serving: 210 Calories; 3.4 g Total Fat (1.5 g Mono, 1.0 g Poly, 0.4 g Sat); 65 mg Cholesterol; 19 g Carbohydrate; 5 g Fibre; 24 g Protein; 482 mg Sodium

CHOICES: 1 Vegetables; 3 Meat & Alternatives

Paré Pointer

Dragons sleep all day because they hunt knights.

Cajun-Stuffed Trout

For an impressive dinner, you can't beat a stuffed fish—and you won't believe how quick and easy it is to make! These trout are filled with mildly spiced rice and vegetables.

Whole rainbow trout (7 – 8 oz., 200 – 225 g, each), pan-ready	2	2
Cajun seasoning	1/4 tsp.	1 mL
Canola oil	1 tsp.	5 mL
Chopped onion	1/4 cup	60 mL
Chopped red pepper	1/4 cup	60 mL
Cajun seasoning	1 tsp.	5 mL
Cooked converted rice (about 3 tbsp., 50 mL, uncooked)	1/2 cup	125 mL
Fat-free ranch dressing	1 tbsp.	15 mL

Preheat oven to 400°F (205°C). Sprinkle half of first amount of seasoning inside each fish.

Heat canola oil in small frying pan on medium. Add next 3 ingredients. Cook for about 2 minutes, stirring often, until onion starts to soften.

Add rice. Heat and stir for 1 minute. Remove from heat.

Add dressing. Stir well. Place fish on greased baking sheet. Spoon rice mixture into fish. Spread evenly. Bake for 10 to 12 minutes until fish flakes easily when tested with fork. Serves 4.

1 serving: 205 Calories; 7.1 g Total Fat (2.4 g Mono, 2.2 g Poly, 1.7 g Sat); 69 mg Cholesterol; 10 g Carbohydrate; trace Fibre; 24 g Protein; 269 mg Sodium

CHOICES: 1/2 Grains & Starches; 3 Meat & Alternatives

Scallop And Asparagus Rotini

Asparagus, scallops, and lemon make for one dynamite combination! A sprinkling of fresh dill rounds out the flavour perfectly.

Water	8 cups	2 L
Salt	1 tsp.	5 mL
Whole-wheat rotini	8 oz.	225 g
Canola oil	1 tsp.	5 mL
Fresh asparagus, trimmed of tough ends, cut into 2 inch (5 cm) pieces	1 lb.	454 g
Garlic cloves, minced (or 1/2 tsp., 2 mL, powder)	2	2
Prepared vegetable broth	1 cup	250 mL
Salt	1/2 tsp.	2 mL
Pepper	1/4 tsp.	1 mL
Prepared vegetable broth	2 tbsp.	30 mL
Cornstarch	1 tbsp.	15 mL
Small bay scallops	3/4 lb.	340 g
Lemon juice	2 tbsp.	30 mL
Chopped fresh dill (or 3/4 tsp., 4 mL, dried)	1 tbsp.	15 mL

Combine water and salt in large saucepan. Bring to a boil. Add pasta. Boil, uncovered, for 7 to 9 minutes, stirring occasionally, until tender but firm. Drain. Return to same pot. Cover to keep warm.

Heat wok or large frying pan on medium-high until very hot. Add canola oil. Add asparagus and garlic. Stir-fry for about 1 minute until garlic is fragrant. Add next 3 ingredients. Bring to a boil, stirring occasionally. Reduce heat to medium. Boil gently, uncovered, for about 3 minutes until asparagus starts to soften.

Stir second amount of broth into cornstarch in small cup. Add asparagus mixture to pan. Heat and stir for 1 minute until bubbling and thickened.

Add scallops. Stir. Cook for about 2 minutes, stirring often, until scallops turn opaque.

(continued on next page)

Add lemon juice and dill. Add to pasta. Stir. Makes about 6 cups (1.5 L). Serves 4.

1 serving: 344 Calories; 5.4 g Total Fat (0.7 g Mono, 0.6 g Poly, 0.7 g Sat); 28 mg Cholesterol; 47 g Carbohydrate; 11 g Fibre; 26 g Protein; 574 mg Sodium

CHOICES: 2 Grains & Starches; 2 Meat & Alternatives

Pictured on page 108.

Mustard Shrimp And Leek

Mustard's not just for hotdogs or sandwiches anymore! This spicy condiment adds heat and flavour to a medley of shrimp and leek.

Dijon mustard (with whole seeds)	1/4 cup	60 mL
White wine vinegar	1/4 cup	60 mL
Olive (or canola) oil	1 tbsp.	15 mL
Granulated sugar	1 tsp.	5 mL
Olive (or canola) oil	2 tsp.	10 mL
Sliced leek (white part only)	4 cups	1 L
Garlic clove, minced (or 1/4 tsp., 1 mL, powder)	1	1
Uncooked medium shrimp (peeled and deveined)	1 1/2 lbs.	680 g

Combine first 4 ingredients in small bowl. Set aside.

Heat second amount of olive oil in large frying pan on medium. Add leek and garlic. Cook for about 8 minutes, stirring occasionally, until softened.

Add shrimp and mustard mixture. Stir. Cook, covered, for about 5 minutes until shrimp turn pink. Makes about 6 cups (1.5 L). Serves 4.

1 serving: 318 Calories; 10.0 g Total Fat (4.6 g Mono, 1.8 g Poly, 1.4 g Sat); 259 mg Cholesterol; 20 g Carbohydrate; 3 g Fibre; 37 g Protein; 580 mg Sodium

CHOICES: 2 Vegetables: 5 Meat & Alternatives; 1 Fats

Tuscan Sole

Delicate, crumb-crusted fish fillets are served with a flavourful medley of roasted vegetables. This dish has definitely got sole!

TUSCAN VEGETABLES

Chopped zucchini (with peel), 1/2 inch (12 mm) pieces	2 cups	500 mL
Chopped onion	1 cup	250 mL
Grape tomatoes	24	24
Chopped fresh white mushrooms	1 cup	250 mL
Italian seasoning	2 tsp.	10 mL
Olive (or canola) oil	2 tsp.	10 mL
Pepper	1/4 tsp.	1 mL

CRUMB-TOPPED SOLE

Sole fillets (about 2 oz., 57 g, each), any small bones removed	8	8
Lemon juice	4 tsp.	20 mL
Crushed multigrain crackers	1/2 cup	125 mL

Tuscan Vegetables: Set oven racks on bottom and upper positions (see Note 1). Preheat oven to 475°F (240°C). Combine first 7 ingredients in large bowl. Toss until coated. Arrange in single layer on greased baking sheet with sides. Bake on lower rack for about 16 minutes, stirring at halftime, until vegetables start to brown. Makes about 3 cups (750 mL).

Crumb-Topped Sole: Meanwhile, arrange fillets on separate greased baking sheet (see Note 2). Sprinkle with lemon juice. Press 1 tbsp. (15 mL) cracker crumbs evenly on top of each fillet. Bake on upper rack for about 8 minutes until crumbs are golden and fish flakes easily when tested with fork. Serve with Tuscan Vegetables. Serves 4.

1 serving: 271 Calories; 6.4 g Total Fat (2.0 g Mono, 0.8 g Poly, 0.7 g Sat); 54 mg Cholesterol; 27 g Carbohydrate; 4 g Fibre; 25 g Protein; 349 mg Sodium

CHOICES: 1 Grains & Starches; 1 Vegetables; 3 Meat & Alternatives

Note 1: Upper rack is the position second from the top (about 7 inches, 18 cm, from element) in oven.

Note 2: Sole comes in various sizes and the tail end is usually thinner than the middle. To ensure even cooking, fold the thinner tail portion underneath and group smaller fillets together to create portions of uniform size and thickness.

Chili Ginger Salmon

Kick your taste buds into overdrive with chili and ginger, then cool them down with a burst of fresh lime. Serve with a side of colourful stir-fried or steamed veggies.

Sweet chili sauce	3 tbsp.	50 mL
Lime juice	1 tbsp.	15 mL
Finely grated gingerroot (or 1/4 tsp., 1 mL, ground ginger)	1 tsp.	5 mL
Salt, just a pinch		
Salmon fillets (4 – 5 oz., 113 – 140 g, each), skin removed	4	4
Chopped fresh basil	4 tsp.	20 mL
Lime wedges	4	4

Preheat broiler. Combine first 4 ingredients in small bowl.

Arrange salmon on baking sheet, lined with greased foil. Brush with chili sauce mixture. Broil on top rack in oven for about 5 minutes until fish flakes easily when tested with fork. Transfer to serving plate.

Sprinkle with basil. Serve with lime wedges. Serves 4.

1 serving: 226 Calories; 11.9 g Total Fat (5.1 g Mono, 2.4 g Poly, 2.8 g Sat); 75 mg Cholesterol; 5 g Carbohydrate; trace Fibre; 23 g Protein; 166 mg Sodium

CHOICES: 3 Meat & Alternatives

Pictured on page 107.

Pictured on page 107.

Paré Pointer

*You don't need training to be a garbage collector—
you just pick it up as you go along.*

Lime Hazelnut Tilapia

Spicy, nutty and citrusy flavours mingle in these crunchy hazelnut-crusted fillets. The light homemade tartar sauce makes for the perfect accompaniment.

All-purpose flour	1/4 cup	60 mL
Large egg, fork-beaten	1	1
Lime juice	1 tbsp.	15 mL
Tex Mex seasoning	1 tbsp.	15 mL
Grated lime zest	1 tsp.	5 mL
Fine dry bread crumbs	1/4 cup	60 mL
Chopped sliced hazelnuts (filberts)	1/3 cup	75 mL
Tilapia fillets (about 4 – 5 oz., 113 – 140 g, each), any small bones removed	4	4
TARTAR SAUCE		
Light mayonnaise	1/3 cup	75 mL
Chopped green onion	1 tbsp.	15 mL
Tangy dill relish	1 tbsp.	15 mL
Grated lime zest	1/2 tsp.	2 mL

Preheat oven to 425°F (220°C). Measure flour onto plate.

Combine next 4 ingredients in large shallow dish.

Combine bread crumbs and hazelnuts in small cup. Transfer to separate plate.

Press both sides of fillets into flour. Dip into egg mixture. Press both sides of fillets into crumb mixture until coated. Discard any remaining flour, egg mixture and bread crumb mixture. Arrange fillets on greased baking sheet. Bake for about 10 minutes until fish flakes easily when tested with fork.

Tartar Sauce: Combine all 4 ingredients in small bowl. Makes about 6 tbsp. (100 mL) sauce. Serve with fillets. Serves 4.

1 serving: 308 Calories; 16.3 g Total Fat (9.0 g Mono, 3.5 g Poly, 1.5 g Sat); 110 mg Cholesterol; 15 g Carbohydrate; 1 g Fibre; 27 g Protein; 430 mg Sodium

CHOICES: 1/2 Grains & Starches; 3 1/2 Meats & Alternatives; 2 Fats

Kaleidoscope Shrimp

A kaleidoscope of colours and flavours in this dish of fresh vegetables and shrimp, coated with a light lemon sauce and packed with peppery punch. Serve with brown basmati rice to sneak in a little extra fibre.

Prepared vegetable broth	1/3 cup	75 mL
Lemon juice	1/4 cup	60 mL
Sweet chili sauce	2 tbsp.	30 mL
Cornstarch	2 tsp.	10 mL
Coarsely ground pepper	1 tsp.	5 mL
Grated lemon zest	1/2 tsp.	2 mL
Canola oil	1 tbsp.	15 mL
Sugar snap peas, trimmed	2 cups	500 mL
Thinly sliced red pepper	2 cups	500 mL
Thinly sliced orange pepper	2 cups	500 mL
Can of cut baby corn, drained	14 oz.	398 mL
Thinly sliced red onion	1 cup	250 mL
Garlic cloves, minced	2	2
(or 1/2 tsp., 2 mL, powder)		
Uncooked large shrimp	1 lb.	454 g
(peeled and deveined)		

Combine first 6 ingredients in small cup. Set aside.

Heat wok or large frying pan on medium-high until very hot. Add canola oil. Add next 6 ingredients. Stir-fry for about 3 minutes until peppers start to soften.

Add shrimp. Stir-fry for about 3 minutes until shrimp turn pink. Stir broth mixture. Add to shrimp mixture. Heat and stir for about 1 minute until boiling and thickened. Makes about 7 cups (1.75 L). Serves 6.

1 serving: 264 Calories; 4.8 g Total Fat (1.8 g Mono, 1.7 g Poly, 0.6 g Sat); 115 mg Cholesterol; 37 g Carbohydrate; 6 g Fibre; 21 g Protein; 208 mg Sodium

CHOICES: 1 Grains & Starches; 2 Vegetables; 2 Meat & Alternatives; 1/2 Fats

Pictured on page 107.

Warm Mango Salsa Salmon

Don't just spoon cold salsa over salmon—warm your homemade salsa with the fish so the flavours can mingle. A quick and tasty dinner!

Diced frozen mango pieces	1 cup	250 mL
Diced kiwifruit	1/2 cup	125 mL
Finely chopped fresh jalapeño pepper (see Tip, page 130)	2 tbsp.	30 mL
Finely chopped red onion	2 tbsp.	30 mL
Lemon juice	1 tbsp.	15 mL
Lime juice	1 tbsp.	15 mL
Salt	1/2 tsp.	2 mL
Salmon fillets, skin removed, cut into 1 inch (2.5 cm) pieces	1 1/4 lbs.	560 g
Tub margarine	4 tsp.	20 mL
Light mayonnaise	2 tbsp.	30 mL
Chopped fresh parsley	1 tbsp.	15 mL

Preheat oven to 425°F (220°C). Combine first 7 ingredients in large bowl. Add salmon. Toss. Spread evenly in greased 9 x 13 inch (22 x 33 cm) baking dish.

Spoon margarine, in 1/2 tsp. (2 mL) amounts, over salmon mixture. Bake, uncovered, for about 12 minutes until fish flakes easily when tested with fork.

Add mayonnaise and parsley. Stir gently. Makes about 4 1/2 cups (1.1 L). Serves 4.

1 serving: 360 Calories; 21.4 g Total Fat (9.3 g Mono, 5.3 g Poly, 4.1 g Sat); 96 mg Cholesterol; 13 g Carbohydrate; 2 g Fibre; 29 g Protein; 475 mg Sodium

CHOICES: 1/2 Fruits; 4 Meat & Alternatives; 1 Fats

1. Kaleidoscope Shrimp, page 105
2. Mango Jicama Scallops, page 95
3. Chili Ginger Salmon, page 103

Props courtesy of: Casa Bugatti
Danesco Inc.

Mexican-Spiced Halibut

This incredibly easy dish, enlivened with the flavours of Mexico, packs a punch that will send your taste buds south of the border. Olè!

Olive (or canola) oil	1 1/2 tbsp.	25 mL
Paprika	1 tbsp.	15 mL
Dried oregano	1 1/2 tsp.	7 mL
Grated lime zest	1/2 tsp.	2 mL
Ground cumin	1/2 tsp.	2 mL
Dried crushed chilies	1/4 tsp.	1 mL
Salt	1/4 tsp.	1 mL
Pepper	1/2 tsp.	2 mL
Halibut fillets (about 4 – 5 oz., 113 – 140 g, each), any small bones removed	4	4

Preheat broiler. Combine first 8 ingredients in small bowl.

Rub fillets with spice mixture. Place on greased baking sheet. Broil on top rack in oven for about 5 minutes until fish flakes easily when tested with fork. Serves 4.

1 serving: 178 Calories; 8.0 g Total Fat (4.6 g Mono, 1.4 g Poly, 1.1 g Sat); 36 mg Cholesterol; 2 g Carbohydrate; 1 g Fibre; 24 g Protein; 209 mg Sodium

CHOICES: 3 Meat & Alternatives; 1 Fats

1. Strawberry Wafer Layers, page 148
2. Greek Bread Salad, page 31
3. Scallop And Asparagus Rotini, page 100

Props courtesy of: Danesco Inc.

Santa Fe Salmon Stew

This saucy stew is full of salmon and potatoes with just a hint of heat. Enjoy with a slice of crusty whole-wheat bread to soak up the delicious sauce.

Small red baby potatoes, cut in half	3/4 lb.	340 g
Canola oil	1 tsp.	5 mL
Chopped onion	1 cup	250 mL
Chopped celery	1/2 cup	125 mL
Canned black beans, rinsed and drained	1 cup	250 mL
Frozen kernel corn	1 cup	250 mL
Grated carrot	1/2 cup	125 mL
Can of diced green chilies	4 oz.	113 g
Chili powder	1 tsp.	5 mL
Finely chopped chipotle pepper in adobo sauce (see Tip, page 40)	1 tsp.	5 mL
Salt	1/4 tsp.	1 mL
All-purpose flour	2 tbsp.	30 mL
Prepared vegetable broth	2 cups	500 mL
Salmon fillets, skin removed, cut into 1 inch (2.5 cm) cubes	1 lb.	454 g
Skim evaporated milk	1/2 cup	125 mL

Put potatoes into medium microwave-safe bowl. Microwave, covered, on high (100%) for about 4 minutes until almost tender. Cover to keep warm.

Meanwhile, heat canola oil in large saucepan on medium-high. Add onion and celery. Cook, uncovered, for about 2 minutes, stirring often, until starting to soften.

Add next 7 ingredients. Stir. Cook, uncovered, for about 2 minutes, stirring occasionally, until fragrant.

Add flour. Heat and stir for 1 minute. Slowly add broth, stirring constantly, until boiling and thickened.

Add salmon, evaporated milk and potatoes. Stir. Bring to a boil. Reduce heat to medium-low. Simmer, covered, for about 5 minutes until fish flakes easily when tested with fork and potatoes are tender. Makes about 8 cups (2 L). Serves 4.

(continued on next page)

1 serving: 434 Calories; 13.7 g Total Fat (5.8 g Mono, 2.8 g Poly, 3.0 g Sat); 76 mg Cholesterol; 46 g Carbohydrate; 7 g Fibre; 32 g Protein; 802 mg Sodium

CHOICES: 2 Grains & Starches; 1 Vegetables; 3 1/2 Meat & Alternatives

---

Grilled Salmon With Ginger Cream

Fresh and flavourful! A simple, satisfying supper of fresh salmon, dressed up in a pretty pink and green-speckled sauce.

Salmon fillets (4 – 5 oz., 113 – 140 g, each), skin removed	4	4
Olive (or canola) oil	2 tsp.	10 mL
Salt, sprinkle		
Pepper, sprinkle		
GINGER CREAM		
Light mayonnaise	1/4 cup	60 mL
Light sour cream	1/4 cup	60 mL
Finely chopped celery	2 tbsp.	30 mL
Chopped fresh parsley	1 tbsp.	15 mL
Finely chopped pickled ginger slices	1 tbsp.	15 mL
Sliced green onion	1 tbsp.	15 mL

Preheat gas barbecue to medium. Brush salmon with olive oil. Sprinkle with salt and pepper. Cook on greased grill for about 2 minutes per side until fish flakes easily when tested with fork.

Ginger Cream: Combine all 6 ingredients in small bowl. Serve with salmon. Serves 4.

1 serving: 300 Calories; 20.4 g Total Fat (9.2 g Mono, 4.1 g Poly, 3.9 g Sat); 85 mg Cholesterol; 4 g Carbohydrate; trace Fibre; 24 g Protein; 217 mg Sodium

CHOICES: 3 Meat & Alternatives; 1 1/2 Fats

Mixed-Bean Tagine

Although a tagine is traditionally simmered for a long period of time, this meatless version cooks up tangy and tasty in less than 30 minutes. Serve this saucy stew of tomato and beans over couscous, rice or pasta.

Canola oil	2 tsp.	10 mL
Chopped celery	1 cup	250 mL
Chopped onion	1 cup	250 mL
Garlic cloves, minced	2	2
(or 1/2 tsp., 2 mL, powder)		
Ground ginger	1 tsp.	5 mL
Ground cumin	1/2 tsp.	2 mL
Ground cinnamon	1/4 tsp.	1 mL
Salt	1/4 tsp.	1 mL
Pepper	1/4 tsp.	1 mL
Can of diced tomatoes (with juice)	28 oz.	796 mL
Can of mixed beans, rinsed and drained	19 oz.	540 mL
Liquid honey	1 tbsp.	15 mL
Lemon juice	2 tsp.	10 mL

Heat canola oil in large saucepan on medium. Add next 8 ingredients. Cook, uncovered, for about 5 minutes, stirring often, until onion is softened.

Add remaining 4 ingredients. Stir. Bring to a boil. Boil gently, partially covered, for 5 minutes to blend flavours. Makes about 5 1/2 cups (1.4 L). Serves 4.

1 serving: 201 Calories; 3.0 g Total Fat (1.4 g Mono, 0.7 g Poly, 0.2 g Sat); 0 mg Cholesterol; 38 g Carbohydrate; 6 g Fibre; 10 g Protein; 869 mg Sodium

CHOICES: 1 Grains & Starches; 2 Vegetables; 1 Meat & Alternatives

Pictured on page 126.

Edamame Curry Bowl

Edamame, cauliflower and sweet potato are tossed in a flavourful and spicy sauce. Serve with pasta or rice.

Canola oil	1 tsp.	5 mL
Cauliflower florets	2 cups	500 mL
Chopped onion	1 cup	250 mL
Brown sugar, packed	1 tsp.	5 mL
Thai red curry paste	1/2 tsp.	2 mL
Salt	1/2 tsp.	2 mL
Pepper	1/4 tsp.	1 mL
Prepared vegetable broth	2 cups	500 mL
Frozen shelled edamame (soybeans)	1 1/2 cups	375 mL
Garlic cloves, minced (or 1/2 tsp., 2 mL, powder)	2	2
Can of sweet potatoes, drained and chopped	19 oz.	540 mL
Prepared vegetable broth	1 tbsp.	15 mL
Cornstarch	1 tbsp.	15 mL

Heat canola oil in large frying pan on medium-high. Add next 6 ingredients. Cook for about 5 minutes, stirring often, until onion is softened.

Add next 3 ingredients. Stir. Bring to a boil. Reduce heat to medium. Cook, covered, for about 5 minutes until cauliflower is tender.

Add sweet potato. Stir second amount of broth into cornstarch in small cup. Add to cauliflower mixture. Heat and stir for about 2 minutes until sweet potato is heated through and sauce is boiling and thickened. Makes about 5 cups (1.25 L). Serves 4.

1 serving: 300 Calories; 5.0 g Total Fat (0.7 g Mono, 0.6 g Poly, 0.5 g Sat); 0 mg Cholesterol; 56 g Carbohydrate; 10 g Fibre; 11 g Protein; 646 mg Sodium

CHOICES: 2 1/2 Grains & Starches; 1 Vegetables

Orzo-Stuffed Peppers

Orzo for everyone! Keep the whole family happy when they each get their own portion of orzo, packed into tender-crisp red peppers with pecans, veggies and Parmesan cheese.

Diced zucchini (with peel)	1 cup	250 mL
Prepared vegetable broth	1 cup	250 mL
Chopped onion	1/2 cup	125 mL
Grated carrot	1/2 cup	125 mL
Orzo	1/2 cup	125 mL
Garlic and herb no-salt seasoning	1/2 tsp.	2 mL
Pepper	1/8 tsp.	0.5 mL
Chopped pecans, toasted (see Tip, below)	1/4 cup	60 mL
Grated light Parmesan cheese	2 tbsp.	30 mL
Water	2 tbsp.	30 mL
Large red peppers, halved lengthwise	2	2

Combine first 7 ingredients in medium microwave-safe bowl. Microwave, covered, on high (100%) for about 15 minutes, stirring every 5 minutes, until orzo is tender and liquid is absorbed.

Add pecans and cheese. Stir.

Pour water into greased 2 quart (2 L) casserole. Arrange pepper halves in casserole. Fill with orzo mixture. Microwave, covered, on high (100%) for about 5 minutes until peppers are tender-crisp. Makes 4 stuffed peppers.

1 stuffed pepper: 211 Calories; 6.6 g Total Fat (3.0 g Mono, 1.8 g Poly, 0.6 g Sat); 2 mg Cholesterol; 34 g Carbohydrate; 4 g Fibre; 7 g Protein; 167 mg Sodium

CHOICES: 1 1/2 Grains & Starches; 1 Vegetables; 1 Fats

 When toasting nuts, seeds or coconut, cooking times will vary for each type of nut—so never toast them together. For small amounts, place ingredient in an ungreased frying pan. Heat on medium for 3 to 5 minutes, stirring often, until golden. For larger amounts, spread ingredient evenly in an ungreased shallow pan. Bake in a 350°F (175°C) oven for 5 to 10 minutes, stirring or shaking often, until golden.

Quinoa Lentil Simmer

Cooking the veggies and spices separate from the quinoa allows for full-flavour impact. Combine the two to create one super-powered meatless main course!

Prepared vegetable broth	2 cups	500 mL
Quinoa, rinsed and drained	1 cup	250 mL
Canola oil	2 tsp.	10 mL
Sliced fresh white mushrooms	4 cups	1 L
Thai red curry paste	1/2 tsp.	2 mL
Frozen Oriental mixed vegetables	6 cups	1.5 L
Can of lentils, rinsed and drained	19 oz.	540 mL
Thai peanut sauce	1/3 cup	75 mL

Bring broth to a boil in large saucepan. Add quinoa. Stir. Reduce heat to medium. Boil gently, covered, for about 18 minutes, without stirring, until tender.

Meanwhile, heat canola oil in large frying pan on medium-high. Add mushrooms and curry paste. Cook for about 10 minutes, stirring often, until starting to brown.

Add remaining 3 ingredients. Stir. Cook, covered, for about 5 minutes until vegetables are heated through. Add quinoa. Stir. Makes about 9 1/2 cups (2.4 L). Serves 6.

1 serving: 278 Calories; 5.9 g Total Fat (1.3 g Mono, 1.1 g Poly, 0.8 g Sat); 0 mg Cholesterol; 44 g Carbohydrate; 12 g Fibre; 13 g Protein; 576 mg Sodium

CHOICES: 1 1/2 Grains & Starches; 1 Vegetables; 1 Meat & Alternatives

Pictured on page 126.

Chickpea Spinach Fajitas

Looking for a quick lunch or dinner? These family-friendly fajitas will have you saying "that's a wrap!" in no time.

Canola oil	2 tsp.	10 mL
Sliced onion	1 cup	250 mL
Sliced red pepper	1 cup	250 mL
Garlic clove, minced	1	1
(or 1/4 tsp., 1 mL, powder)		
Ground cumin	1/2 tsp.	2 mL
Pepper	1/4 tsp.	1 mL
Can of chickpeas (garbanzo beans),	19 oz.	540 mL
rinsed and drained		
Fresh spinach leaves, lightly packed	2 cups	500 mL
Tomato sauce	1/2 cup	125 mL
Light sour cream	1/2 cup	125 mL
Whole wheat flour tortillas	4	4
(9 inch, 22 cm, diameter)		
Shredded lettuce, lightly packed	2 cups	500 mL
Diced tomato	1 cup	250 mL

Heat canola oil in large frying pan on medium-high. Add next 5 ingredients. Stir-fry for about 2 minutes until onion starts to soften.

Measure 1 cup (250 mL) chickpeas into small bowl. Mash. Add to onion mixture. Add spinach, tomato sauce and remaining chickpeas. Stir. Cook, covered, for about 2 minutes until spinach is wilted. Remove from heat.

Add sour cream. Stir.

Meanwhile, stack tortillas on work surface. Wrap in damp tea towel. Microwave on medium (50%) for about 2 minutes until warmed. Arrange tortillas on work surface. Scatter lettuce and tomato over top. Spoon chickpea mixture over tomato. Fold bottom end of each tortilla over filling. Fold in sides. Fold over from bottom to enclose filling. Makes 4 fajitas.

1 fajita: 322 Calories; 8.6 g Total Fat (1.9 g Mono, 3.0 g Poly, 1.8 g Sat); 10 mg Cholesterol; 51 g Carbohydrate; 10 g Fibre; 13 g Protein; 599 mg Sodium

CHOICES: 2 Grains & Starches; 1 1/2 Vegetables; 1/2 Meat & Alternatives; 1 Fats

Grilled Eggplant Parmigiana

Simple to prepare, yet elegant. This easy grilled casserole is a fun new twist on a hearty Italian classic. Everything is cooked on the grill, so you don't have to run back and forth between barbecue and stove.

Roasted garlic tomato pasta sauce	2 cups	500 mL
Chopped fresh parsley	2 tbsp.	30 mL
(or 1 1/2 tsp., 7 mL, flakes)		
Dried crushed chilies	1/4 tsp.	1 mL
Dried oregano	1/4 tsp.	1 mL
Pepper	1/4 tsp.	1 mL
Medium eggplants (with peel), cut crosswise into 8 slices each	2	2
Olive (or canola) oil	2 tbsp.	30 mL
Grated part-skim mozzarella cheese	2 cups	500 mL

Preheat gas barbecue to medium-high. Combine first 5 ingredients in medium saucepan. Place on 1 side of grill (see Note). Close lid. Cook, covered, for about 10 minutes, stirring occasionally, to blend flavours.

Meanwhile, brush both sides of eggplant slices with olive oil. Place on greased grill. Cook for about 3 minutes per side until tender. Arrange 8 slices of eggplant in bottom of greased 9 x 13 inch (22 x 33 cm) baking pan. Spoon half of sauce over eggplant. Spread evenly.

Sprinkle with half of cheese. Repeat with remaining eggplant slices, sauce and cheese. Place pan on grill. Close lid. Cook for about 5 minutes until sauce is bubbly and cheese is melted. Serves 4.

1 serving: 351 Calories; 18.7 g Total Fat (8.1 g Mono, 1.1 g Poly, 7.9 g Sat); 39 mg Cholesterol; 28 g Carbohydrate; 9 g Fibre; 21 g Protein; 645 mg Sodium

CHOICES: 3 Vegetables; 2 Meat & Alternatives; 1 Fats

Note: If your saucepan doesn't have a heatproof handle, wrap the handle in foil before placing on the grill and try to keep it away from any flames.

Greek Bulgur Burgers

Beef burgers have met their match! These meatless patties are filled with the fabulous flavours of peppers, spinach and oregano. Both delicious and nutritious.

Canola oil	1 tsp.	5 mL
Chopped onion	1 cup	250 mL
Chopped roasted red pepper	1 cup	250 mL
Greek seasoning	1 tsp.	5 mL
Dried oregano	1/2 tsp.	2 mL
Pepper	1/4 tsp.	1 mL
Prepared vegetable broth	3/4 cup	175 mL
Bulgur	1/2 cup	125 mL
Fresh spinach leaves, lightly packed, chopped	4 cups	1 L
Fine dry bread crumbs	2/3 cup	150 mL
Crumbled light feta cheese	1/2 cup	125 mL
Cooking spray		

Preheat broiler. Heat canola oil in large frying pan on medium-high. Add next 5 ingredients. Cook for about 3 minutes, stirring often, until onion and red pepper are softened.

Add broth. Bring to a boil. Add bulgur. Boil, uncovered, for about 2 minutes until bulgur is tender and liquid is absorbed. Remove from heat.

Add spinach. Heat and stir for about 2 minutes until spinach starts to wilt. Transfer to large bowl.

Add bread crumbs and cheese. Stir. Measure 1/2 cup (125 mL) portions onto greased baking sheet. Shape into 1/2 inch (12 mm) thick patties.

Spray with cooking spray. Broil for about 10 minutes per side, turning at halftime, until browned. Makes 6 burgers.

1 burger: 167 Calories; 4.2 g Total Fat (0.8 g Mono, 0.5 g Poly, 1.6 g Sat); 7 mg Cholesterol; 26 g Carbohydrate; 4 g Fibre; 8 g Protein; 568 mg Sodium

CHOICES: 1 Grains & Starches; 1 Vegetables; 1/2 Meat & Alternatives

Spaghetti Squash 'N' Sauce

The most fun you'll ever have with a meatless dish! The pasta-like strands of spaghetti squash offer a truly unique presentation.

Small spaghetti squash (about 1 1/2 – 2 lbs., 680 – 900 g)	1	1
Olive oil	2 tsp.	10 mL
Sliced fresh white mushrooms	2 cups	500 mL
Garlic cloves, minced (or 1/2 tsp., 2 mL, powder)	2	2
Chopped onion	1/2 cup	125 mL
Chopped red pepper	1/2 cup	125 mL
Can of diced tomatoes (with juice)	14 oz.	398 mL
Dried thyme	1/2 tsp.	2 mL
Granulated sugar	1/2 tsp.	2 mL
Salt	1/4 tsp.	1 mL
Pepper	1/8 tsp	0.5 mL
Grated Parmesan cheese	2 tsp.	10 mL

Cut squash in half lengthwise. Remove seeds. Cut squash halves crosswise to make 4 pieces. Arrange in ungreased 3 quart (3 L) casserole. Microwave, covered, on high (100%) for about 15 minutes until squash strands separate easily when tested with fork. Cover to keep warm.

Meanwhile, heat olive oil in large frying pan on medium. Add next 4 ingredients. Cook for about 5 minutes, stirring often, until onion is softened.

Add next 5 ingredients. Cook and stir for 2 minutes to blend flavours.

Loosen squash strands with fork, leaving strands in shells. Spoon tomato mixture over top.

Sprinkle with cheese. Serves 4.

1 serving: 119 Calories; 3.7 g Total Fat (1.8 g Mono, 0.7 g Poly, 0.7 g Sat); 1 mg Cholesterol; 21 g Carbohydrate; 3 g Fibre; 3 g Protein; 469 mg Sodium

CHOICES: 3 Vegetables; 1/2 Fats

Zucchini Chickpea Toss

This hearty blend of roasted veggies has lots of protein from chickpeas, and plenty of flavour from cheese and sun-dried tomato pesto.

Chopped zucchini (with peel), 3/4 inch (2 cm) pieces	4 cups	1 L
Chopped green pepper	1 1/2 cups	375 mL
Chopped red pepper	1 1/2 cups	375 mL
Can of chickpeas (garbanzo beans), rinsed and drained	19 oz.	540 mL
Grated Romano cheese	2 tbsp.	30 mL
Sun-dried tomato pesto	1 tbsp.	15 mL
Red wine vinegar	2 tsp.	10 mL
Pepper	1/4 tsp.	1 mL

Preheat broiler. Arrange first 3 ingredients in single layer on ungreased baking sheet with sides. Broil on top rack in oven for 5 minutes. Stir. Broil for another 3 minutes until tender and starting to turn brown.

Meanwhile, put chickpeas into large microwave-safe bowl. Microwave, covered, on high (100%) for about 3 minutes until heated through. Add vegetables. Toss.

Add remaining 4 ingredients. Toss. Makes about 6 cups (1.5 L). Serves 4.

1 serving: 174 Calories; 3.4 g Total Fat (0.8 g Mono, 1.3 g Poly, 0.7 g Sat); 3 mg Cholesterol; 29 g Carbohydrate; 9 g Fibre; 10 g Protein; 237 mg Sodium

CHOICES: 1 Grains & Starches; 1 Vegetables; 1 Meat & Alternatives

tip If a recipe calls for less than an entire can of tomato paste, freeze the unopened can for 30 minutes. Open both ends and push the contents through one end. Slice off only what you need. Freeze the remaining paste in a resealable freezer bag or plastic wrap for future use.

Mushroom Tofu Ragout

Tofu, the chameleon of the food world, absorbs the flavours of the ingredients it's cooked with—in this case, earthy mushrooms in a rich and savoury stew. Great served over pasta or with fresh bread.

Package of medium tofu, diced	1 lb.	454 g
Canola oil	1 tbsp.	15 mL
Sliced portobello mushrooms	4 cups	1 L
Sliced fresh white mushrooms	2 cups	500 mL
Chopped onion	1 1/2 cups	375 mL
Dried thyme	1/2 tsp.	2 mL
Paprika	1/2 tsp.	2 mL
Seasoned salt	1/2 tsp.	2 mL
Pepper	1/4 tsp.	1 mL
All-purpose flour	3 tbsp.	50 mL
Tomato paste (see Tip, page 120)	2 tbsp.	30 mL
Prepared vegetable broth	2 cups	500 mL
Light sour cream	3 tbsp.	50 mL
Chopped fresh parsley (or 1 1/2 tsp., 7 mL, flakes)	2 tbsp.	30 mL
Dijon mustard	1 tbsp.	15 mL

Put tofu on paper towel-lined plate to drain.

Heat canola oil in large saucepan or Dutch oven on medium-high. Add next 7 ingredients. Cook, uncovered, for about 5 minutes, stirring often, until onion is softened and mushrooms start to brown.

Add flour and tomato paste. Heat and stir for 1 minute. Slowly add vegetable broth, stirring constantly until boiling and thickened. Reduce heat to medium. Boil gently, uncovered, for 5 minutes to blend flavours. Add tofu. Stir. Boil gently, uncovered, for another 2 minutes, stirring occasionally, until heated through.

Add remaining 3 ingredients. Stir. Makes about 7 cups (1.75 L).

1 cup (250 mL): 120 Calories; 4.6 g Total Fat (1.5 g Mono, 1.6 g Poly, 0.8 g Sat); 2 mg Cholesterol; 13 g Carbohydrate; 2 g Fibre; 7 g Protein; 298 mg Sodium

CHOICES: 1 Vegetables; 1/2 Meat & Alternatives

Spicy Chickpea Bulgur

The subtle heat of this peppery bulgur is offset by sweet raisins and cashews.

Olive (or canola) oil	1 tsp.	5 mL
Chopped onion	1 cup	250 mL
Diced green pepper	1/2 cup	125 mL
Diced red pepper	1/2 cup	125 mL
Garlic cloves, minced	2	2
(or 1/2 tsp., 2 mL, powder)		
Chili powder	1 tsp.	5 mL
Dried crushed chilies	1/4 tsp.	1 mL
Ground cinnamon	1/4 tsp.	1 mL
Ground cumin	1/4 tsp.	1 mL
Salt	1/2 tsp.	2 mL
Pepper	1/4 tsp.	1 mL
Prepared vegetable broth	2 cups	500 mL
Can of chickpeas (garbanzo beans), rinsed and drained	19 oz.	540 mL
Bulgur	1 cup	250 mL
Dark raisins	1/2 cup	125 mL
Unsalted, roasted cashews	1/2 cup	125 mL
White vinegar	1 tbsp.	15 mL
Chopped fresh parsley	2 tsp.	10 mL

Heat olive oil in large frying pan on medium. Add next 10 ingredients. Cook for about 5 minutes, stirring often, until onion is softened.

Add broth. Bring to a boil, stirring occasionally. Add next 5 ingredients. Boil gently, uncovered, for about 5 minutes until bulgur is tender and liquid is absorbed.

Sprinkle with parsley. Makes about 6 cups (1.5 L). Serves 4.

1 serving: 451 Calories; 12.2 g Total Fat (6.1 g Mono, 2.8 g Poly, 1.9 g Sat); 0 mg Cholesterol; 77 g Carbohydrate; 13 g Fibre; 15 g Protein; 688 mg Sodium

CHOICES: 2 1/2 Grains & Starches; 1 Fruits; 1 Vegetables; 1 Meat & Alternatives; 2 Fats

Pictured on page 126.

Feta Creamed Spinach

Truly the crème de la crème *of spinach dishes. Here this leafy green is elevated to elegant fare with the addition of feta, mushrooms and back bacon.*

Tub margarine	1 1/2 tbsp.	25 mL
Chopped fresh white mushrooms	1 cup	250 mL
Garlic clove, minced	1	1
(or 1/4 tsp., 1 mL, powder)		
All-purpose flour	1 1/2 tbsp.	25 mL
Pepper, sprinkle		
Skim milk	1 cup	250 mL
Box of frozen chopped spinach,	10 oz.	300 g
thawed and squeezed dry		
Crumbled light feta cheese	1/2 cup	250 mL
Diced back (Canadian) bacon	1/4 cup	60 mL

Melt margarine in medium saucepan on medium. Add mushrooms and garlic. Cook, uncovered, for about 4 minutes, stirring occasionally, until liquid has evaporated.

Sprinkle with flour and pepper. Heat and stir for 1 minute. Slowly add milk, stirring constantly until boiling and thickened. Reduce heat to low.

Add remaining 3 ingredients. Cook, uncovered, for about 3 minutes, stirring occasionally, until heated through. Makes about 2 cups (500 mL). Serves 4.

1 serving: 157 Calories; 8.4 g Total Fat (2.2 g Mono, 1.9 g Poly, 3.0 g Sat); 16 mg Cholesterol; 10 g Carbohydrate; 2 g Fibre; 13 g Protein; 651 mg Sodium

CHOICES: 1 Meat & Alternatives; 1 Fats

Orange Veggie Medley

Add brightness and freshness to your next meal with this colourful and delicious medley of fresh vegetables in a sweet orange glaze.

Butternut squash, cut into 1/2 inch (12 mm) pieces	2 lbs.	900 g
Frozen peas	1 cup	250 mL
Chopped red pepper	1/2 cup	125 mL
Frozen concentrated orange juice, thawed	2 tbsp.	30 mL

Place squash in steamer basket. Place steamer basket in large saucepan. Pour boiling water into saucepan until within 1 inch (2.5 cm) of basket bottom. Cook, covered, on medium for about 7 minutes until squash is tender-crisp.

Add peas. Cook, covered, for about 3 minutes until peas are hot and squash is tender.

Combine red pepper and concentrated orange juice in large bowl. Add squash and peas. Toss. Makes about 4 cups (1 L). Serves 6.

1 serving: 99 Calories; 0.3 g Total Fat (trace Mono, 0.1 g Poly, 0.1 g Sat); 0 mg Cholesterol; 24 g Carbohydrate; 4 g Fibre; 3 g Protein; 33 mg Sodium

CHOICES: 3 Vegetables

Pictured at right.

1. Orange Veggie Medley, above
2. Eat Your Greens, page 134
3. Lemon Oregano Vegetables, page 131

Props courtesy of: Danesco Inc.
Totally Bamboo

Oven-Roasted Parsnips

Roasting brings out a deliciously sweet, almost candy-like quality in parsnips. An absolutely perfect side dish for a weekday supper, but classy enough for company.

Large peeled parsnips, halved lengthwise and cut into 1/2 inch (12 mm) pieces (about 3 cups, 750 mL)	4	4
Water	2 tbsp.	30 mL
Canola oil	2 tbsp.	30 mL
Dried sage	1 tsp.	5 mL
Salt	1/4 tsp.	1 mL
Pepper	1/8 tsp.	0.5 mL

Preheat oven to 450°F (230°C). Put parsnip into large microwave-safe bowl. Sprinkle with water. Microwave, covered, on high (100%) for about 5 minutes until tender-crisp.

Add remaining 4 ingredients. Toss. Spread in single layer on greased baking sheet with sides. Bake for about 15 minutes, stirring twice, until tender and golden. Makes about 2 cups (500 mL). Serves 4.

1 serving: 136 Calories; 7.1 g Total Fat (4.1 g Mono, 2.1 g Poly, 0.6 g Sat); 0 mg Cholesterol; 18 g Carbohydrate; 3 g Fibre; 1 g Protein; 156 mg Sodium

CHOICES: 3 Vegetables; 1 Fats

1. Quinoa Lentil Simmer, page 115
2. Mixed-Bean Tagine, page 112
3. Spicy Chickpea Bulgur, page 122

Props courtesy of: Pfaltzgraff Canada
Cherison Enterprises Inc.
The Bay

Roasted Broccoli

Why not bring out broccoli's naturally earthy flavour by roasting it? Add a drizzle of Dijon and garlic vinaigrette and you've got a very flavourful side.

Broccoli florets	5 cups	1.25 L
Canola oil	1 tbsp.	15 mL
Salt	1/4 tsp.	1 mL
Canola oil	1 tbsp.	15 mL
Red wine vinegar	1 tbsp.	15 mL
Dijon mustard	1/4 tsp.	1 mL
Garlic powder	1/4 tsp.	1 mL
Pepper	1/4 tsp.	1 mL

Preheat oven to 450°F (230°C). Put broccoli into large bowl. Drizzle with first amount of canola oil. Sprinkle with salt. Toss. Spread evenly on greased baking sheet with sides. Bake for about 15 minutes until browned and tender. Transfer to large serving bowl.

Meanwhile, combine remaining 5 ingredients in small cup. Drizzle over broccoli. Toss. Makes about 3 cups (750 mL). Serves 4.

1 serving: 86 Calories; 7.1 g Total Fat (4.0 g Mono, 2.2 g Poly, 0.5 g Sat); 0 mg Cholesterol; 5 g Carbohydrate; 3 g Fibre; 3 g Protein; 174 mg Sodium

CHOICES: 1 Fats

Broiled Tomatoes

Why mess with nature's perfection? Fresh, juicy tomatoes are at their finest when topped with a simple combination of cheese and onion.

Medium tomatoes	2	2
Finely chopped onion	2 tbsp.	30 mL
Grated Romano cheese	2 tbsp.	30 mL
Light mayonnaise	2 tbsp	30 mL

Preheat broiler. Cut tomatoes in half horizontally. Place, cut-side up, on ungreased baking sheet.

(continued on next page)

Combine next 3 ingredients in small bowl. Spread on tomatoes. Broil on centre rack in oven for about 4 minutes until cheese is golden and bubbly. Makes 4 tomatoes.

1 tomato: 57 Calories; 3.6 g Total Fat (1.5 g Mono, 0.8 g Poly, 0.5 g Sat); 6 mg Cholesterol; 5 g Carbohydrate; 1 g Fibre; 2 g Protein; 103 mg Sodium

CHOICES: 1/2 Vegetables; 1/2 Fats

Citrus Cauliflower

With fabulous flavour and a unique presentation that uses a whole head of cauliflower, it'll be easy to get your family to eat their vegetables!

Canola oil	2 tbsp.	30 mL
All-purpose flour	1 tbsp.	15 mL
Low-sodium prepared chicken broth	1/3 cup	75 mL
Milk	1/3 cup	75 mL
Lemon juice	1 tbsp.	15 mL
Grated lemon zest	1 tsp.	5 mL
Dried dillweed	1/4 tsp.	1 mL
Medium head of cauliflower, outer leaves trimmed (about 1 1/4 lbs., 560 g)	1	1
Low-sodium prepared chicken broth	1/4 cup	60 mL

Put canola oil into small microwave-safe bowl. Microwave, covered, on high (100%) for 15 seconds. Add flour. Stir until smooth. Add first amount of broth to flour mixture, stirring constantly, until smooth. Add milk. Stir. Microwave, covered, on medium (50%) for about 2 minutes, stirring every 45 seconds, until thickened.

Add next 3 ingredients. Stir. Cover to keep warm. Set aside.

Place cauliflower in deep 2 quart (2 L) casserole. Pour second amount of broth over top. Cover tightly. Microwave on high (100%) for about 8 minutes until tender-crisp. Pour sauce over cauliflower. Microwave, uncovered, on high (100%) for about 1 minute until heated through. Serves 4.

1 serving: 116 Calories; 7.0 g Total Fat (4.1 g Mono, 2.0 g Poly, 0.6 g Sat); 2 mg Cholesterol; 10 g Carbohydrate; 3 g Fibre; 4 g Protein; 143 mg Sodium

CHOICES: 1 Vegetables; 1 Fats

Couscous Mexicana

This colourful Mexican-inspired couscous is a fiesta for your taste buds.

Olive (or canola) oil	2 tsp.	10 mL
Chopped onion	1/2 cup	125 mL
Garlic clove, minced	1	1
(or 1/4 tsp., 1 mL, powder)		
Ground cumin	1/2 tsp.	2 mL
Prepared chicken broth	1 cup	250 mL
Couscous	3/4 cup	175 mL
Canned diced tomatoes, drained	1/2 cup	125 mL
Chopped green pepper	1/4 cup	60 mL
Chopped jalapeño pepper, seeds and ribs	2 tbsp.	30 mL
removed (see Tip, below)		
Chopped fresh cilantro	2 tbsp.	30 mL

Combine olive oil and onion in medium microwave-safe bowl. Microwave, covered, on high (100%) for about 2 minutes, stirring twice, until softened.

Add garlic and cumin. Stir. Microwave, covered, on high (100%) for about 1 minute until garlic is softened.

Add next 5 ingredients. Stir. Microwave, covered, on high (100%) for about 3 minutes, stirring occasionally, until couscous is tender and broth is absorbed.

Add cilantro. Stir. Makes about 3 cups (750 mL). Serves 6.

1 serving: 117 Calories; 1.9 g Total Fat (1.2 g Mono, 0.3 g Poly, 0.3 g Sat); 0 mg Cholesterol; 21 g Carbohydrate; 1 g Fibre; 4 g Protein; 299 mg Sodium

CHOICES: 1 Grains & Starches

 tip Hot peppers contain capsaicin in the seeds and ribs. Removing the seeds and ribs will reduce the heat. Wear rubber gloves when handling hot peppers and avoid touching your eyes. Wash your hands well afterwards.

Lemon Oregano Vegetables

What a smart idea! Use the cooking liquid from the vegetables to make a shiny lemon glaze. This helps to retain nutrients and flavour and adds some great visual appeal to these tasty, tender-crisp veggies.

Prepared chicken broth	1 cup	250 mL
Dried oregano	1 tsp.	5 mL
Baby carrots	1 cup	250 mL
Broccoli florets	1 cup	250 mL
Chopped red pepper	1 cup	250 mL
Lemon juice	1 tbsp.	30 mL
Cornstarch	1 tsp.	5 mL
Pepper, sprinkle		

Combine broth and oregano in medium saucepan. Bring to a boil. Add carrots. Cook, uncovered, for about 5 minutes until starting to soften.

Add broccoli and red pepper. Reduce heat to medium. Cook, covered, for about 5 minutes until vegetables are tender-crisp. Remove to medium bowl with slotted spoon. Bring liquid to a boil.

Stir lemon juice into cornstarch in small cup. Add to boiling liquid. Heat and stir until thickened. Drizzle over vegetables.

Sprinkle with pepper. Toss. Makes about 2 1/2 cups (625 mL). Serves 4.

1 serving: 47 Calories; 0.8 g Total Fat (0.1 g Mono, 0.3 g Poly, 0.2 g Sat); 0 mg Cholesterol; 9 g Carbohydrate; 2 g Fibre; 2 g Protein; 397 mg Sodium

CHOICES: 1 Vegetables

Pictured on page 125.

Paré Pointer

Pulling a few strings will help you get ahead—especially if you're a puppeteer.

Cranberry Sweet Potatoes

Even though this combination of spice-scented sweet potatoes and tart cranberries has a holiday feel, you can serve it any time of year as a tasty, healthy side dish.

Tub margarine	1 tbsp.	15 mL
Diced onion	1 cup	250 mL
Cubed fresh peeled orange-fleshed sweet potato (about 1 lb., 454 g)	3 cups	750 mL
Frozen (or fresh) cranberries	1 cup	250 mL
Brown sugar, packed	3 tbsp.	50 mL
Orange juice	2 tbsp.	30 mL
Grated orange zest	1 tsp.	5 mL
Ground cinnamon	1/4 tsp.	1 mL
Ground ginger	1/4 tsp.	1 mL
Ground nutmeg	1/4 tsp.	1 mL
Salt	1/4 tsp.	1 mL

Melt margarine in 2 quart (2 L) casserole. Add onion. Stir. Microwave, covered, on high (100%) for about 3 minutes, stirring at halftime, until softened.

Add remaining 9 ingredients. Stir. Microwave, covered, on high (100%) for about 12 minutes, stirring twice, until sweet potato and cranberries are tender. Makes about 3 cups (750 mL). Serves 4.

1 serving: 184 Calories; 3.1 g Total Fat (1.2 g Mono, 1.2 g Poly, 0.5 g Sat); 0 mg Cholesterol; 38 g Carbohydrate; 5 g Fibre; 2 g Protein; 245 mg Sodium

CHOICES: 1 Grains & Starches; 1/2 Other Choices; 1/2 Fats

Paré Pointer
A grandfather clock is actually an old timer.

Potato Apple Cakes

Everyone loves potato cakes, but these have the added fresh flavour and goodness of apple.

Grated peeled baking potato	1 1/2 cups	375 mL
Grated peeled tart apple (such as Granny Smith)	1 cup	250 mL
Finely chopped celery	1/2 cup	125 mL
Chopped green onion	1/4 cup	60 mL
Seasoned salt	1 tsp.	5 mL
Grated lemon zest	1/2 tsp.	2 mL
Pepper	1/4 tsp.	1 mL
Large egg, fork-beaten	1	1
Whole-wheat flour	2 tbsp.	30 mL
Canola oil	2 tbsp.	30 mL

Squeeze potato and apple in paper towels to remove excess moisture. Put into medium bowl.

Add next 5 ingredients. Stir well.

Whisk egg and flour in small bowl until smooth. Add to potato mixture. Stir.

Meanwhile, heat 1 tbsp. (15 mL) canola oil in large frying pan on medium. Drop 4 portions of potato mixture, using about 1/4 cup (60 mL) for each, into pan. Flatten slightly. Cook for about 3 minutes per side until browned. Transfer to plate. Cover to keep warm. Repeat with remaining canola oil and potato mixture. Makes 8 cakes. Serves 4.

1 serving: 158 Calories; 11.8 g Total Fat (6.2 g Mono, 2.7 g Poly, 2.3 g Sat); 47 mg Cholesterol; 18 g Carbohydrate; 2 g Fibre; 3 g Protein; 396 mg Sodium

CHOICES: 1 Grains & Starches; 1 Fats

Eat Your Greens

You'd better believe your family will eat their greens when you dish up this tasty combination of crisp snap peas and asparagus.

Olive (or canola) oil	1 tbsp.	15 mL
Sliced green onion	1/2 cup	125 mL
Garlic clove, minced	1	1
(or 1/4 tsp., 1 mL, powder)		
Fresh asparagus, trimmed of tough ends, cut into 2 inch (5 cm) pieces	1 lb.	454 g
Sugar snap peas, trimmed	1 cup	250 mL
Low-sodium prepared chicken broth	1/4 cup	60 mL
Soy sauce	1 tsp.	5 mL
Coarsely ground pepper	1/2 tsp.	2 mL
Cornstarch	1/2 tsp.	2 mL

Heat olive oil in large frying pan on medium. Add green onion and garlic. Cook for about 2 minutes, stirring often, until onion is softened.

Add next 3 ingredients. Stir. Cook, covered, for about 3 minutes, stirring occasionally, until vegetables are tender-crisp.

Combine remaining 3 ingredients in small cup. Add to vegetables. Heat and stir until bubbling and vegetables are coated. Makes about 4 cups (1 L). Serves 6.

1 serving: 63 Calories; 2.3 g Total Fat (1.7 g Mono, 0.2 g Poly, 0.3 g Sat); trace Cholesterol; 7 g Carbohydrate; 3 g Fibre; 3 g Protein; 73 mg Sodium

CHOICES: 1 Vegetables; 1/2 Fats

Pictured on page 125.

Roasted Vegetable Quinoa

This light, flavourful Mediterranean-inspired side will have you yearning for the canals of Venice.

Water	1 1/2 cups	375 mL
Salt	1/8 tsp.	0.5 mL
Quinoa, rinsed and drained	1 cup	250 mL
Chopped red pepper	1 cup	250 mL
Chopped zucchini (with peel)	1 cup	250 mL
Chopped onion	1/2 cup	125 mL
Olive (or cooking) oil	2 tbsp.	30 mL
Dried rosemary, crushed	1/2 tsp.	2 mL
Salt	1/2 tsp.	2 mL
Pepper	1/4 tsp.	1 mL
Cherry tomatoes	10	10
Garlic clove, minced	1	1
(or 1/4 tsp., 1 mL, powder)		
Balsamic vinegar	3 tbsp.	50 mL
Liquid honey	2 tbsp.	30 mL
Olive (or canola) oil	1 tbsp.	15 mL

Preheat oven to 400°F (205°C). Combine water and salt in large saucepan. Bring to a boil. Add quinoa. Stir. Reduce heat to medium-low. Simmer, covered, for about 20 minutes, without stirring, until quinoa is tender and liquid is absorbed. Transfer to medium bowl. Fluff with fork. Cover to keep warm.

Meanwhile, put next 3 ingredients into medium bowl. Drizzle with olive oil. Sprinkle with next 3 ingredients. Toss until coated. Spread in single layer on greased baking sheet with sides. Bake for about 15 minutes until starting to brown.

Add tomatoes and garlic. Toss. Bake for another 5 minutes until tomatoes are hot and vegetables are tender-crisp. Add to quinoa. Toss.

Drizzle with remaining 3 ingredients. Toss until coated. Makes about 4 cups (1 L).

1/2 cup (125 mL): 161 Calories; 6.4 g Total Fat (4.1 g Mono, 1.0 g Poly, 0.8 g Sat); 0 mg Cholesterol; 23 g Carbohydrate; 2.4 g Fibre; 3.5 g Protein; 192 mg Sodium

CHOICES: 1 Grains & Starches; 1/2 Vegetables; 1 Fats

Spinach Feta Bulgur

*Bulgur is livened up with spinach, feta, olives and a bright lemon finish.
Fresh, flavourful and nutritious, too!*

Canola oil	1 tsp.	5 mL
Chopped onion	1 cup	250 mL
Garlic cloves, minced,	2	2
(or 1/2 tsp. 2 mL, powder)		
Dried oregano	1/2 tsp.	2 mL
Pepper	1/4 tsp.	1 mL
Prepared vegetable broth	1 1/2 cups	375 mL
Bulgur	1/2 cup	125 mL
Fresh spinach leaves, lightly packed	4 cups	1 L
Crumbled light feta cheese	1/3 cup	75 mL
Sliced black olives	1/4 cup	60 mL
Grated lemon zest	1/2 tsp.	2 mL

Heat canola oil in large frying pan on medium. Add next 4 ingredients.
Cook for about 5 minutes, stirring often, until onion is softened.

Add broth. Bring to a boil. Add bulgur. Stir. Boil gently, covered, for about
5 minutes, stirring occasionally, until bulgur is tender and broth
is absorbed.

Add spinach. Heat and stir for about 2 minutes until wilted. Remove
from heat.

Add remaining 3 ingredients. Stir. Makes about 3 cups (750 mL). Serves 4.

*1 serving: 152 Calories; 4.7 g Total Fat (1.4 g Mono, 0.6 g Poly, 1.6 g Sat); 7 mg Cholesterol;
22 g Carbohydrate; 4 g Fibre; 8 g Protein; 524 mg Sodium*

CHOICES: 1 Grains & Starches; 1/2 Meat & Alternatives

Rapid Ratatouille

Being in a hurry is no reason to settle for a second-rate side. This dish comes together quickly, and mixed vegetables have never tasted so good!

Chopped fresh basil (or 1 1/2 tsp., 7 mL, dried)	2 tbsp.	30 mL
Olive (or canola) oil	2 tbsp.	30 mL
Lemon juice	1 tbsp.	15 mL
Sweet chili sauce	1 tbsp.	15 mL
Garlic clove, minced (or 1/4 tsp., 1 mL, powder)	1	1
Salt	1/4 tsp.	1 mL
Pepper	1/4 tsp.	1 mL
Olive (or canola) oil	2 tsp.	10 mL
Sliced red pepper	2 cups	500 mL
Sliced Asian eggplant (with peel)	1 cup	250 mL
Sliced fresh white mushrooms	1 cup	250 mL
Sliced zucchini (with peel)	1 cup	250 mL

Combine first 7 ingredients in small bowl.

Heat wok or large frying pan on medium-high until very hot. Add second amount of olive oil. Add remaining 4 ingredients. Stir-fry for about 5 minutes until vegetables are tender-crisp. Add lemon juice mixture. Toss. Remove from heat. Let stand, covered, for 5 minutes to blend flavours. Makes about 4 cups (1 L). Serves 4.

1 serving: 130 Calories; 9.4 g Total Fat (6.7 g Mono, 1.0 g Poly, 1.3 g Sat); 0 mg Cholesterol; 12 g Carbohydrate; 4 g Fibre; 2 g Protein; 188 mg Sodium

CHOICES: 1 Vegetables; 1 Fats

Paré Pointer

A chicken lays an egg because if she dropped it, it would break.

Feta Ruby Chard

Introduce your family to this delicious and nutritious green with a simple sauté of chard, garlic and feta cheese.

Tub margarine	2 tsp.	10 mL
Sliced onion	1/2 cup	125 mL
Garlic clove, minced	1	1
(or 1/4 tsp., 1 mL, powder)		
Coarsely chopped ruby chard, lightly packed	9 cups	2.25 L
Prepared vegetable broth	2 tbsp.	30 mL
Crumbled feta cheese	1/4 cup	60 mL

Melt margarine in large saucepan on medium. Add onion and garlic. Cook, uncovered, for about 5 minutes, stirring often, until onion is softened and starting to brown.

Add chard and broth. Stir. Cook, covered, for about 4 minutes until chard starts to wilt. Stir. Cook for another 4 minutes until chard is wilted. Transfer to plate.

Sprinkle with cheese. Makes about 3 1/2 cups (875 mL). Serves 4.

1 serving: 66 Calories; 3.3 g Total Fat (0.9 g Mono, 0.8 g Poly, 1.1 g Sat); 4 mg Cholesterol; 7 g Carbohydrate; 2 g Fibre; 4 g Protein; 350 mg Sodium

CHOICES: 1 Vegetables

Pictured on divider.

Creamy Polenta

This creamy polenta with hints of pepper and cheese is true comfort food. Try using it as a base for serving with stews or other saucy dishes.

Prepared vegetable broth	3 1/4 cups	800 mL
Yellow cornmeal	1 cup	250 mL
Grated Italian cheese blend	1/3 cup	75 mL
Coarsely ground pepper	1/2 tsp.	2 mL

(continued on next page)

Combine broth and cornmeal in 1.5 quart (1.5 L) casserole. Microwave, covered, on high (100%) for about 12 minutes, stirring every 3 minutes, until cornmeal is tender and broth is absorbed.

Add cheese and pepper. Stir. Makes about 4 cups (1 L). Serves 6.

1 serving: 123 Calories; 2.2 g Total Fat (0.1 g Mono, 0.2 g Poly, 1.1 g Sat); 4 mg Cholesterol; 21 g Carbohydrate; 2 g Fibre; 4 g Protein; 288 mg Sodium

CHOICES: 1 Grains & Starches

Edamame Succotash

Don't like lima beans? We've swapped them for a whole new legume in this familiar side. Edamame is high in protein and fibre and is a good source of vitamins and minerals. If you like, you could add a sprinkle of simulated bacon bits for a smoky flavour.

Canola oil	2 tsp.	10 mL
Chopped onion	1 cup	250 mL
Chopped red pepper	1/2 cup	125 mL
Garlic clove, minced	1	1
(or 1/4 tsp., 1 mL, powder)		
Can of diced tomatoes (with juice)	14 oz.	398 mL
Frozen kernel corn	1 1/2 cups	375 mL
Frozen shelled edamame (soybeans)	1 1/2 cups	375 mL
Prepared vegetable broth	1/4 cup	60 mL
Chili powder	2 tsp.	10 mL

Heat canola oil in large frying pan on medium. Add next 3 ingredients. Cook for about 5 minutes, stirring occasionally, until onion and red pepper start to soften.

Add remaining 5 ingredients. Bring to a boil. Reduce heat to medium-low. Cook, covered, for about 5 minutes, stirring occasionally, until edamame is tender-crisp. Makes about 4 cups (1 L). Serves 6.

1 serving: 119 Calories; 3.8 g Total Fat (0.9 g Mono, 0.6 g Poly, 0.3 g Sat); 0 mg Cholesterol; 17 g Carbohydrate; 3 g Fibre; 6 g Protein; 215 mg Sodium

CHOICES: 1/2 Grains & Starches; 1 Vegetables; 1/2 Meat & Alternatives

Ginger Biscuits
With Orange Cream

*Finish a heavy meal with something sweet and light—delicate biscuits studded
with crystallized ginger and served with a fresh orange-flavoured cream.*

ORANGE CREAM		
Can of mandarin orange segments, drained	10 oz.	285 g
Light sour cream	1/2 cup	125 mL
Frozen light whipped topping, thawed	1/2 cup	125 mL
Grated orange zest	1 tsp.	5 mL
GINGER BISCUITS		
All-purpose flour	1 cup	250 mL
Whole-wheat flour	1/4 cup	60 mL
Granulated sugar	2 tbsp.	30 mL
Minced crystallized ginger	1 tsp.	5 mL
Baking powder	1/2 tsp.	2 mL
Baking soda	1/2 tsp.	2 mL
Ground ginger	1/2 tsp.	2 mL
Salt	1/4 tsp.	1 mL
Tub margarine	1/4 cup	60 mL
Large egg, fork-beaten	1	1
1% buttermilk	1/4 cup	60 mL

Orange Cream: Combine first 4 ingredients in small bowl. Chill for about
20 minutes. Makes about 2 cups (500 mL) cream.

Ginger Biscuits: Preheat oven to 425°F (220°C). Combine first 8 ingredients
in medium bowl.

Cut in margarine until mixture resembles coarse crumbs.

Add egg and buttermilk. Stir until just moistened. Turn out onto lightly floured
surface. Knead 4 or 5 times until dough just comes together. Roll out to
6 x 6 inch (15 x 15 cm) square. Transfer to greased baking sheet. Score
4 squares into dough, about 1/2 inch (12 mm) deep, using greased sharp
knife. Cut each square into 2 triangles, for a total of 8 triangles. Bake for about
12 minutes until wooden pick inserted in centre comes out clean. Let stand on
baking sheet for 5 minutes to cool. Makes 8 biscuits. Serve with Orange Cream.

(continued on next page)

1 biscuit with 1/4 cup (60 mL) Orange Cream: 187 Calories; 8.2 g Total Fat (2.7 g Mono, 2.4 g Poly, 2.3 g Sat); 29 mg Cholesterol; 24 g Carbohydrate; 1 g Fibre; 4 g Protein; 272 mg Sodium

CHOICES: 1 Grains & Starches; 1 1/2 Fats

Tropical Twist Iced Treat

What's the twist? This iced treat includes beans, which add protein and fibre, but the smooth, creamy texture will make you think you're eating soft-serve.

Canned navy beans, rinsed and drained	1 cup	250 mL
Orange juice	1/2 cup	125 mL
Package of fat-free instant white chocolate pudding powder (4-serving size)	1	1
Frozen mango pieces, chopped (do not thaw)	1 1/2 cups	375 mL
Frozen raspberries (do not thaw)	1 1/2 cups	375 mL

Process beans and orange juice in food processor, scraping down sides if necessary, until smooth.

Add pudding powder. Process until combined.

Add mango and raspberries. Process until smooth, scraping down sides if necessary. Serve immediately. Makes about 3 1/3 cups (825 mL). Serves 4.

1 serving: 247 Calories; 0.9 g Total Fat (0.1 g Mono, 0.2 g Poly, 0.2 g Sat); 0 mg Cholesterol; 56 g Carbohydrate; 7 g Fibre; 6 g Protein; 444 mg Sodium

CHOICES: 1/2 Grains & Starches; 1 Fruits; 1 1/2 Other Choices; 1/2 Meat & Alternatives

Chocolate Berry Parfaits

A light delight with layers of berries, chocolate pudding and creamy whipped topping.

Skim milk	2 cups	500 mL
Box of fat-free instant chocolate pudding powder (4-serving size)	1	1
Sliced fresh strawberries	1 cup	250 mL
Fresh blueberries	1 cup	250 mL
Frozen light whipped topping, thawed	1/4 cup	60 mL

Beat milk and pudding powder in small bowl for about 2 minutes until thickened. Chill for about 5 minutes until set.

Put strawberries into 4 tall glasses. Spoon half of pudding over strawberries. Scatter blueberries over pudding. Top with remaining pudding.

Spoon whipped topping over pudding. Makes 4 parfaits.

1 parfait: 193 Calories; 1.0 g Total Fat (0.1 g Mono, 0.1 g Poly, 0.7 g Sat); 2 mg Cholesterol; 43 g Carbohydrate; 2 g Fibre; 5 g Protein; 234 mg Sodium

CHOICES: 1/2 Fruits; 2 Other Choices; 1/2 Milk & Alternatives

1. Berry Ricotta Custards, page 146
2. Triple-Chocolate Shortcakes, page 149
3. Crustless Cheesecake Bites, page 146

Props courtesy of: The Bay

Grilled Peaches And Strawberries

Elegance can be this easy! The sweetness of grilled peaches and strawberries blend with the tanginess of honey and balsamic vinegar for the perfect combination.

Balsamic vinegar	1/4 cup	60 mL
Liquid honey	2 tbsp.	30 mL
Olive oil	2 tsp.	10 mL
Ground cinnamon	1/4 tsp.	1 mL
Ground ginger	1/2 tsp.	2 mL
Fresh peaches, halved and pitted	2	2
Large fresh strawberries	8	8

Preheat gas barbecue to medium-high. Whisk first 5 ingredients in large bowl.

Add peaches and strawberries. Toss until coated. Place peaches, cut-side down, on greased grill. Place strawberries on greased grill. Cook for about 6 minutes, turning once and brushing with vinegar mixture, until fruit is tender but firm. Transfer to 4 plates. Drizzle with remaining vinegar mixture. Serves 4.

1 serving: 97 Calories; 2.4 g Total Fat (1.7 g Mono, 0.3 g Poly, 0.3 g Sat); 0 mg Cholesterol; 19 g Carbohydrate; 2 g Fibre; 1 g Protein; 5 mg Sodium

CHOICES: 1/2 Fruits; 1/2 Other Choices; 1/2 Fats

1. Pumpkin Power Puffs, page 51
2. Chocolate Chip Softies, page 47
3. Quick PB Cookies, page 59
4. Cocoa Coconut Macaroons, page 52

Crustless Cheescake Bites

Craving cheesecake? These rich chocolate bites are loaded with cheesy goodness. This is one cheesecake you can indulge in, guilt-free!

95% fat-free cream cheese	8 oz.	250 g
Granulated sugar	1/3 cup	75 mL
All-purpose flour	2 tbsp.	30 mL
Cocoa powder, sifted if lumpy	1 tbsp.	15 mL
Large egg	1	1
Chocolate syrup	1/4 cup	60 mL

Preheat oven to 350°F (175°C). Beat first 4 ingredients in medium bowl until combined. Add egg. Beat until smooth. Divide into 12 greased muffin cups. Bake for about 12 minutes until set. Let stand in pan for 5 minutes. Carefully remove from pan and place on serving plate.

Drizzle with chocolate syrup. Makes 12 bites.

1 bite: 67 Calories; 0.7 g Total Fat (0.3 g Mono, 0.1 g Poly, 0.3 g Sat); 17 mg Cholesterol; 12 g Carbohydrate; trace Fibre; 4 g Protein; 112 mg Sodium

CHOICES: 1/2 Other Choices

Pictured on page 143.

Berry Ricotta Custards

Fresh berry flavour is complemented by light lemon in this comforting custard. Berry good!

Frozen mixed berries, thawed and drained	1 1/2 cups	375 mL
Large eggs	2	2
Light ricotta cheese	1 cup	250 mL
Granulated sugar	3 tbsp.	50 mL
Cornstarch	2 tbsp.	30 mL
Lemon juice	2 tsp.	10 mL
Grated lemon zest	1 tsp.	5 mL
Salt	1/8 tsp.	0.5 mL

(continued on next page)

Preheat oven to 400°F (205°C). Spoon berries into 4 greased 6 oz. (170 mL) ramekins.

Whisk remaining 7 ingredients in small bowl. Spoon over berries. Bake for about 20 minutes until knife inserted in centre of custard comes out clean. Makes 4 custards.

1 custard: 174 Calories; 5.0 g Total Fat (1.1 g Mono, 0.4 g Poly, 2.3 g Sat); 108 mg Cholesterol; 22 g Carbohydrate; 2 g Fibre; 8 g Protein; 159 mg Sodium

CHOICES: 1/2 Fruits; 1/2 Other Choices; 1 Meat & Alternatives

Pictured on page 143.

Blueberry Frozen Yogurt

Craving ice cream? This frosty frozen dessert combines the creaminess of pudding with the tanginess of yogurt and lemon—and it's virtually fat-free!

Box of fat-free instant vanilla pudding powder (4-serving size)	1	1
Non-fat plain yogurt	1 cup	250 mL
Frozen blueberries (do not thaw)	3 cups	750 mL
Lemon juice	1 tbsp.	15 mL

Process pudding powder and yogurt in food processor or blender for about 15 seconds, scraping down sides if necessary, until combined.

Add blueberries and lemon juice. Process, scraping down sides if necessary, until smooth. Spoon into 4 chilled dessert cups. Serve immediately. Makes about 2 1/2 cups (625 mL). Serves 4.

1 serving: 164 Calories; 0.8 g Total Fat (0 g Mono, 0 g Poly, trace Sat); 1 mg Cholesterol; 40 g Carbohydrate; 3 g Fibre; 3 g Protein; 172 mg Sodium

CHOICES: 1/2 Fruits; 1 1/2 Other Choices; 1/2 Milk & Alternatives

Strawberry Wafer Layers

Bring a little freshness to your dinner table with this layered dessert of sweet strawberry mousse and crisp cookie wafers.

WAFER COOKIES

Egg white (large), room temperature	1	1
Icing (confectioner's) sugar	1/4 cup	60 mL
All-purpose flour	2 1/2 tbsp.	37 mL
Tub margarine, melted	2 tbsp.	30 mL
Water	1 tsp.	5 mL
Vanilla extract	1/4 tsp.	1 mL

STRAWBERRY CREAM

Frozen fat-free whipped topping, thawed	1 1/2 cups	375 mL
Frozen sliced strawberries in light syrup, thawed (with syrup)	1/2 cup	125 mL
Frozen sliced strawberries in light syrup, thawed (with syrup)	1/2 cup	125 mL

Wafer Cookies: Preheat oven to 400°F (205°C). Whisk all 6 ingredients in small bowl until smooth. Spoon 8 portions of batter, using 2 tsp. (10 mL) for each, onto parchment paper-lined baking sheet. Spread to 3 inch (7.5 cm) circles. Bake for about 7 minutes until edges are browned and crisp. Transfer to wire rack to cool. Makes 8 cookies.

Strawberry Cream: Meanwhile, combine whipped topping and first amount of strawberries in small bowl. Makes about 2 cups (500 mL). Place 4 cookies on plates. Spoon half of strawberry mixture onto wafers. Repeat with remaining wafers and strawberry mixture.

Top with second amount of strawberries. Serves 4.

1 serving: 179 Calories; 5.8 g Total Fat (2.4 g Mono, 2.3 g Poly, 0.8 g Sat); 0 mg Cholesterol; 29 g Carbohydrate; trace Fibre; 2 g Protein; 106 mg Sodium

CHOICES: 1/2 Fruits; 1/2 Other Choices; 1 Fats

Pictured on page 108.

Triple-Chocolate Shortcakes

Three times the chocolate! Light-flavoured chocolate biscuits are filled with white chocolate pudding and topped with a dark chocolate drizzle.

All-purpose flour	1 1/4 cups	300 mL
Brown sugar, packed	3 tbsp.	50 mL
Cocoa powder, sifted if lumpy	2 tbsp.	30 mL
Baking powder	1 tsp.	5 mL
Baking soda	1/4 tsp.	1 mL
Salt	1/8 tsp.	0.5 mL
Tub margarine	2 tbsp.	30 mL
1% buttermilk	1/2 cup	125 mL
Vanilla extract	1 tsp.	5 mL
Box of fat-free instant white chocolate pudding powder (4-serving size)	1	1
Skim milk	2 cups	500 mL
Chocolate syrup	2 tbsp.	30 mL

Preheat oven to 450°F (230°C). Combine first 6 ingredients in large bowl. Cut in margarine until mixture resembles coarse crumbs.

Add buttermilk and vanilla. Stir until just moistened. Drop 6 portions of batter, using 3 tbsp. (50 mL) for each, about 2 inches (5 cm) apart onto greased baking sheet. Bake for about 10 minutes until wooden pick inserted in centre of biscuit comes out clean. Transfer to wire rack to cool slightly.

Meanwhile, beat pudding powder and milk in small bowl for about 2 minutes until thickened. Chill for about 5 minutes until set. Cut biscuits in half horizontally. Transfer to plates. Spoon about 1/4 cup (60 mL) pudding onto each biscuit bottom. Set biscuit tops over pudding. Spoon 1 tbsp. (15 mL) pudding over top of each.

Drizzle with chocolate syrup. Makes 6 shortcakes.

1 shortcake: 275 Calories; 4.4 g Total Fat (1.7 g Mono, 1.5 g Poly, 0.9 g Sat); 3 mg Cholesterol; 53 g Carbohydrate; 1 g Fibre; 7 g Protein; 381 mg Sodium

CHOICES: 1 Grains & Starches; 2 Other Choices; 1/2 Milk & Alternatives; 1 Fats

Pictured on page 143.

Measurement Tables

Throughout this book measurements are given in Conventional and Metric measure. To compensate for differences between the two measurements due to rounding, a full metric measure is not always used. The cup used is the standard 8 fluid ounce. Temperature is given in degrees Fahrenheit and Celsius. Baking pan measurements are in inches and centimetres as well as quarts and litres. An exact metric conversion is given below as well as the working equivalent (Metric Standard Measure).

Spoons

Conventional Measure	Metric Exact Conversion Millilitre (mL)	Metric Standard Measure Millilitre (mL)
1/8 teaspoon (tsp.)	0.6 mL	0.5 mL
1/4 teaspoon (tsp.)	1.2 mL	1 mL
1/2 teaspoon (tsp.)	2.4 mL	2 mL
1 teaspoon (tsp.)	4.7 mL	5 mL
2 teaspoons (tsp.)	9.4 mL	10 mL
1 tablespoon (tbsp.)	14.2 mL	15 mL

Cups

Conventional Measure	Metric Exact Conversion Millilitre (mL)	Metric Standard Measure Millilitre (mL)
1/4 cup (4 tbsp.)	56.8 mL	60 mL
1/3 cup (5 1/3 tbsp.)	75.6 mL	75 mL
1/2 cup (8 tbsp.)	113.7 mL	125 mL
2/3 cup (10 2/3 tbsp.)	151.2 mL	150 mL
3/4 cup (12 tbsp.)	170.5 mL	175 mL
1 cup (16 tbsp.)	227.3 mL	250 mL
4 1/2 cups	1022.9 mL	1000 mL (1 L)

Dry Measurements

Conventional Measure Ounces (oz.)	Metric Exact Conversion Grams (g)	Metric Standard Measure Grams (g)
1 oz.	28.3 g	28 g
2 oz.	56.7 g	57 g
3 oz.	85.0 g	85 g
4 oz.	113.4 g	125 g
5 oz.	141.7 g	140 g
6 oz.	170.1 g	170 g
7 oz.	198.4 g	200 g
8 oz.	226.8 g	250 g
16 oz.	453.6 g	500 g
32 oz.	907.2 g	1000 g (1 kg)

Oven Temperatures

Fahrenheit (°F)	Celsius (°C)
175°	80°
200°	95°
225°	110°
250°	120°
275°	140°
300°	150°
325°	160°
350°	175°
375°	190°
400°	205°
425°	220°
450°	230°
475°	240°
500°	260°

Pans

Conventional Inches	Metric Centimetres
8x8 inch	20x20 cm
9x9 inch	22x22 cm
9x13 inch	22x33 cm
10x15 inch	25x38 cm
11x17 inch	28x43 cm
8x2 inch round	20x5 cm
9x2 inch round	22x5 cm
10x4 1/2 inch tube	25x11 cm
8x4x3 inch loaf	20x10x7.5 cm
9x5x3 inch loaf	22x12.5x7.5 cm

Casseroles

CANADA & BRITAIN Standard Size Casserole	Exact Metric Measure	UNITED STATES Standard Size Casserole	Exact Metric Measure
1 qt. (5 cups)	1.13 L	1 qt. (4 cups)	900 mL
1 1/2 qts. (7 1/2 cups)	1.69 L	1 1/2 qts. (6 cups)	1.35 L
2 qts. (10 cups)	2.25 L	2 qts. (8 cups)	1.8 L
2 1/2 qts. (12 1/2 cups)	2.81 L	2 1/2 qts. (10 cups)	2.25 L
3 qts. (15 cups)	3.38 L	3 qts. (12 cups)	2.7 L
4 qts. (20 cups)	4.5 L	4 qts. (16 cups)	3.6 L
5 qts. (25 cups)	5.63 L	5 qts. (20 cups)	4.5 L

Recipe Index

151

152

154

156

Recipe Notes

Recipe Notes

Recipe Notes

Recipe Notes